SECURITY, RELIGION, AND THE RULE OF LAW

Security, Religion, and the Rule of Law argues that true, substantive, and sustainable national security is only possible through respect for the rule of law, human rights, and religious freedom.

Despite the emphasis on national security and the war on terror that has preoccupied governments for over two decades, nations – and the world – seem to be more divided than ever, with a concomitant impact of increasing the risk of terrorism and religious and political violence. The national security paradigm, previously reserved primarily for foreign threats, has been turned increasingly inwards, focusing on a state's own citizens as potential threats. This is often along religious lines, threatening fundamental human freedoms. This book provides a series of critical engagements on some of the most pressing issues at the interface of religion and security today, including proposing a deeper engagement with theology when dealing with freedom of religious belief, exploring a better understanding between domestic peace and international relations, abiding by the rule of law while countering terrorism, and developing a broader understanding of identities and of the nature of citizenship. It provides the resources to further reflect upon and address these topics, as well as stimulate further discussions on religion and security matters across a range of different disciplines. Wide-ranging case studies consider Australia, China, Europe, the Kurdish people, Nigeria, Russia, Ukraine, the United Nations, and the United States.

This book will appeal to students and scholars across a range of disciplines, including international relations, law, philosophy, political science, religious studies, security studies, and theology. It will also appeal to human rights lawyers, judges, NGO researchers, governmental agency specialists, and policy makers.

Tania Pagotto is a Postdoctoral Researcher in Law and Religion at the University of Milan-Bicocca, Italy.

Joshua M. Roose is an Associate Professor of Politics at the Alfred Deakin Institute for Citizenship and Globalisation in the School of Humanities and Social Sciences at Deakin University, Australia.

G. P. Marcar is a Research Affiliate and former Harold Turner Research Fellow with the Centre for Theology and Public Issues at the University of Otago, New Zealand.

Security, Religion, and the Rule of Law: International Perspectives offers a multidisciplinary and multidimensional analysis of relationships between the paradigms of national security and freedom of religion. Employing rigorous argument through overarching chapters and a selection of case studies, the authors signal moves towards a positive understanding of the potential of freedom of religion to function as a healing mechanism in fractured polities, contextualising and undermining simplistic perceptions of religion as a threat to national and international security. This 'flipping of the coin' of voguishly negative discourse on the role of religion in society is important, overdue, and deserving of the widest readership.

Patrick Thornberry CMG, *Emeritus Professor of International Law at Keele University, UK, and Fellow of Kellogg College, University of Oxford, UK*

Routledge Studies in Religion and Politics

Edited by Jeffrey Haynes, London Metropolitan University, UK

This series aims to publish high quality works on the topic of the resurgence of political forms of religion in both national and international contexts. This trend has been especially noticeable in the post-cold war era (that is, since the late 1980s). It has affected all the 'world religions' (including Buddhism, Christianity, Hinduism, Islam, and Judaism) in various parts of the world (such as the Americas, Europe, the Middle East and North Africa, South and Southeast Asia, and sub-Saharan Africa).

The series welcomes books that use a variety of approaches to the subject, drawing on scholarship from political science, international relations, security studies, and contemporary history.

Books in the series explore these religions, regions, and topics both within and beyond the conventional domain of 'church-state' relations to include the impact of religion on politics, conflict and development, including the late Samuel Huntington's controversial – yet influential – thesis about 'clashing civilisations'.

In sum, the overall purpose of the book series is to provide a comprehensive survey of what is currently happening in relation to the interaction of religion and politics, both domestically and internationally, in relation to a variety of issues.

Security, Religion, and the Rule of Law
International Perspectives
Edited by Tania Pagotto, Joshua M. Roose and G. P. Marcar

For more information about this series, please visit: https://www.routledge.com/Routledge-Studies-in-Religion-and-Politics/book-series/RSRP

SECURITY, RELIGION, AND THE RULE OF LAW

International Perspectives

Edited by
Tania Pagotto, Joshua M. Roose and G. P. Marcar

Routledge
Taylor & Francis Group
LONDON AND NEW YORK

First published 2024
by Routledge
4 Park Square, Milton Park, Abingdon, Oxon OX14 4RN

and by Routledge
605 Third Avenue, New York, NY 10158

Routledge is an imprint of the Taylor & Francis Group, an informa business

British Library Cataloguing-in-Publication Data
A catalogue record for this book is available from the British Library

Library of Congress Cataloging-in-Publication Data
Names: Pagotto, Tania, editor. | Roose, Joshua M., 1980– editor. | Marcar, G. P., editor. | Souza Alves, Rodrigo Vitorino, contributor.
Title: Security, religion, and the rule of law : international perspectives / edited by Tania Pagotto, Joshua M. Roose, and G.P. Marcar ;
contributors, Rodrigo Vitorino Souza Alves [and five others].
Description: Abingdon, Oxon [UK] ; New York, NY : Routledge, 2023. |
Series: Routledge studies in religion and politics | Includes
bibliographical references and index.
Identifiers: LCCN 2023037705 (print) | LCCN 2023037706 (ebook) |
ISBN 9781032591261 (hardback) | ISBN 9781032591247 (paperback) |
ISBN 9781003453086 (ebook)
Subjects: LCSH: Religion and state. | Freedom of religion. | Religious law and legislation. | Rule of law | National security—Law and legislation. | International law and human rights.
Classification: LCC K3280 .S43 2023 (print) | LCC K3280 (ebook) | DDC 342.08/52—dc23/eng/20230926
LC record available at https://lccn.loc.gov/2023037705
LC ebook record available at https://lccn.loc.gov/2023037706

ISBN: 978-1-032-59126-1 (hbk)
ISBN: 978-1-032-59124-7 (pbk)
ISBN: 978-1-003-45308-6 (ebk)

DOI: 10.4324/9781003453086

Typeset in Sabon
by codeMantra

CONTENTS

ACKNOWLEDGEMENTS

The genesis of this book lies in the 2019 Young Scholars Fellowship programme, organized by the International Center for Law and Religious Studies at BYU Law, and hosted by Christ Church College at Oxford. The project owes an enormous debt of gratitude to those who organized and ran this programme – in particular, Brett G. Scharffs, Jane Wise, Mary Jensen, Kim Pearson, Blythe Moffitt Shupe, Holly Hinckley Lesan, and Deborah Wright. As the book developed, the support of these scholars remained invaluable. We would like to especially thank Jane Wise, whose support and assistance were unwavering throughout the editorial process. Finally, we would like to thank Nathanael Sederholm for assistance in proofreading, and Amy Andrus for her continuous support since becoming the ICLRS Associate Director in 2021.

CONTRIBUTORS

Rodrigo Vitorino Souza Alves is Professor at the Faculty of Law of the Federal University of Uberlandia, Brazil, and Leading Scholar of the Brazilian Center of Studies in Law and Religion – CEDIRE. He is a member of Steering Committees of the International Consortium for Law and Religion Studies – ICLARS – and the Latin American Consortium for Religious Freedom – CLLR. He is also a member of the International Academic Advisory Board of the Religion and the Rule of Law at Oxford Program.

Azizat Omotoyosi Amoloye-Adebayo is a Reader in the Department of Islamic Law in the Faculty of Law at the University of Ilorin, Nigeria. She is a Barrister and Solicitor of the Supreme Court of Nigeria; a Commonwealth Scholar; an Associate of the Chartered Institute of Arbitrators in Nigeria and the UK; and a Research Fellow at the Research Institute for Theology and Religion at the University of South Africa. She researches and publishes in areas including Islamic law, international human rights law, and issues corncerning law, gender, and religion.

Renae Barker is a Senior Lecturer in the School of Law, and an Associate Research Fellow at the Centre for Muslim States and Societies, at the University of Western Australia.

Michelle Flynn is an Irish barrister and an Associate at the Max Planck Institute for Social Anthropology, Halle, Germany.

Elena López Ruf is a lawyer who graduated from the Faculty of Law at the Pontifical Catholic University of Argentina (UCA). She teaches Philosophy of Law at UCA and "Religion and the Global World" at Austral University. Elena has extensive experience promoting interreligious and ecumenical relationships at the local, regional, and international levels. She has worked in faith-based organizations, UNDP, and government entities. She is a member of several organizations, including the International Consortium for Law and Religion Studies (ICLARS) and the Latin American Consortium for Religious Freedom (CLLR).

Maksym Vasin is Executive Director of the Institute for Religious Freedom, Ukraine. He is a researcher at LYN Community, United States, and a member of the International Consortium for Law and Religion Studies – ICLARS. He researches and publishes in areas including interfaith relations, church-state cooperation, international human rights law, and religious freedom.

FOREWORD

Brett G. Scharffs
Director, International Center for Law and Religion Studies
Jane Wise
Associate Director, International Center for Law and Religion Studies

The International Center for Law and Religion Studies (ICLRS) is based at Brigham Young University Law School in Provo, Utah, USA, and is a pioneering academic centre focused on law and religion from an international and comparative law perspective. It has created and participated in many international programmes and projects, bringing together people and international networks interested in the study of law and religion in nearly every part of the world.

Along with its programme host, Christ Church, Oxford, and institutions providing expertise, ICLRS sponsors an annual three-week workshop at Oxford for international faculty, graduate students, and government officials focusing on freedom of thought, conscience, religion, and belief, and more specifically on the intersections of law and religion. This course of study focuses on freedom of religion or belief (FoRB) as a human right and a constitutional right. Participants learn to teach a course in law and religion from an international and comparative law perspective, participate in writing tutorials helping them hone an English-language scholarly article on FoRB topics for academic journals, become 'visiting fellows' of BYU Law School, receive training in civic engagement and law reform, and present their research to and network with other scholars.

The group of scholars who participated in the 2019 Oxford Workshop proposed writing a book together addressing international perspectives on how national security is impacted by religion and the rule of law. This book is the outcome of those discussions, which began around a seminar table and continued at pubs and restaurants around Oxford. Scholar contributors to this volume are from Italy, Australia, New Zealand, Ireland, Nigeria, Brazil, Argentina, and Ukraine.

This extraordinary and important work came about through the connections made between 15 international scholars who share a commitment to the principles of FoRB. One of our primary goals at the ICLRS is to promote the creation and maintenance of networks of scholars who are interested in the field of law and religion, and, so you can imagine, it is with great satisfaction that we welcome this book that focuses on the important intersections of religion and national security, from a comparative law perspective. We are fortunate that this group of scholars has found such a meaningful project to pursue together, and we are grateful that our Center can help facilitate good work in this area. We feel a bit like proud parents.

INTRODUCTION

From Spaces of Tension, to Spaces of Conversation: Freedom of Religion or Belief and National Security

Tania Pagotto and G. P. Marcar

1 The Inward Flexion of National Security[1]

The question about the interrelation between the exercise of freedom of religion or belief (FoRB) and national security stretches far beyond the halls of academia (Marsden, 2019). While national security has preoccupied governments since the 9/11 attacks – although this is considered a conventional date – a worrying trend has arisen in the context of the global war on terror and, above all, the (re)emergence of global populism and authoritarian leadership (Scandian, 2022; Morieson, 2021; DeHanas and Shterin, 2020; Huq, 2016).

The term "security" has been defined as an "ambiguous symbol" (Wolfers, 1952). For Lippman, for example, "a nation has security when it does not have to sacrifice its legitimate interests to avoid war and is able, if challenged, to maintain them by war" (Lippman, 1943, p. 51). Historian Melvyn P. Leffler (2004, p. 123) noted that "national security policy encompasses the decisions and actions deemed imperative to protect domestic core values from external threats." Moreover, he adds an important point: the perception of these foreign threats involved not only material elements (objective threats to peace and acts of aggression), but also ideologies, cultural symbols, and, often, misperceptions (Leffler, 2004).

In the last two decades, in fact, the focus of national security has been deflected inward and has changed target.

National security legislation and restrictions now focus more on individuals and groups of people: States increasingly face immediate threats directly from violent groups and by extension from the diverse communities considered to house them, including religious congregations. In this way, State governments make national security policies that consider their own citizens

DOI: 10.4324/9781003453086-1

as potentially hostile. Citizens are both the objects *and subjects* of national security strategies: indeed, decisions on securitization and surveillance often rely upon a duty of loyalty that demands universal political, social, and religious conformity of citizens and third-country nationals alike.

Framed as such, the "inward turn" of the national security paradigm impinges upon many of the most fundamental civil and political rights, enshrined in many international human rights treaties and conventions that flourished in the aftermath of the Second World War, such as free speech, freedom of movement, freedom of assembly and of association, and – most notably – FoRB.

This no doubt constitutes a major change. First, according to the standard international human rights approach, national security is not listed as a legitimate aim for restricting the manifestation of FoRB (Art. 9 ECHR; Art. 18 ICCPR; Art. 10 CFREU). The UN Human Rights Committee, in its *General Comment No. 22: Article 18 (Freedom of Thought, Conscience or Religion)*, observed in 1993 that "restrictions are not allowed on grounds not specified there, even if they would be allowed as restrictions to other rights protected in the Covenant, such as national security" (*UN Human Rights Committee*, 1993, para. 8). Recently, moreover, the 2019 OSCE Report *Freedom of Religion or Belief and Security: Policy Guidance* has more expressly stated that "'security' or 'national security' are not recognized by international law as permissible grounds for restricting the manifestation of freedom of religion or belief" (*OSCE/ODHIR*, 2019, para 18; see also *OSCE/ODHIR*, 2014). Public order or public safety (among a few others)[2] may represent legitimate aims by which to limit the exercise of fundamental rights and freedoms, but only under strict conditions, i.e. the measures shall be prescribed by law and necessary in a democratic society, and proportionate to achieve the legitimate aim concerned.

By contrast, as Silvio Ferrari has noted, there have been at least three ways in which States have restricted religious freedom as a result of political pressure to impinge upon FoRB on the grounds of national security. Governments have (1) enacted new legislation limiting human rights in general; (2) indirectly scrutinized religious organizations; and (3) directly intervened in the internal affairs or beliefs of religious communities (Ferrari, 2004). It therefore seems that national security has become a fluid and unclear *modus operandus* of modern States. In the wake of amorphous and far-reaching notions of security, governments have adopted policies and restrictions of fundamental rights, national interest, or public safety (Ferrari, 2004).

Second, the national security paradigm understands FoRB as particularly and intrinsically challenging. Not only do governments perceive the bonds of solidarity that religious believers share as competitors to the State's supremacy, but they also look at religious pluralism as something to screen through the narrow lens of acceptability, rather than as a value to cherish.

While scientific literature shows the contribution of FoRB in building peace, ensuring security, and contributing to social and political cohesion, the religious element has become a point of contention among decision-makers and nations. Too often, the religious dimension is oversimplified and misunderstood, "leading some observers to use the label 'religion' broadly and loosely" and overlooking a "careful, contextualized analysis of all relevant factors" (Bielefeldt, 2014).

2 FoRB and National Security Is Not a Trade-Off

Against this background, the essential assumption of the present collection is that true, substantive, and sustainable national security is only possible through respect for human rights in general and FoRB in particular.

The cost of increasing antagonisms within societies calls for us to urgently re-examine States' rule-of-law compliance and the need for them to implement strategies, policies, and laws that, while operating in the area of security, simultaneously reinforce governments' commitment to human rights and both the positive and negative obligations of FoRB. As Jonathan Shaw put it, religion "must be at the table if national security policy is to embrace the fullness of the human situation, formulate effective concepts, and yield enduring results" (Shaw, 2011, p. 2). In other words: both security and religious freedom are in the interest of social peace.

Commentators have identified the crucial link between religion and security. Moreover, after the release of the 2019 OSCE Report *Freedom of Religion or Belief and Security: Policy Guidance*, recent books have provided additional insights on the need to reflect upon effective and human-rights-compliant strategies addressing national security (Marchei and Milani, 2023; Alicino, 2020; Bialasiewicz and Gentile, 2019; Annicchino, 2017; Murphy, 2013; Seiple, Hoover, and Otis, 2013; Wellman and Lombardi, 2012; Shaw, 2011).

A sound and bold reflection on these crucial issues needs and entails a wide variety of perspectives to stimulate involvement at all levels of society. The intersection of national security, religion, and the rule of law is a multifaceted, complex, and immensely challenging topic, and constitutes one of the leading political, moral, and ethical dilemmas of our time with real-world violence, targeting religious communities having geostrategic implications (Mazzola, 2017; de Vergottini, 2004).

This is why the ideas put forward in this volume represent a multidisciplinary synthesis, with contributing authors coming from a variety of backgrounds, giving this collection both theoretical grounding and interdisciplinary depths. The editors themselves have worked together not only from different locations (Italy, Australia, New Zealand) but also by blending different academic disciplines: law, political sociology, philosophy, and theology. In this way, the anthology contributes to academic knowledge by inviting scholars and policymakers to reflect upon a variegated approach to the question of religion and national security.

In addition, while the field of law and religion has been dominated by leading scholarship scrutinizing multiple implications of constitutional law and the human right to freedom of religion, this book tries to pluralize the points of observation, but sheds light on the nature and the various forms that the relationships between national security and FoRB can take.

The conversation about this monograph started in 2019 at Oxford, under the auspices of the summer program *Young Scholar Fellowship on Religion and the Rule of Law*. The entire project, including an online conference titled *Religion and Security: Sharing Perspectives* that took place in the midst of the Covid-19 pandemic, was sponsored by the International Center for Law and Religious Studies at Brigham Young University.

While gathering at Oxford and back in their home countries, the authors kept examining and reflecting on a series of critical questions on some of the most pressing issues at the interface of religion and security today. What place should religion or theology have in relation to the nature and development of civil laws? How might States and their people best negotiate conflicting national and religious identities? How might the goals of internal civic cohesion and security be best achieved alongside the goal of religious-cultural diversity?

The collection explores these questions by addressing them from both religious and secular perspectives, as well as by appealing to international case studies, with chapters focused on Ukraine, Nigeria, Europe, Australia, the United States, and the United Nations.

3 Spaces of Tension: Theology, Geopolitics, and Identities

Perhaps the most important lesson learned from this ongoing conversation and inquiry is that there are different spaces where tensions underpinning the nexus between security and FoRB manifest.

The first space of tension is located at a theoretical level.

In this section, **G. P. Marcar** sketches some conceptual and psychological tensions between security, toleration, and religious beliefs, before highlighting some important differences between Locke's and Rousseau's visions of religion and the State.

Elena López Ruf explores the relationship between religious freedom and human security within the United Nations system. While Marcar's chapter looks at this question from a secular perspective, López Ruf's contribution addresses the normative dimensions of religious teachings in promoting human security. By revisiting the parable of the Good Samaritan as a religious narrative of human insecurity, she analyzes the notion of "Human Fraternity" as a complementary framework to the "Human Security" for "living together in diversity" and "in a spirit of fraternity."

The second space of tension is geopolitics.

In this section, **Rodrigo Vitorino Souza Alves** addressed FoRB in the context of counter-terrorism in the United Nations system and argues that anti-terrorism legislation (or judicial and administrative measures) restricting FoRB on the grounds of terrorism shall contain a series of inherent qualities. In particular, these measures shall be scrutinized under a strict necessity test and, accordingly, the author enumerates conditions that can guide legal interpreters to assess the necessity of a measure.

Michelle Flynn locates her contribution within the context of US national security as framed by the National Security Strategy (NSS) Reports, issued over the course of two decades. She examines these documents commencing with the 1997 NSS Report, wherein religion was first identified as a matter of concern in respect of national security, and traces the broader development of the role of religion in US national security matters.

Maksym Vasin considers the amended religious legislation promulgated in Ukraine as a response to the Russian aggression, paying particular attention to the measures that interfere with FoRB of the Orthodox Church. Vasin's chapter delineates the limits of permissible state intervention in the internal affairs of religious organizations in a situation that has developed in Ukraine, under the influence of external geopolitical factors.

The third space of tension is identities.

This section, in particular, considers the extent to which a particular religion as such (i.e. Islam) has been problematized across different contexts.

Azizat Omotoyosi Amoloye-Adebayo presents the case of the "third identity" in Nigeria and uses this country as an example of a religiously pluralistic and culturally divergent context under a national constitution and Islam, as the religious context, to argue that Nigerian constitutional provisions are not sufficiently instructive for Nigerian Muslims to forge a religious identity that is compatible with national ideals.

Renae Barker focuses on case law and is concerned with arguments relating to public safety and security, often raised to support bans or restrictions on wearing religious dress and symbols. She examines cases where the courts have rejected security, public safety, and public order and explains when and why security has been rejected as a legitimate justification for bans and restrictions on wearing religious dress and symbols.

The chapter of **Tania Pagotto** explores the mutual interaction between addressing migration flows and regulating citizenship acquisition under the lens of security concerns. She explores the practice of pre-entry tests and citizenship tests, carried out in some EU countries, by focusing on the religious factor. She underlines that in regulating both migration and citizenship, countries often conflate concerns on security with concerns on potential clashes over values and identity.

Finally, **Joshua Roose** analyzes the issue of foreign fighters and the question of the relationship between citizenship and loyalty by focusing on the legislative, jurisprudential, and liberal philosophical challenges of decisions relating to stripping citizenship undertaken by some Western States. In particular, Roose assesses the potential legal implications for religious minorities belonging to diasporas with contested foreign territorial claims and explores the questions around FoRB and participation in foreign conflicts that remain largely unaddressed in contemporary literature.

4 A Space of Conversation: The Rule of Law

This collection, finally, has a twofold ultimate goal.

First, it aims to provide the resources to reflect upon and stimulate further discussions on religion and national security matters across a range of different disciplines. Second, the book represents a choir of different voices, with different expertise, geared toward creating a space of conversation where not only is the picture which emerges more nuanced, but different perspectives are also subject to public scrutiny.

In this respect, the editors chose the concept of the "rule of law" to include, under the same umbrella, several perspectives and many different angles – all unified by a very simple idea, yet complex to implement, that

> (1) the people (including, one should add, the government) should be ruled by, and obey, the law and obey it and (2) that the law should be such that people will be able (and, one should add, willing) to be guided by it.
>
> *(Walker, 1988)*

If a "good" law is the one that makes people able and *willing* to follow, then FoRB should be balanced against security and not annihilated in the name of it. The second purpose of this work, as deepened in the Conclusion, is to underline the need to urgently define FoRB against (re)emergent forms of authoritarianism: in fact, "when measures that limit freedom of religion or belief are necessary to ensure security in specific cases, comprehensive and sustainable security can be attained only if these measures respect human dignity and human rights" (*OSCE/ODIHR*, 2019, p. 56).

Notes

1 Although the Introduction reflects the common view of the authors, Parts 1 and 2 were written by Tania Pagotto and Parts 3 and 4 by G. P. Marcar.

2 Art. 9, para 2, ECHR: "Freedom to manifest one's religion or beliefs shall be subject only to such limitations as are prescribed by law and are necessary in a democratic society in the interests of public safety, for the protection of public order, health or morals, or for the protection of the rights and freedoms of others." Art. 18, para 3, ICCPR: "Freedom to manifest one's religion or beliefs may be subject only to such limitations as are prescribed by law and are necessary to protect public safety, order, health, or morals or the fundamental rights and freedoms of others."

References

Alicino, F. (ed) (2020) Terrorismo di Ispirazione Religiosa: Prevenzione e Radicalizzazione nello Stato Laico, Rome, APES.

Annicchino, P. (2017) 'Sicurezza nazionale e diritto alla libertà religiosa. Alcune considerazioni alla luce della recente esperienza statunitense', Stato, Chiese e Pluralismo Confessionale, 13 February.

Bialasiewicz, L., and Gentile, V. (eds) (2019) Spaces of Tolerance: Changing Geographies and Philosophies of Religion in Today's Europe, London, Routledge.

Bielefeldt, H. (2014) Report of the Special Rapporteur on Freedom of Religion or Belief, New York, United Nations General Assembly.

DeHanas, D. N., and Shterin, M. (eds) (2020) Religion and the Rise of Populism, Abingdon, Routledge.

de Vergottini, G. (2004) 'La difficile convivenza fra libertà e sicurezza. La risposta delle democrazie al terrorismo. Gli ordinamenti nazionali', Boletìn Mexicano de Derecho Comparado, vol. 37, no. 111, pp. 1185–1211.

Ferrari, S. (2004) 'Individual Religious Freedom and National Security in Europe after September 11', BYU Law Review, vol. 2004, no. 2, pp. 357–84.

Huq, A. Z. (2016) 'The Uses of Religious Identity, Practice, and Dogma in "Soft" and "Hard" Counterterrorism', University of Chicago Public Law Working Papers, no. 609.

Leffler, M. P. (2004) 'National Security', in Hogan, M. J. and Paterson, T. G. (eds) Explaining the History of American Foreign Relations, Cambridge, Cambridge University Press, pp. 123–136.

Lippmann, W. (1943) US Foreign Policy: Shield of the Republic, Boston, MA, Little Brown and Company.

Marchei, N., and Milani, D. (eds.) (2023) Freedom of Religion, Security and the Law: Key Challenges for a Pluralistic Society, Abingdon, Routledge.

Marsden, L. (2019) Religion and International Security, Hoboken, NJ, John Wiley & Sons.

Mazzola, R. (2017) '"Stato d'urgenza", "ragion di stato" e fattore religioso', in Martino, R., Alicino, F. and Barone, A. (eds) L'impatto delle Situazioni di Urgenza Sulle Attività Umane Regolate dal Diritto, Milan, Giuffré, pp. 15–39.

Morieson, N. (2021) Religion and the Populist Radical Right: Secular Christianism and Populism in Western Europe, Wilmington, DE, Vernon Press.

Murphy, K. (2013) State Security Regimes and the Right to Freedom of Religion and Belief: Changes in Europe Since 2001, Abingdon, Routledge.

OSCE/ODIHR (2019) Freedom of Religion or Belief and Security: Policy Guidance, Vienna [Online]. Available at https://www.osce.org/odihr/429389 (Accessed 1 March 2023).

OSCE/ODIHR (2014) Preventing Terrorism and Countering Violent Extremism and Radicalization that Lead to Terrorism: A Community-Policing Approach, Vienna [Online]. Available at https://www.osce.org/secretariat/111438 (Accessed 1 March 2023).

Scandian, E. (2022) Populism and Securitization of Migration in Europe, Masters Thesis, Adelaide, Flinders University.

Seiple, C., Hoover, D., and Otis, P. (2013) The Routledge Handbook of Religion and Security, Abingdon, Routledge.

Shaw, J. E. (2011) The Role of Religion in National Security Policy Since September 11, 2001, Carlisle, PA, Strategic Studies Institute, U.S. Army War College.

UN Human Rights Committee (1993) CCPR General Comment No. 22: Article 18 (Freedom of Thought, Conscience or Religion), New York, United Nations [Online]. Available at https://www.refworld.org/docid/453883fb22.html (Accessed 1 March 2023).

Walker, Geoffrey de Q. (1988) The Rule of Law: Foundation of Constitutional Democracy, Melbourne, Melbourne University Press.

Wellman, J. K., and Lombardi, C. (2012) Religion and Human Security: A Global Perspective, Oxford, Oxford University Press.

Wolfers, A. (1952) '"National Security" as an Ambiguous Symbol', Political Science Quarterly, vol. 67, no. 4, pp. 481–502.

PART I

Religion, Security, and Theology

1

DOUBTFUL CIVIL BELIEF

Or, Tolerating One's Damned Neighbours with Jean-Jacques Rousseau

G. P. Marcar

1 Introduction: Contours of Tension between Security, Toleration, and Religion

Any attempt to investigate the conceptual and normative relationships between religion and security is fated to be difficult for at least two reasons. First, the relationship between religion and security has a long and complicated backstory (see, for instance, Engh 2010). For much of history, religious persons have been prosecuted, penalised, or even executed for their beliefs, or lack thereof, under the pretence of security. Prominent examples of this include Socrates (executed in 399 BC) and Jesus Christ. Indeed, the context in which "religious liberty" (*libertas religionis*) was coined by the 2nd-century theologian Tertullian was one of early Christian persecution for posing an apparent threat to the *Pax Romana*. From the outset then, it is worth noting that freedom of religion and security—to an equal or perhaps even greater extent than other rights or freedoms—have a particularly long and fraught history.

Second, there is no firm scholarly consensus on the definition of either religion or security; both remain "essentially contested" concepts, with a plurality of understandings and continuing disagreement about their respective normative moorings (see generally Gallie 1955, 167–198). Before questions concerning religion and security are—or can be—addressed, some conceptual housekeeping must take place. To begin with "security," the meaning of this concept has been neither univocal nor static. Security may refer to an internal state or disposition (as in the early Greek and Roman thought) or to an external condition characterised by the absence of threat; additionally, "secure" may describe a state of being, or it may refer to a socio-political *process*

DOI: 10.4324/9781003453086-3

by which this state is achieved (see Herington 2012). For our purposes here, the most inclusive and "common denominator" definition of security will be used: namely, security as the absence of, or "freedom from," threat (see for instance Buzan 2008, 11). The definition of "religion," meanwhile, is no less disputed, and varies widely between social scientists, theologians, philosophers, and legal scholars. As with security, I will adopt a broad and inclusive conceptualisation, capable of encompassing any system—from Christianity to Buddhism and atheistic Humanism—which has at its core values and beliefs which are non-empirical and morally evaluative in nature.

Security and freedom may be said, in general, to have an inverse relationship: to turn the dial up on one is to decrease it on the other, and *vice versa*. As a result, the goal of policymakers and courts is often framed as one of finding the right "balance" between the two. Conflict between security and religious freedom may be direct or indirect. Examples of *indirect* conflict might include someone being asked to remove religious clothing or items for identification and security purposes within a bank, or for health and safety reasons at a hospital. In such situations, the security measure being required (e.g. that the faces of all bank visitors be visible) does not imply a link between religiosity *per se* and threat: the concern that underlies the security policy is not people's beliefs, but their level of identifiability in an environment where personal concealment presents a particular risk. In situations of *direct* conflict, by contrast, a person's beliefs are the subject of a security concern. Two of the most prominent historical victims of such conflict—Socrates and Jesus Christ—have already been noted. Further examples might include the experience of Jehovah's Witnesses in many jurisdictions or Rohingya Muslims in Myanmar. It is the contours of direct tension and conflict which will be explored below.

1.1 The Perceived Value and Foundational Status of Security

While the attainment of proportionality or "balance" may be the intended goal of policymakers, theorists, and legal courts, the reality more often resembles a trumping of freedom by security. Theoretically, this prioritisation can be traced to political philosophy, where security has long been posited as the ontological antecedent to freedom, as well as its precondition and necessary entailment. In his *Two Treatises of Government* for instance, John Locke makes it clear that although human beings in their pre-contractual "State of nature" enjoyed freedom and rights by virtue of natural law and reason, they nevertheless lacked safety or security, and therefore consented to State governance "for the mutual preservation of their lives, liberties and estates" (Locke 2003, 325). Although Locke perhaps also intends this to constitute a limiting principle on civil power, it remains the case that security is both the foundation of and *raison d'être* for State government. Locke is often contrasted with the notoriously more pessimistic Thomas Hobbes; on this point, however, they appear to agree: the desire for personal security, and the necessity of such security for the enjoyment of liberty, is the catalyst for humanity's transition from the "State of nature" to the "social contract" of the State.

Under such framing, security acquires an existential significance and weighting. This resonates with common discourses on "security," in which the descriptive and the evaluative are readily conflated: simply to *describe* something as "secure," it is often presumed, is to detail something desirable as a *good*. Security as an empirical state—in terms of how things stand in relation to risks and threats—is therefore rarely distinguished from security as a normative state. As the "social contract" which underwrites the State is predicated upon the need to safeguard individuals' security, moreover, it follows that responding to significant security threats should logically take priority over other considerations, including other rights or liberties.

1.2 The Conceptual Entanglement of Security and Toleration with Trust

A further dimension of difficulty for toleration in relation to security concerns the conceptual and psychological entanglement of security and toleration with trust. The first element of this entanglement is that both toleration and a sense of security require *trust*. Put differently, a security concern is commonly understood to be underpinned by fear or *mis*trust: indeed, given this chapter's working definition of security as an absence of threat, it is almost tautologous to say that where trust is lacking in someone who can constitute a threat, others will perceive themselves to lack security.

In a similar vein, an attitude of toleration requires "at least a minimal level of trust" towards the other, *qua* other (Dees 1998, 83; see also Webb 1997, 420). Speaking of the rationality of toleration in terms of game theory (the well-known hypothetical of "prisoners' dilemma"), Richard H. Dees thus notes that if "two sides cannot trust each other at all, then they cannot form even the distant relationship that mere toleration demands" (Dees 1998, 83). A rational actor is highly unlikely to tolerate another if the trust which this involves is likely to result in a costly betrayal (Ibid). Moreover, as Diego Gambetta points out in his work on trust and game theory, for two parties to choose cooperation (or toleration) towards one another, the trust between them must be explicitly understood as mutual; otherwise, "the mere expectation that the second player might choose to defect can lead the first player to do so" (Gambetta 1990, 216). The danger, then, is not simply that of one party distrusting the other, but of either party wrongly second-guessing his counterpart's *perceptions* of his trustworthiness. On a conceptual and psychological level, one might say that for toleration to be possible, there must be trust all the way down.

Trust, therefore, appears to be necessary for security or toleration. However, whereas toleration requires trust, it is further argued that trust *entails* security. In "Trust as Noncognitive Security about Motives," Lawrence C. Becker posits that although trust may take various forms in different contexts—for instance, as interpersonal reliance (an ability to depend upon someone) or credulity (a belief in the veracity of someone else's reports)—trust as a "sense of security" (experiencing someone else's agency to be benevolent) is trust's primary and implicit form (Becker 1996, 45–46). Becker notes that when trust is conceived in terms of either *reliance* or *credulity*, it is too easily reducible to a function of deficiency in either power (reliance) or knowledge (credulity) between people: "trust" in these cases simply denotes that at least one person is either dependent or ignorant in relation to another (ibid, 47–52). Trust as a sense of security, by contrast, is a non-reducible and basic form which logically *precedes* both reliance and credulity in another.

Interrogating the concept of trust and its relationship to security in this way reveals another reason why a concern for security will often outweigh an interest in freedom and toleration. As we have seen, toleration requires trust. Trust, however, is predicated upon a "sense of security." Given such a dynamic, the odds in any conflict between security and toleration appear to be stacked against the latter. Insofar as mistrust both underpins and entails a concern for security and is antithetical to toleration, its presence in the public mind is highly likely to be a serious problem for toleration in any socio-political conflict with security.

1.3 The Compounding Factor of Religion

So far, little has been said about how religion (rather than that of security or toleration *per se*) might contribute towards the contours of tension between it and security. Here, I will sketch two points which I hope will subsequently be brought into clearer focus and detail.

First, compounding the problem of trust's necessity for toleration is the way in which religious beliefs have the potential to attract, and even cause, mistrust. The adjective "religious"—unlike, perhaps, "secure"—is not necessarily assumed to be positive in an evaluative sense; for some, religiosity carries negative connotations. In itself, this difference between "secure" and "religious" may be responsible for a socio-political centre of gravity which is inherently disfavourable to religion. Perhaps even more consequential, however, are some of the reasons for this disparity. In *Why Tolerate Religion?* Brian Leiter alleges that respect should not be the default attitude towards religion because religiosity entails not only "*false* or at least *unwarranted*" beliefs (Leiter 2014, xviii), but also beliefs which are "*perniciously* false," insofar as they have behavioural consequences which seem pernicious to unbelievers (ibid, 76). As others have noted, Leiter may here represent an outsider perspective on religion which does not necessarily track religious understandings (Devine 2013, 595–597; McConnell 2013, 770–810). It is worth noting, however, that even for those who self-identify as religious, Leiter's description is likely to be true for (at least *some*) *other* faiths. To connect this to our above focus, one broader observation from Leiter's account is that religious beliefs may undermine one person's capacity to sympathetically understand the reasons, intentions, or character of another's actions. Parsed differently, religious actors may present particular obstacles to trust, and therefore also to both toleration and security.

Second, Dees points out that where situations involve a conflict of irreconcilable and fundamental values, toleration may *itself* be intrinsically undesirable. If, for example, tolerating another is viewed as entailing a risk to the community's salvation or freedom, then the safeguarding of these fundamental values will entail an unwillingness to tolerate the other, regardless even of his/her trustworthiness (Dees 1998, 86–87). In such a situation, rejecting toleration *per se* would not be irrational, as toleration would itself entail a threat to fundamental values. Without a complete change in perspective or "moral conversion," Dees notes that to tolerate the other here would be an "act of lunacy" (ibid, 91). As Dees' example here of communal salvation (as a concern which renders toleration impossible) helps illuminate, certain religious beliefs constitute a serious security-*esque* impasse to tolerating others with contrary viewpoints (see also Waldron 2003).

This chapter will seek to explore the problematic depths of this situation with two very different philosophical attempts to navigate the tension between religious toleration and mistrust: John Locke and Jean-Jacques Rousseau, respectively.

2 Locke's Toleration and Rousseau's Civil Religion

2.1 The Mutual Separation of State and Belief: John Locke's Defence of Toleration

John Locke (1632–1704) is widely recognised as one of the original champions of "toleration" towards religious belief by civil government. The historical backdrop of Locke's arguments was a particularly turbulent period in England. Prior to writing both *An Essay Concerning Toleration* (*ECT*) (written in 1667; published posthumously) and *A Letter Concerning Toleration* (*LCT*) (1689), Locke experienced sectarian social-religious tensions which culminated in the English Civil War (1642–1651), the execution of

King Charles I, and a period of republic before the restoration of the monarchy in 1660. Such events during Locke's formative years no doubt motivated *ECT* and *LCT*, in which Locke presents a series of arguments for why religious beliefs amongst the citizenry should not be the object of governmental legislation or force.

The crux of Locke's arguments which do not explicitly appeal to religious axioms is that beliefs, *qua* beliefs, cannot be formed or altered through the coercive means of civil government. For Locke, the spheres of government and religion are wholly separate. While the former is concerned with the "civil interests" of "Life, Liberty, Health, and Indolency of Body"—which, Locke stresses, are wholly "confined to the care of the things of this World; and hath nothing to do with the World to come"—religion "consists in the inward and full persuasion of the mind" by which individuals concern themselves with their own moral character in this life, and their salvation in the next (Locke 2010, 12–15). The business of religion, Locke holds, is intrinsically individualistic, voluntarist, and self-regarding. Locke defines a Christian church as "a free and voluntary society" wherein "[n]o body is born a Member" and "every one joins himself voluntarily to that Society in which he believes he has found that Profession and Worship which is truly acceptable unto God" (ibid, 15). Those who believe in infant baptism (whereby pre-linguistic children are admitted to a religion), or who see church membership as a matter of ancestry, may take issue here with Locke's partisan, quintessentially Protestant conception of religious belief. Such objections notwithstanding, Locke's contention here is that civil government cannot affect religious beliefs, and religious beliefs, in turn, do not bear upon civil society; consequently, a policy of toleration towards belief is justified.

Before proceeding to offer a critique of Locke's framework, two notable exceptions to toleration within his argument should be underscored: atheists and Roman Catholics. Individuals in these classes are not afforded the same toleration as others because Locke believes that they cannot be trusted to keep oaths or promises. In the case of atheists, Locke writes that "[t]hose are not at all to be tolerated who *deny the Being of a God*. Promises, Covenants, and Oaths, which are the Bonds of Humane Society, can have no hold upon an Atheist" (ibid, 52–53 [emphasis original]). For Locke, the meta-ethical operating system of atheists—in particular, their explicit rejection of an absolute grounding for morality in a law-giving God, or of any post-mortem accountability for their actions—means that one cannot be confident that they will have sufficient moral motivation to keep their promises.

Similarly, because Roman Catholics have allegiance to a foreign figure whom they believe can be infallible (the Pope), Locke maintains in *ECT* that they must be considered "irreconcilable enemies [of the government]...whose fidelity you can never be secured," as they "can upon occasion dispense with all their oaths, promises and the obligations" (ibid, 123). In a letter to Henry Stubbe (whose 1659 work, *Essay in Defence of the Good Old Cause,* defended tolerating Catholics), Locke explicitly frames this exclusion of Catholics as a matter of "*the security of the Nation (the end of government)*" (Locke 2003, 138 [emphasis added]). The sticking point, for Locke, is Catholicism's belief in the divinely guaranteed infallibility of a foreign authority (ibid). This is also evident in Locke's more recently discovered manuscript, "Reasons for tolerateing [sic] Papists equally with others." In this work, which dates from 1667 to 1668 (significantly prior to *LCT*, but contemporaneous with *ECT*), Locke notably entertains reasons why Catholics *might* be tolerated. One should be cautious, however, of viewing this as evidencing an entirely different paradigm in Locke's thought: rather, implicit in most of Locke's "reasons" appears to be a utilitarian consideration of whether a policy of toleration might, in fact, be a good *strategy* for hastening Catholicism's *departure* from the State (for instance, by increasing Protestants' dislike of, and unity against, Catholics!) (see Walmsley and Waldmann 2019, 1111–1112). Although Catholics may be "sincerely conscientious," the case remains that because they believe themselves subject to "an authority supposed infallible," Catholics on Locke's view hold "dangerous & factious tenents in reference to the state" and cannot, therefore, be tolerated on the same terms as others (ibid, 1113–1115).

In the alleged untrustworthiness of atheists and Roman Catholics, then, Locke finds a ground to exclude a sizeable demographic (even in his time) from toleration.[1] In this, Locke concedes that people operating according to certain metaphysical and meta-ethical frameworks may, due to these frameworks, be reasonably distrusted—and thereby exempted from toleration on the grounds that they constitute a security threat. This concession constitutes a loose thread which once probed, I will now posit, causes Locke's defence of toleration to unravel.

To return to this defence, it has been observed that Locke's argumentation hinges upon two claims: first, that coercive means are not affective on belief, and, second, that true religious belief is sufficiently otherworldly and individualistic, such that it is not concerned with, or consequential upon, temporal matters. Unfortunately for Locke, both of these contentions may be challenged. Concerning the first, it is not at all clear that civil government cannot—even in a limited way—effectively impact upon belief: for instance, by curtailing the citizenry's exposure to particular beliefs or by tailoring their exposure to particular characterisations of these beliefs. Insofar as Locke's argument is predicated upon the view that the State *cannot* (rather than could, but *should not*) coerce beliefs; therefore, his perspective may be disconcertingly compatible with a State agenda of religious persecution (Waldron 1988; see also Bou-Habib 2003).

Perhaps even more significantly, Locke's argument also misconceives the potential impact of *belief* upon the civil sphere. For Locke, it will be recalled, the proper subject and remit of belief is individuals' personal salvation. In this, Locke's argument not only requires a narrow and specifically Protestant conception of religiosity and its boundaries but also hinges upon an eminently contestable proposition—even in relation to Protestant Christianity! Belief in an omnipotent and providential God, a transcendental ideal of goodness, eternal life, and the divine judgement of one's neighbours, all carry significant potential implications for how someone normatively relates to others in society and the civic apparatus of the State itself. For one thing, a belief in God clearly makes a substantial difference to a person's modal framework; if an all-powerful and conscious force operates within the universe, the perimeters of what is possible or impossible must be fundamentally redrawn: as the Christian scriptures put it, "with God all things are possible" (Matthew 19:26). Similarly, belief in an agent of transcendental goodness who can command or forbid certain acts may well have a significant bearing on the believer's meta-ethical calculus. Unlike the person who does not believe in an omnipotent and morally prescriptive agency, the religious believer may not act according to commonly held axioms of self-interest or altruism, thereby making his moral decision-making difficult to anticipate.

To give a more concrete example and bring this point into focus, while Protestant Christians may not believe in the infallibility of the Pope, they *do* commonly hold that God's will is infallible and that God might communicate His will directly to individuals. Given the possibility that this divine will might conflict with someone's ethical, social, or political obligations to others or civil authorities, it would seem to follow (on Locke's logic) that those who might consider themselves potential recipients of God's infallible instructions should also be excluded from toleration. The overall import of this, I argue, is not only that religious believers may interact with the public square in markedly different ways than their non-religious counterparts; it also bears upon the question of whether religious believers (of a non-Catholic variety) might have superseding metaphysical and moral reasons for breaking public oaths or promises, thereby rendering them untrustworthy.

In making a trust-based exception to toleration of atheists and Catholics, therefore, Locke inadvertently renders almost any religious faith a potential candidate for exemption. Put in the terms of this chapter's previous section, under Locke's argument, religious belief remains vulnerable against, and must defer to, security-orientated concerns about the trustworthiness of those operating according to religious principles. Such an outcome should perhaps be unsurprising, given the political theory that undergirds Locke's argument for toleration. As noted above, Locke sees individuals' mutual concern for the "preservation of their lives, liberties and estates" as the driving force behind humanity's departure from the State of nature. Civil authorities are entrusted with power not to "provide for the Truth of Opinions," but to ensure that individuals enjoy liberty within "the Safety and Security of the Commonwealth" (Locke 2010, 44–45; See also ibid, 105–106 and 113). Seen thus, one might say that Locke's "social contract" is in fact a "social-*security* contract." If the internal logic of the Lockean State is not to be undermined, therefore, *any* group who might threaten such security—for instance, by subscribing to beliefs which would make them unreliable underwriters of their own public declarations—cannot be tolerated.

2.2 The Need for Unity and the Intolerability of Intolerance: Jean-Jacques Rousseau's Case for Civil Religion

I now turn to a fundamentally different approach: Jean-Jacques Rousseau (1712–1778) and his case for a "civil religion." First, however, a fundamental contrast with Locke's political philosophy should be noted. In contradistinction to Locke, Rousseau in his *Discourse on the Origin and Foundation of Inequality among Mankind* (1753) describes humanity's "State of nature" as one of happiness, freedom, and solicitude. It is only after it becomes necessary to live in close relation to other humans, in Rousseau's view, that problems arise. Once in physical proximity, human beings "begin to consider different objects, and to make comparisons...jealousy kindles with love; discord triumphs; and the gentlest of passions requires sacrifices of human blood to appease it" (Rousseau 2002, 118). For Rousseau, the self-love (*amour de sui*) which characterises pre-societal human beings is non-pathological, whereas the comparison-based love (*amour-propre*) which arises from communal living is a "factitious sentiment" which frequently leads to conflicts that require resolution: either in the aforementioned "sacrifices" or in the advent of a form of collective belonging which is strong enough to override the factiousness generated by *amour-propre* (ibid, 146).

Unlike Locke then, Rousseau's rationale for civil government is not physical security *per se*, but the need for human beings to maintain a sense of cohesion and unity sufficient to offset comparison-derived resentment. While one might also characterise this as a concern for security, the cause of socio-political *in*security, for Rousseau, is significantly different. For Rousseau, beliefs—along with the desires which arise *from* those beliefs—constitute a cause of human beings' problems and must therefore be incorporated into the civic solution. It is in this context that Rousseau discusses the "social contract" which must pertain between human beings, as well as the need for a shared "civil religion" (*religion civile*) within the State.

Rousseau begins his case for a *religion civile* in the fourth book of *The Social Contract* by outlining a typology of religious beliefs and explicating how, in each case, these different types of belief (as he sees them) interface with the internal and external security of the State. With regard to Roman

Catholicism, Rousseau does not fundamentally disagree with Locke. Catholicism, as per Rousseau's view, is paradigmatic of a "religion of the priest," which endangers the social unity required for the State because it "gives men two codes of law, two rulers, and two countries, imposes contradictory duties on them, and makes it impossible for them to be believers and citizens" (Rousseau 2018, 70). What sets Rousseau apart from Locke, however, is that he also considers the possible security implications of a far broader set of belief systems.

Previously, Rousseau claims, religions and States went hand in hand, such that "there were as many gods as peoples" (ibid, 67). Put differently, Rousseau holds that all ancient (or pre-Christian) religions were *national* religions. From Rousseau's perspective, this conflation of religion and the State has both positive and negative aspects. On the positive side of the ledger, national religions ferment social unity and cohesion, as well as guarantee adherence to national laws, *qua* sacred dictates. This allegiance, however, comes at a steep cost, insofar as people can easily become violently exclusive and intolerant of others, resulting in a "*natural state of war* with everyone else, so that its security is deeply endangered" (ibid, 70 [emphasis original]).

Within Rousseau's schema, the advent of Christianity marks a dramatic change to humanity's religious landscape: for the first time, a "universal religion" existed which sought allegiance from all human beings, regardless of their social or geographic setting. In his *Letters Written from the Mountain* (*LWM*), Rousseau summarises the core message of Christianity thus:

> Embracing all men equally in his limitless charity, its divine Author came to lift the barrier that was separating Nations, and to unite the whole human race in a people of brothers...Such is the true spirit of the Gospel.
>
> *(Rousseau 2013a, 147)*

In its original and un-institutionalised form, Christianity on Rousseau's view represents a return to the "natural compassion" that human beings possessed before society and the State (Rousseau 2002, 126). Under Rousseau's conception, this universal "religion of man" is essentially the mirror image of "national religion," both in its advantages and in its security-related costs. Concerning the latter, Rousseau postulates that in the absence of any other political or metaphysical framework, Christian society would be "in a sense too sociable...inspiring humanity rather than patriotism, and tending to fashion men rather than Citizens" (Rousseau 2013a, 149). Christianity detaches people's desires from "all earthly things," which for Rousseau is "more contrary to the social spirit" than any other attitude (ibid). One prominent security danger which arises from this, for Rousseau, is that a single "self-seeker or hypocrite" could take advantage of the

Christians' apathy towards temporal matters, and rise to power (Rousseau 2018, 71). Once this occurs, the public would have difficulty rousing the animosity necessary to depose the usurper, as "Christian charity doesn't make it easy for a man to think ill of another man" (ibid). In short, Rousseau suggests that, in the absence of any other framework which might anchor believers in the temporal world and selectively channel their benevolence towards others, the "universal" religion of Christianity cannot provide the cohesion, unity, and temporal commitment necessary for the preservation and security of the State.

With this backdrop established, Rousseau makes his case for a shared "civil religion." In *LWM*, Rousseau responds to accusations that he is attempting to set up a rival religious camp to Protestant Christianity, by insisting that his proposal merely augments and *supplements* a (de-nationalised) Protestantism with additional faith-like commitments (Rousseau 2013a, 157–159). Among the "positive" dogmas of Rousseau's civil religion are belief in a providential and benevolent deity, the afterlife, moral justice, and "the sanctity of the social contract" (Rousseau 2018, 73). In *LWM*, Rousseau glosses these as "dogmas truly useful to either a universal or a particular society" (Rousseau 2013a, 148). As for what one *cannot* believe under the auspices of the civil religion, Rousseau lists only one dogmatic ground: the "exclusion of intolerance" (Rousseau 2018, 73; cf. Rousseau 2013a, 154 and 157). Civil and theological intolerance, Rousseau rules, cannot ultimately be separated:

> You can't possibly live at peace with people you regard as damned; loving them would be hating God who punishes them: we absolutely must either reform them or torment them...Anyone who ventures to say: "[o]utside the Church is no salvation" should be driven from the state.
>
> *(Rousseau 2018, 73)*

Rousseau thus advocates for a common commitment to particular beliefs in order to avoid the social-political insecurity which he perceives as endemic to internal features of "national religion," (pre-Christian religion) "religion of the priest" (Roman Catholicism), and "universal religion" (Christianity in its original form). In this, Rousseau considers the potential trust and security implications of a broader set of belief systems than Locke. Despite this, however, Rousseau's prescribed cure for the issues he perceives has its own difficulties—most notably, in the homogeneity it demands, the conscientious disobedience it rejects, and the severity of punishment it recommends. While the State cannot compel anyone to believe in the civil religion, Rousseau holds that it can and should "banish" unbelievers (Rousseau 2018, 72). Further, Rousseau holds that any individual who feigns adherence to the civil religion's "social sentiments," but proceeds to behave "as if he doesn't believe them" can be executed for having committed "the worst of all crimes—lying before the law" (ibid, 72–73). By professing to subscribe to the civil religion while behaving in a way which contradicts this claim, individuals reveal a dissonance between their words and actions: here too, it is evident that without trust, there can be no toleration.

Such a high civil liberties cost has rendered Rousseau's proposal deeply unpalatable for many commentators. In *Rousseau and the Modern State,* for instance, Alfred Cobban alleges that to assert that every individual must either subscribe to the civil religion or else find an alternative body politic is simply "ridiculous, and shows that Rousseau is still not fully emancipated from an artificial conception of the state" (Cobban 2019, 53). In sentiments which echo those of other commentators, Cobban concludes from this that

> in the end, one cannot pretend to regard the chapter on the Civil Religion as other than unfortunate: though so short...it helps us to understand why its author should have been so often regarded as the apostle of tyranny and an enemy to liberty in the state.
>
> *(ibid, 56)*

Furthermore, it may be objected that Rousseau's approach in fact ends up failing along similar lines to Locke. While Locke's defence of toleration may be said to demand a narrow (and specifically Protestant) form of religious belief, Rousseau's "civil religion" may be seen to require a similarly attenuated, denominationally partisan form of religiosity. Specifically, in claiming that because one cannot "live in peace" with others they regard as damned, "[a]nyone who ventures to say: '[o]utside the Church is no salvation' should be driven from the state," Rousseau's civil religion appears to amount to a prescriptive "civil universalism," under which only those religious belief systems that do not include any discriminating features or criteria for salvation can be tolerated. Seen on these terms, Rousseau's proposal requires a conception of religious belief which is as narrow and artificial as that required by Locke's defence of toleration.

In order to further examine this issue, the remainder of this chapter will scrutinise the theological lineage of Rousseau's provocative (yet often overlooked) "damned" and "damning" neighbour claims: namely, that no one can tolerate neighbours they believe are damned, and then that because of this, those who hold to such salvifically exclusory beliefs cannot themselves be tolerated; indeed, those who hold that "outside the church no salvation" exists should be "driven from the state."

3 The Intolerability of Rousseau's Damned Neighbours Further Explored

To begin by reiterating Rousseau's assertion in book 4 of *The Social Contract*:

> You can't possibly live at peace with people you regard [*croit*] as damned; loving them would be hating God who punishes them: we absolutely must either reform them or torment them.
>
> *(Rousseau 2018, 73)*

The sentiment closely echoes Rousseau's earlier sentiment in his epistolary novel, *Julie* (1761):

> [I]t is impossible for intolerance not to harden the soul. How can one tenderly cherish people whom one reproves? What charity can one retain among the damned? To love them would be to hate God who punishes them.
>
> *(Rousseau 1997, 573)*

Finally, in book 4 of *Emile* (1762) Rousseau similarly exclaims, in the voice of his "Savoyard Vicar," "God forbid that I ever preach the cruel dogma of intolerance to them, that I ever bring them to detest their neighbor, to say to other men, 'You will be damned'" (Rousseau 1979, 309).[2] Rousseau attaches a footnote to this declaration:

> It is this horrible dogma which arms men against one another and makes them all enemies of mankind [*ennemis du genre humain*]. The distinction between civil tolerance and theological tolerance is puerile and vain… Even angels would not live in peace with men they regarded as enemies of God [*ennemis de Dieu*].
>
> *(ibid)*

Rousseau does not elaborate on *why* he supposes that people cannot tolerate those they believe to be damned by God. In order to explore the possible underpinnings of Rousseau's claim, a detour into theology is necessary. Such a detour might admittedly seem strange, particularly to those who would be more inclined to describe Rousseau as an *anti*-theologian (see Armenteros 2016). To be sure, Rousseau's relationship with theology is a complicated one. Although as a young adult Rousseau spent approximately two months at a theological seminary with the intention of training to become a priest, he likens this experience to voluntarily seeking to be tortured, and confesses that during his instruction at the seminary, "I pretend to understand…and I understand nothing" (Rousseau 2013b, 100). Notwithstanding Rousseau's characterisation of his seminary experience, however, I posit that this background, along with Rousseau's continued engagement with church authorities later in life, nonetheless strongly suggests that he was familiar with the theological perspectives of his time, a familiarity, I further submit, which is evidenced in Rousseau's association in *Emile* of "the damned" with "enemies of God."

The descriptive association of the damned and "enemies of God" is immediately reminiscent of 16th–18th-century Calvinism, according to which human beings are predestined to be either one of the "elect"—destined by God to be saved through their faith in Him—or one of the damned. In his *Institutes of Christian Religion*, the founder of this tradition and Geneva's most famous figure from the Reformation, John Calvin (1509–1564), divides humanity into the "elect" (*elus*), on the one hand, and the damned or reprobates (*reprouves*), on the other. Without being called, chosen, or elected by God, the common fate of human beings is to be "darkness, the heirs of death, and the enemies of God" (Calvin 1863b, 78). This emphasis continues to manifest in the thought of Calvin's successors, including (as will be explored further below) one of the most prolific representatives of 18th-century Calvinism, the American theologian Jonathan Edwards (1703–1758). With this theological schema in mind, we can identify several ways in which the damned, *qua* damned, cannot be tolerated.

3.1 "Enemies of God": Trust, Toleration, and the (Im)moral Anthropology of the Damned

The damned, by definition, stand in a relation of opposition to God. In a sermon delivered in August 1736, Edwards gives an extensive account of how "Men Naturally Are God's Enemies." On Edwards' view, the default setting for human beings—that is, their state in the absence of special grace—is one of complete and irreparable cognitive, emotional, and volitional alienation from God. This alienation pervades every human faculty, including the affections, the understanding, and the will (Edwards 1974, 354–356). In each of these, human beings' enmity manifests in their failure to orientate towards God as the proper object of desire, attention, or obedience. Following the Christian tradition, Edwards traces the origins of this condition to humanity's "fall" from an original state of grace, to one of sinfulness and separation from God:

> [W]hen man fell, he departed from the true God, and the union that was between his heart and his Creator was broken: he wholly lost his principle of love to God. And henceforward man clave to other gods...When God

> ceased to be the [human being's] object of supreme love and respect, other things of course became the objects of it.
>
> *(Edwards 1974, 357)*

As the object of every human desire is always ultimately either God or an idol, the human heart displays its enmity towards God whenever it is orientated towards the latter (ibid). Human beings are thus naturally God's enemies, Edwards asserts, regardless of whether or not they consciously register this state (Edwards 1974, 360). Seen from a different angle, it might be said that even if the damned do not consciously and explicitly identify themselves as God's opponents, it remains true that God as their punisher opposes *them*. Opposition to God, moreover, constitutes enmity against someone who is infallible and morally perfect. In a sermon on Deuteronomy 13:5 (which states that "Prophets or dreamers of dreams shall be put to death"), Calvin thus warns against those who are "traitors to God" and "defacers of his majesty" (Calvin 2020). By virtue of the fact that such people present an affront to God, such people are *ipso facto* "enemies of mankind" and "worse than murderers" (ibid). As Rousseau's abovementioned comments in *The Social Contract*, *Julie*, and *Emile* appear to understand, such a theology presents an acute obstacle to the faithful's toleration of the damned. Insofar as believers align themselves in obedience and love with the will of God, they cannot (without dissonance) simultaneously tolerate those existing in a relation of enmity towards God.

A dominant theological rationale for not tolerating perceived heretics within the Church or civil society has been the potentially contaminating effects of their beliefs on others. Insofar as people may be attracted to the beliefs (or sinful behaviour) of the damned, the damned's presence within the community may pose a threat to their status as un-damned. For this reason, the damned (along with the heretical beliefs they are believed to purvey) have historically been likened to fire, corrupting ingredients, pestilence, or predatory animals, whose removal from the community is necessary for the defence of those who might otherwise be vulnerable to their salvation-threatening effects. Writing in the 4th century, the early church theologian Jerome (347–420) asserts that "perverse doctrine begins with one person and at first finds a favorable audience of barely two or three people," after which

> the cancer gradually festers in the body and, according to the familiar proverb, one sheep's disease pollutes the entire flock. Therefore, the ember must be extinguished as soon as it appears so that the house does not burn down. Yeast must be kept far from the batch [of flour] so that it does not spoil. Putrid flesh must be amputated so that the body does not rot. And

> the diseased animal must be sequestered from the sheepfolds so that the flocks do not die.
>
> *(Jerome and Hieronymus 2010, 210–211)*[3]

Such a concern is arguably compounded if (as in much of the Calvinist theological tradition) the condition of damnable sinfulness is viewed as a form of bondage, wherein the damned no longer have the volitional capacity to leave this state. From this perspective, the sinner no longer serves the interests of even himself; rather, he is in service to sin itself or to God's adversary, Satan. The damned, according to this view, are not self-regulating agents, but have instead become utilities of sin and the devil. Calvin thus likens sinfulness to a form of "dominion," in which the human being's will is entirely enslaved (Calvin 1863a, 246–247). From this perspective, the damned's dangerousness is heightened, as they lack control of themselves and are effectively functions of forces (sin/Satan) which are hostile to God and desirous that others also be damned. In relation to the issue of trust, it is difficult to understate the obstacles this belief presents. In a similar vein to Jerome, Calvin thus speaks of how

> Satan cometh with his poison and plagues, that he may destroy all. We see the flock of God troubled and tormented with ravenous wolves, that devour and destroy whatsoever they can. Must we be moved with mercy towards a wolf: and in the meantime let the poor sheep and lambs…perish? When we see any wicked man troubling the church either by offences or false doctrine, we must prevent him as much as lieth in our power…this I say, is our duty.
>
> *(Luther and Calvin 1829, 65–66)*

A belief that the damned are volitionally hostage to sin and/or Satan—and therefore existentially dangerous—would thus seem to constitute a further de facto reason against tolerating them. Even without such a belief, however, it may be argued that the doctrine of damnation always entails a certain "im(moral) anthropology" of the damned, which in turn undermines any prospect for mutual understanding or trust between the damned and the un-damned. If, for instance, it is held that with the same (or at least, an essentially equivalent) set of external circumstances, different people will make diametrically opposed decisions—such that one group will justly deserve eternal punishment, while the other will not—one might well ask: to what extent *can* those who believe themselves to be "saved" trust those they believe to be in the "other" category? For trust to be possible, people must believe that they are at least capable of understanding others' reasons for action. Given a belief in others' damnation, however, the possibility for such understanding would seem greatly compromised.

The demarcation of human beings into "saved" and "unsaved" implies two essentially and qualitatively different moral categories or classes. Indeed, under the auspices of theologies with which Rousseau would be familiar, these divisions are divinely predetermined from the moment of creation. This raises the spectre that those who are predestined for damnation and those who are not (the "elect") do not simply *become* different over the course of their lives; they are *created* differently by God. Clearly, a prenatal difference of this kind puts enormous strain on any notion that all human beings are, in some respect, essentially equal—or perhaps even *comparable*—in their moral nature. From this, it follows that a belief in others' damnation will be undermining for human solidarity and trust—and hence also for security and toleration.

In summation, although Rousseau's comments in *The Social Contract*, *Julie* and *Emile* that people cannot tolerate others whom they believe to be damned may appear cursory, they point towards an internal theological logic and coherence which may arguably deserve attention within a wider discussion of religion, civil society, and security. Within the context of 16th–18th-century Calvinism, it has been noted that for those who subscribe to this religious framework, proximity to the damned may be very difficult to tolerate, both because of the threat they may pose to the salvation of others and because they constitute an affront to the character or sovereignty of God. Seen in this light, Rousseau's insistence that those who believe their neighbours to be damned cannot themselves be tolerable perhaps becomes much more understandable (if not justified). I now turn to a possible way of reinterpreting the nature of Rousseau's remarks.

3.2 Rousseau's Condemnation of "no salvation outside the Church": Prescriptive Universalism, or a Question of Epistemology?

In the paragraph which follows Rousseau's claim in *The Social Contract* that people cannot tolerate others they believe to be damned and so cannot *themselves* be tolerated, Rousseau writes that "[a]nyone who ventures to say: 'Outside the Church is no salvation' [*Hors de l'Église, point de salut*] should be driven from the state," unless of course the State is co-extensive with the Church and under the Pontiff's control (Rousseau 2018, 73). Rousseau's subsequent aside reference to the Pope here appears to suggest that his chief interlocutor might be the Roman Catholic Church, to which the doctrinal maxim that there is "no salvation outside the Church" (*extra Ecclesiam nulla salus*) was commonly ascribed. To take one prominent example, in his defence of the Catholic faith the theologian (and former bishop of Geneva) St. Francis De Sales likens the Church to the biblical "Ark" on which a select number of creatures were saved from a global flood: "[O] utside the true Church there is no salvation, out[side] of this Ark every one is lost" (de Sales 1886, 59). On this view—which in one form or another has been expressed by Roman Catholic doctrine since at least the 13th century—there can be no salvation outside the Church, as it is this institutional structure which is the sole vehicle through which salvation is communicated and transmitted by God.

The contention that there is "no salvation outside the Church" was not, however, exclusive to Roman Catholic thought; it was also found in Calvin.[4] As observed above, Calvin's theological framework divides humanity into the "elect" who are preordained by God for salvation, on the one hand, and the damned who are "enemies of God," on the other. Such a stark divide raises the urgent question: how can a person *discern* who is a member of the elect, and is an enemy of God? In the fourth book of his *Institutes*, Calvin provides the resources for answering this question. Although absolute knowledge of the elect (the "invisible Church") is reserved for God alone, "[t]he knowledge of his body [the Church], inasmuch as he knew it to be more necessary for our salvation, [God] has made known to us by surer marks": namely, the external operations of the "visible Church" (Calvin 1863b, 289). The visible Church, for Calvin, is the best means of discerning insiders and outsiders of the Christian faith. For this reason, Calvin also opines that those who leave the Church "deserve to be crushed by the full thunder of [God's] anger. No crime can be imagined more atrocious" (ibid, 290).

Membership of the Church, for both Catholics such as de Sales and Protestants such as Calvin, was thus regarded as the best available metric of someone's salvific status: in other words, the doctrine of *extra Ecclesiam nulla salus* provided a yardstick by which the damned and the saved could be identified and counted. It is in large part for this reason, I suggest, that Rousseau objects to the doctrine and why he states that anyone who holds it deserves banishment from the State. Rousseau does not deny that God will justly inflict punishment on the wicked while rewarding the good; indeed, these are beliefs which he explicitly mentions in *The Social Contract* as being *components* of his civil religion. What Rousseau contests is not belief in the damned, perhaps, but confidence in their identities. Prior to condemning the sentiment that "you are damned" on similar terms to *The Social Contract*, Rousseau's Savoyard Priest cautions Emile that "[o]ne ought always to be modest and circumspect, my child—to respect in silence what one can neither reject nor understand, and to humble oneself before the great Being *who alone knows the truth*" (Rousseau 1979, 308 [emphasis added]). Rousseau's concern here and in *The Social Contract*, it might be argued, is not that doctrinal beliefs be either prescribed or excluded *per se*, but that they be held with enough epistemic humility that the "saved" and "damned" (and thus enemies of God) cannot be clearly demarcated: such knowledge belongs to God, "who alone knows the truth."

This case is further strengthened by consideration of Rousseau's comments in *Julie*. After stating that one cannot tolerate those one reproves or regards as "damned," Rousseau's Julie goes on to write, "Do we then wish to be human? Let us judge deeds and not men" (Rousseau 1997, 573). Rather than judging the moral nature of others according to a theological metric, Rousseau's character here urges us to "leave aside the subtle interpretation of dogmas" and instead orientate ourselves according to truths ascertained through practical reasoning about how we should behave (ibid). Instead of immersing oneself in the "bottomless and shoreless abysses of metaphysics" and engaging in "disputations over [God's] essence," one should be content with the more modest affirmation that "[w]e do not know what [God] is, but we know that it is" (ibid, 574). Although Rousseau is often characterised as an anti-religious figure, his sentiments here resonate with a long tradition within Christian theology of negative or "apophatic" theology, which places its emphasis on the unknowability and transcendence of God *qua* God, even while affirming His existence.

Rousseau's plea for epistemic humility echoes that of the Genevan universalist theologian Marie Huber (1695–1753), whose work influenced Rousseau's "Confession of a Sayoyard Priest" in *Emile* and whose 1733 État des âmes séparées des corps ("State of souls separated from their bodies") was owned by Rousseau. In her *Letters Concerning the Religion Essential of Man* (1738), Huber posits to the reader, "[l]et us grant it, we should be ignorant of many things…Men would not damn one another; that Privilege would be unknown to them. They would be as little acquainted with that [as] of tyrannizing over the Consciences of Men" (Huber 1830, 68–69). Such an angle, I suggest, provides the resources for nuancing Rousseau's claims and thus of potentially salvaging his civil religion—at least, in this respect. From this, I further propose that this aspect of Rousseau's civil religion may be reformatted as a form of "doubtful civil belief," or perhaps even as "civil apophatism."[5]

4 Conclusion

As outlined above, Locke and Rousseau represent two very different attempts to navigate the potential for tension and conflict between religion and security. In Locke's theory of toleration, on the one hand, we have the grandfather of attempts within Western liberalism to assert that religious individuals and churches can co-exist within a religiously inert State. Under this view, religious belief and civic power can be separated into two distinct, hermetically sealed spheres of agency. As the salvific concerns of religion and the civic toolkit of the State do not—and indeed, *cannot*—impact upon one another, they need not conflict. Against this, it has been argued that Locke's paradigm succeeds only on a narrow, denominationally specific, attenuated view of religious belief *qua* belief. Certain beliefs, particularly those which entail fundamentally different framings of human identity or nature, will inevitably have implications for the level of trust—and therefore tolerance—between members of the same citizenry. The content of belief or disbelief matters. In positing two trust-based exceptions to toleration in Roman Catholicism and atheism, Locke may be said to implicitly recognise this, but fails to adequately extend the logic of his own thought further.

Rousseau, on the other hand, provides the foundations for a more communitarian attempt to broker the tension between religion and security. Unlike Locke, Rousseau presents a typology of religious belief which, however sociologically flawed or incomplete, nevertheless perceives that forms of religious belief may have potentially problematic implications for civic security. Although Rousseau's proposal is not without its own difficulties—particularly in the civic enforcement he recommends—it nevertheless arguably recognises and frames the problem of religion and security in a way which is more intriguing than Locke. Religious beliefs, from Rousseau's perspective, *do* have effects within the civil sphere, including the level of trust between citizens and their sense of security. As explored above, this is perhaps most poignantly the case with one particular belief that Rousseau singles out: namely, the belief that others are "damned" by God. While Rousseau's apparent prescription of intolerance towards those who hold this belief first appears to render his model of religious belief just as narrow and theologically partisan as Locke's, I have suggested by tracing the theological backdrop to his thought that Rousseau's emphasis is not necessarily upon the belief *per se*, but upon the epistemological certainty with which it is held concerning others' salvation. While space here, unfortunately, does not allow for further development of this point, it may be suggested that thus recasting Rousseau's proposal as one of "doubtful civil belief" might at least lend itself to more promising directions.

Notes

1 In relation to both atheists (see, for instance, John Stewart Mill's *On Liberty*) and Roman Catholics (as in the abovementioned Henry Stubbe), Locke's contentions about trustworthiness may of course be empirically challenged.

2 Some later French editions of *Emile* and their English translations here add: "no salvation outside of the church." This sentence, however, does not appear to have been in editions during Rousseau's lifetime, and may have been added later to further the impression that Rousseau's critique was specifically or exclusively aimed at the Roman Catholic Church.

3 See also Thomas Aquinas (1225–1274) in his *Summa Theologica*, II-II, q. 11, a. 3. Citing Jerome in support, Aquinas argues that unrepentant heretics should not be tolerated.

4 See also Article 28 of Protestant Christianity's *Belgic Confession* (1561), which states that "We believe, since [the Church] is the assembly of the redeemed and there is no salvation outside of it [*qu'il n'y a point de salut hors*]" (French in parenthesis from the 1580 translation).

5 For a brief account of the "mystical sensibilities" which may be discerned within Rousseau's thought, see Armenteros (2016, 596–599).

References

Armenteros, C. (2016) 'The Anti-Theological Theology of Jean-Jacques Rousseau', in *The Oxford Handbook of Early Modern Theology, 1600–1800*, edited by Lehner, U.L., Muller, R.A. and Roeber, A.G. Oxford: Oxford University Press, 594–600.

Becker, L.C. (1996) 'Trust as Noncognitive Security about Motives', *Ethics*, 107 (1): 43–61.

Bou-Habib, P. (2003) 'Locke, Sincerity and the Rationality of Persecution', *Political Studies*, 51 (4): 611–626.

Buzan, B. (2008) *People, States & Fear: An Agenda for International Security Studies in the Post-Cold War Era*. Colchester: ECPR.

Calvin, J. (1863a) *Institutes of the Christian Religion: Volume 1*, translated by Beveridge, H. Edinburgh: T. & T Clark.

Calvin, J. (1863b) *Institutes of the Christian Religion: Volume 2*, translated by Beveridge, H. Edinburgh: T. & T Clark.

Calvin, J. (2020) *The Collected Works of John Calvin*, translated by Beveridge, H. et al. Hastings: Delphi Classics.

Cobban, A. (2019) *Rousseau and the Modern State*. London: Routledge.

Dees, R.H. (1998) 'Trust and the Rationality of Toleration', *Noûs*, 32 (1): 82–98.

de Sales, S.F. (1886) *The Catholic Controversy*. London: Burns and Oates.

Devine, P. (2013) 'Why Tolerate Religion? By Brian Leiter', *Analysis*, 73 (3): 595–597.

Edwards, J. (1974) *The Works of Jonathan Edwards: Volume Two*. Edinburgh: Banner of Truth Trust.

Engh, M.J. (2010) *In the Name of Heaven: 3000 Years of Religious Persecution*. Amherst, NY: Prometheus.

Gallie, W.B. (1955) 'Essentially Contested Concepts', *Proceedings of the Aristotelian Society*, 56 (1): 167–198.

Gambetta, D. (ed.). (1990) *Trust: Making and Breaking Cooperative Relations*. Oxford: Blackwell.

Herington, J. (2012) 'The Concept of Security', in *Ethics and Security Aspects of Infectious Disease Control: Interdisciplinary Perspectives*, edited by Selgelid, M. and Enemark, C. Farnham: Ashgate, 7–26.

Huber, M. (1830). *Letters Concerning the Religion Essential to Man*, translated from the French [translator not given]. London: Printed by Millar, A.

Jerome, St. and Hieronymus, S.E. (2010) *Commentary on Galatians*, translated by Cain, A. Washington, DC: Catholic University of America Press.

Leiter, B. (2014) *Why Tolerate Religion?* Princeton, NJ: Princeton University Press.

Locke, J. (2003) *Political Writings*. Indianapolis, IN: Hackett Publishing.

Locke, J. (2010) *A Letter Concerning Toleration and Other Writings*. Indianapolis, IN: Liberty Fund.

Luther, M. and Calvin, J. (1829) *A Selection of the Most Celebrated Sermons of M. Luther and J. Calvin*. New York: Compiled and published by Bentley, R.

McConnell, M.W. (2013) 'Why Protect Religious Freedom?', *The Yale Law Journal*, 123 (3): 770–810.

Rousseau, J.-J. (1979) *Emile or On Education*, edited and translated by Bloom, A. New York: Basic Books.

Rousseau, J.-J. (1997) *Julie or the New Heloise: Letters of Two Lovers Who Live in a Small Town at the Foot of the Alps*, translated by Stewart, P. and Vache, J. Hanover, NH: Dartmouth College Press.

Rousseau, J.-J. (2002) 'Second Discourse: Discourse on the Origen and Foundations of Inequality Among Mankind', in *The Social Contract: And, The First and Second Discourses*, edited by Dunn, S. New Haven, CT: Yale University Press, 69–148.

Rousseau, J.-J. (2013a) *Letter to Beaumont, Letters Written from the Mountain, and Related Writings*, edited by Kelly, C. and Grace, E., translated by Kelly, C. and Bush, J.R. Hanover, NH: University Press of New England.

Rousseau, J.-J. (2013b) *The Confessions and Correspondence, Including the Letters to Malesherbes*, edited by Kelly, C. et al., translated by Kelly, C. Hanover, NH: University Press of New England.

Rousseau, J.-J. (2018) *On the Social Contract*. The Augustine Press.Waldron, J. (1988) 'Locke: Toleration and the Rationality of Persecution', in *Justifying Toleration: Conceptual and Historical Perspectives*, edited by Susan Mendus. Cambridge: Cambridge University Press, 61–68.

Waldron, J. (2003) 'Toleration and Reasonableness', in *The Culture of Toleration in Diverse Societies: Reasonable Tolerance*, edited by McKinnon, C. and Castiglione, D. Manchester: Manchester University Press, 13–37.

Walmsley, J.C. and Waldmann, F. (2019) 'John Locke and the Toleration of Catholics: A New Manuscript', *The Historical Journal*, 62 (4): 1093–1115.

Webb, M.O. (1997) 'Trust, Tolerance, and the Concept of a Person', *Public Affairs Quarterly*, 11 (4): 415–429.

2

RELIGIOUS FREEDOM, HUMAN SECURITY, AND HUMAN FRATERNITY

Is Religious Freedom a Forgotten Freedom within the Human Security Framework?

Elena López Ruf

1 Introduction. Human Insecurity: Eclipse of Humanity or of God?

At the end of the Second World War, there was a sense that humanity had been forsaken by God. From the deepest silence of existence, David's Psalm 22, "My God, my God, why have you abandoned me?" (Psalm 22: 1) resonated strongly from the abyss of human suffering. This feeling was expressed by the Jewish philosopher Martin Buber as the *eclipse of God*, expressing the idea that God had hidden from humanity and became an inscrutable mystery for it: "Eclipse of the light of heaven, eclipse of God – such is indeed the character of the historic hour through which the world is passing" (2016, pp. 49–50).

A few years later, Rabbi Heschel, one of the most influential voices of Jewish post-Holocaust theology, stated that this historical hour was characterized by the *eclipse of humanity* rather than the *eclipse of God*:

> Today, it is the humanity of man that is no longer self-evident, and the issue we face is how can a human being achieve certainty of his humanity.
>
> *(1965, p. 25)*

From one of the darkest nights of history, the reality that human beings, forsaken by God, had been left alone to their own devices and vulnerable to any threat became stronger. Unprotected, without knowing how to keep faith before a "silent God" (Schorsch, 2005),[1] and with almost no faith in the "humanity of man" (Heschel, 1965, p. 25), the peoples of the world discovered together a renewed spirit of union and trust that forged a promise

DOI: 10.4324/9781003453086-4

for a "world made new" (Glendon, 2002). Philosophers, politicians, legal experts, diplomats, economists, and scientists started to work as designers of the international architecture for a new world order by developing the legal, political, and economic framework to carry on the promise of protection, security, peace, and freedom.

A legal revolution was taking place with a new world order in which: (1) war was outlawed; (2) human rights became the "Magna Carta" of international relations; and (3) a new framework of international cooperation was set for the development and the flourishing of humanity (Hathaway and Shapiro, 2017).

Peace and the promotion of human welfare were the main issues of the postwar period, and the responses in advancing them were the seeds of two reconceptualized and evolved concepts central to the present global agenda: (1) sustainable development and (2) human security.

During this same period, new religious dynamics were simultaneously emerging, characterized, by (1) the emergence of new religious actors[2]; (2) the association of religion to violence and conflicts; and (3) religious institutions' openness to interreligious and ecumenical dialogue as well as the institutionalization of multiple joint initiatives and encounters.

Many of these new religious organizations were relief services involved in assisting the postwar humanitarian crisis and have today become key pillars of the global humanitarian system and of the cooperation for the development of peoples within the framework of international cooperation.

At that time, however, there was no attempt *to take religion seriously* because of secularism. The secularist thesis coined in modern times stated that the development and modernization of societies would be marked by secularization and, therefore, the disappearance of religion. Thus, the remaining premise was, "Being modern means being secular, and in consequence, being religious means not to be completely modern" (Casanova, 2014, p. 24). Religion has been traditionally excluded and marginalized even more in international relations. Based on the secularism of the State(s) and the "Westphalia presumption" (Thomas, 2005, p. 75), the Western model of the relationship between the state and religions has been replicated within the international realm (Calo, 2009).

Since the Cold War and especially after the Twin Towers attacks in 2001, the view of religion's resurgence as a cause of terrorism, violence, and international instability has been reinforced. Furthermore, the global discourse has been fragmented by identity politics (Fukuyama, 2018), religious nationalism (Neo and Scharffs, 2020, p. 10), and civilizational narratives (Huntington, 1993), fueling discrimination, hate speech, and conflicts.

But it was not until recent decades that scholars acknowledged that the post-Cold War period was also characterized by the so-called process of "post-secularism" (Habermas, 2006), "the return from exile" (Hatzopoulos and Petito, 2003), or "the resurgence of religion" (Thomas, 2010). After the Twin Towers terrorist attack in 2001, two basic attitudes have emerged. First, many scholars and policymakers reinforced a negative view of the religious phenomenon as they saw it as a cause of international instability on the global scene, mainly from the association of terrorism with religious fundamentalisms, as a "Revenge of God" (Gilles, 1994), or the concretization of the "Clash of Civilizations" (Huntington, 1993). Second, and an opposite view, Appleby featured the resurgence as the "Ambivalence of the Sacred" (1999). This approach has been recognized as a remarkable contribution as it has given space to the flourishing of fields around religion and peace, "religion and development" (Deneulin and Rakodi, 2011), "religion and international relations" (Kulbálková, 2009), and initiatives for a "dialogue of civilizations" (Petito, 2016).

More recently, the fields of law, policy, and religion studies have witnessed a profound transformation over the last three decades, looking beyond the traditional approach focused on the paradigms of the relationship between the State and religious communities, to include the right of religious freedom, the role of religion in the public space, and the formulation and implementation of a variety of measures, policies, and laws to ensure both freedoms of religion or belief and security. To pursue this, a prolific and consistent contribution has been made to advance the understanding of the right of religious freedom and how it interrelates with human rights at the international and national levels. Sometimes their contesting claims have been characterized as a "clash of universalisms" (Sachedina, 2007), and both religion and human rights "became a problem for the courts" (McCrudden, 2018, p. 4). To face the challenge of living together in diversity and promote a better understanding, there is a remarkable comparative analysis concerning the interplay between religious rules, state law, and legal pluralism (Bottoni et al., 2016) and, on the other hand, more focus on knowing and understanding the religious legal systems and studying the regulatory instruments of religious communities (Doe, 2018).

These initiatives and studies have revealed a new approach to policy in the relationship between religion and security. Religious actors are not seen solely as the cause of political instability, as historically believed, but as partners in the promotion of security and peace. Moreover, as Petito highlights, this approach moves beyond the securitization of religion, in which religion is a problematic issue for the nation-state that needs to manage and control; it also strengthens the promotion of religious freedom, recognizing religious actors as partners and responsible protagonists (Petito et al., 2021, p. 16).

At this point, we could agree with Koskenniemi that "Today religion is everywhere" (2017, p. 4). However, the study of the relationship between international law and religion has not been explored in-depth and is still uncharted territory.

This chapter explores the role of religion in promoting human security from the normative dimension of its teachings and its interplay with the corpus of international law regarding security issues.

Part I analyzes the dynamic and multifaceted notion of security with the human security approach when it emerged within the framework of the United Nations (UN) system and international law. Part II explores the relationship between religious freedom and human security in three different directions: (1) religion as a driver of insecurity, (2) how religious actors contribute to human security, and (3) the normative dimension that refers to the teachings of religious traditions and their intersection with security issues. Part III examines the notion of human fraternity based on the Human Fraternity Document for World Peace and Living Together, jointly signed by Sheikh Ahmed Al-Tayeb and Pope Francis in 2019 to promote "a culture of tolerance, acceptance of others, and of living together peacefully." The Document of Abu Dhabi inspired Pope Francis's encyclical Fratelli Tutti, in which he explains the meaning of human fraternity from the Catholic Church's teaching. I will consider this by revisiting the parable of the Good Samaritan as a religious narrative of human insecurity. Finally, it highlights that Human Security and Human Fraternity could be complementary frameworks for the design and the implementation of concrete and new creative strategies and policies for "living together in diversity" and "in spirit of fraternity."

PART I

2 Striving for Survival: From Outlawing War to Freedom from Fear and Want

As Jeremy Waldron suggested, if there is any interest in finding a "theorist of security" in history, look to Thomas Hobbes (Waldron, 2006, p. 456). Modern states have been built on the theory of Hobbes' *Leviathan* that guaranteed security by protecting individuals from the violence of others, and it was seen as the only alternative for the survival of the individual in a scenario of total war. The Hobbesian Leviathan works where the power of the sovereign state is circumscribed. It monopolizes the distinction between the legitimate or nonlegitimate use of force, and within its extension, it defends its own citizens and national interests from foreign or hostile threats. Traditional studies of security highlight the connection between national security policies with sovereignty and the use of military force to defend the integrity of borders, fight crimes, and suppress internal violent conflicts that threaten public order. In this framework, security is related to self-preservation and protection from violent death from insiders or outsiders. The state controls what happens within its territory, and war is a legitimate weapon to defend or attack any enemy. Even more, "War was an instrument of justice" (Hathaway and Shapiro, 2017, p. xv).

But in 1928 after the devastation of the First World War, the Paris Peace Pact was signed (also known also as the Briand–Kellog Pact and the General Pact for the Renunciation of War). For the first time in the history of the world, war was declared illegal. Skeptics dismissed it thinking it was unenforceable or "singularly vacuous" (Hathaway and Shapiro, 2017, p. xii). Therefore, the Pact failed to end wars. It went unnoticed at the time that the Pact was a powerful and inspiring force because as Shapiro and Hathaway explain, as states renounced the principal means they had used to resolve their disputes – war – the challenge was to discover what would fill that vacuum and how they should respond to illegal behavior with novel measures and mechanisms. The Pact "did not end war between states, but marked the beginning of the end – and, with it, the replacement of one international order with another" (2017, p. xiii).

Throughout the process of outlawing war, international law began a world-creating momentum, and legal philosophers, diplomats, and politicians played a key role. But it took more than 20 years to see it finally realized.

> The period between the First and Second World Wars was not the intellectual vacuum it is often thought to be. During this period international relations scholars believed that democracy, international understanding, arbitration, national self-determination, disarmament, and collective security were the most important ways to promote international peace and security. They therefore tended to emphasize international law and organization rather than military force.
>
> *(Baldwin, 1995, p. 119)*

As the Second World War was coming to an end, many questions arose as to how to consolidate international peace. How could the Peace Pact be enforced without brute strength? In what circumstances would war be legitimate? Did the Pact reformulate the neutrality doctrine? How should states deal with war criminals? Did an international court have the authority to prosecute war criminals? Were there moral limits to the law? Could extreme injustice be legislated? What are the legal and moral foundations of societies?

Many draft proposals, scholarly papers, legal memos, and political speeches were formulated that shaped a continuum conversation among lawyers, statesmen, and philosophers with different visions of law and how to design for the new world order.

Roosevelt's "Four Freedoms" speech, the Peace Pact, the Atlantic Charter, the UN Charter, the Universal Declaration of Human Rights (UDHR), Bretton Woods, and the Marshall Plan were many of the different legal and political responses to the Second World War and have framed the international architecture of today's global (dis)order.

The Charter of the UN was signed on 25 June 1945, in San Francisco, and the "peoples of the United Nations" affirmed in the Preamble their "faith in fundamental human rights," and announced the "advent of a world in which human beings shall enjoy the freedom of speech and belief and freedom from fear and want" (*United Nations General Assembly*, 1948b).

On that same occasion, Great Britain, the Soviet Union, and the United States introduced their collective security arrangement for the postwar period and what would become the main purpose of the UN: to provide mechanisms for settling disputes between nations and to forestall future aggression. But as the conference started, some critics from Latin America[3] and Asia came up with a broader vision: that the new international organization would protect human rights[4] even in peacetime (Glendon, 2003). As Glendon points out, it was the Lebanese philosopher Charles Malik who expressed that the proposed agenda was too narrow and stressed that measures for the maintenance of peace and security would not be sufficient if the causes of conflict and aggression were not addressed (Glendon, 2011). What were the underlying causes of conflict and aggression that Malik refers to?

> Men and women throughout the broken world were yearning not only for peace, but for a better and freer existence. By destroying lives, leveling cities, and displacing peoples, the two world wars had unsettled fixed, familiar patterns of living.(…) More than 250 million people were still living under colonial rule, and millions more belonged to disadvantaged minorities in the United States, Latin America, and the Soviet Union.
>
> *(Glendon, 2002, p. 10)*

Throughout these discussions, tensions about the understanding and scope of security issues were evident. These differences would later be known as, on the one hand, the traditional paradigm of security, and, on the other, the new paradigms that conceived a broader notion of security or comprehensive security (Baldwin, 1995, pp. 133–135).

The traditional security paradigm was characterized by conceiving the national security of the sovereign state as the main subject; the object of security issues was focused on the use of military force, conflicts between states, and the use of weapons of mass destruction. In this sense, national security, confined to domestic affairs of states, is differentiated from international security, which refers to issues of concern that transcend the spheres of the state, for example, the atomic bomb and nuclear arms, and the proliferation of weapons of mass destruction, among other threats.

As countries faced the transition to the post-bipolar world era, the nature of security threats changed, which permeated the limits of the nation-state, and there was an increasing acknowledgment of their mutual interdependence. The traditional understanding of security was changing.

3 Human Security: From Freedom from Fear and Want to Freedom from Indignity

The roots of the paradigm shift, from the traditional to a more comprehensive notion of security, can be traced back to 1941, when President Roosevelt delivered his famous speech, "The Four Freedoms," sharing his liberal vision of a world in which the four fundamental human freedoms would prevail: freedom from want, freedom from fear, freedom of expression, and freedom of religion (1941). Based on this speech, as Lombardi and Wellman suggest, a new movement of human security emerged (2012, p. 3) with the objective "to protect the vital core of all human lives from critical pervasive threats, in a way that is consistent with long-term human fulfillment" (Alkire, 2003).

However, it was difficult to arrive at a definition of human security, which has oscillated between narrow and broad definitions.

Today, it provides a "multidimensional analytical framework". It is a "comprehensive methodology" approach that allows for a broad perspective and "a new way of thinking about the range of challenges the world faces in the 21st century and how the global community responds to them" (*United Nations Trust Fund for Human Security*, 2016, pp. 6–7). It has five fundamental principles which are mutually reinforced: people-centered; comprehensive; context-specific; prevention-oriented; protection and empowerment.

First, the Human Security approach is people-centered, as it considers the broad range of conditions that threaten the survival, livelihood, and dignity of people and their communities. Second, by recognizing the complexity and interconnectedness of the challenges and threats that people face today, this approach seeks a comprehensive response, ensuring coherence, eliminating duplication, and advancing integrated solutions that result in more effective improvements in people's lives and communities. Third, as a dynamic and flexible framework that captures variations over time and within and across countries in addressing people's insecurities, the Human Security approach enables the development of context-specific responses embedded in local realities. Fourth, by addressing the root causes behind ongoing and future challenges, the human security approach goes beyond quick responses. The prevention-oriented principle helps to build sustainable and resilient responses and promotes the development of early warning mechanisms that help to mitigate the impact of current threats and prevent future challenges. For this to happen, it is crucial that people and their communities respond to their needs and those of others. And, fifth, the principle of protection and empowerment evidence the dual policy framework of human security which combines top-down norms including the establishment of the rule of law and good governance, with a bottom-up focus supporting the important roles of individuals and communities as key stakeholders in defining and implementing their essential freedoms. While governments retain the primary role and responsibility for ensuring the survival, livelihood, and dignity of their citizens, since human security is not a substitute for state security, the human security approach seeks partnerships between governments, international and regional organizations, and civil society, creating synergies that can achieve far greater impact in addressing contemporary threats and challenges (*United Nations Trust Fund for Human Security*, 2016).

An in-depth analysis of the history of this paradigm would clearly exceed the purpose of this chapter. It is relevant, however, to highlight at least four milestones in its development: the Human Development Report 1994; the Commission on Human Security (*CHS*, 2003) created after 2000; the General Assembly Resolution in 2012; and the Human Development 2022 Special Report (SR) on Human Security.

The *Human Development Report: New Dimensions of Human Security*, released by the UN in 1994, introduced the concept of human security within the broader framework of human development and proposed that as "the dark shadows of cold war recede" (*United Nations Development Program*, 1994, p. 2), it was time to focus attention on the daily insecurities that people were facing. The Sen-Ottawa Commission enriched and deepened this vision (*Commission on Human Security*, 2003). But it was not until the UN-GA Resolution 66/290 in 2012 that the notion of Human Security was mainstreamed by stating "human security is an approach to assist Member States in identifying and addressing widespread and cross-cutting challenges to the survival, livelihood, and dignity of people" (2012). Furthermore, after the adoption of Agenda 2030 for Sustainable Development in 2015 (*United Nations General Assembly*, 2015b), the Sendai Framework for Risk Disasters (*United Nations General Assembly*, 2015a), and the Agenda for Humanity of the World Humanitarian Summit in 2016 (*United Nations*, 2016), Human Security has been revitalized and understood as an approach to be integrated into policy design which, rather than being a competing approach, enhances and reinforces Sustainable Development Goals (SDGs) "to ensure that no one is left behind" (*United Nations General Assembly*, 2015b).

In January 2022, United Nations Development Programme (UNDP) released its 2022 Special Report on Human Security entitled *New Threats to Human Security in the Anthropocene: Demanding Greater Solidarity* (*United Nations Development Program*, 2022). If the 1994 Report refocused the debate on security from territorial security to the security of people inviting us to look beyond the protection of the nation-state, this SR aims to update the definition of human security and understand what it implies for the context of the Anthropocene, in which humans are driving planetary change and alteration of the biosphere.

The SR identifies a new generation of interacting threats: the downsides of digital technology, violent conflicts, horizontal inequalities, and evolving challenges to healthcare systems. Analyzing these threats to human security, one of the surprising findings of the report is the low sense of safety and security perception in six out of seven people worldwide – including the wealthiest countries – just before the outbreak of the Covid-19 pandemic (*United Nations Development Program*, 2022, p. 13). It is also interesting to note that the perceptions of human insecurity are associated with low interpersonal trust which could affect the implementation of responses and cooperation (*United Nations Development Program*, 2022, p. 20).

In response to these threats, the SR hopes to set the foundations for a new generation of human security strategies by proposing two elements to enrich the human security framework: the agency approach and solidarity. First, the agency approach refers to the understanding that everyone could drive changes by having meaningful participation at different levels of decision-making (*United Nations Development Program*, 2022, p. 25). Second, solidarity is added to the human security strategies of protection and empowerment, so that the three working together could strengthen the interdependence across people and between people and the planet. It is important to highlight that for the context of the SR, solidarity is rooted in the recognition of a shared humanity and is understood "as a commitment to work together to navigate the challenges of the Anthropocene" (*United Nations Development Program*, 2022, p. 29). Des Gasper and Gómez affirmed that the report presents solidarity "as a required commitment to others, globally; as an implication of interconnectedness; and as a required response to uncertainty states," but, at the same time, they point out that solidarity has not been theorized in-depth in the SR and thus provides an open door to subsequent work (Gómez and Gasper, 2023, p. 4).

This section has shown that the notion of security is dynamic and there are varying perspectives on it and the scope of security issues. When the UN was created, the main issue was how to consolidate international peace. While for some outlawing war and creating alternative mechanisms to dispute resolutions was the way forward, for others this was a narrow vision, as people want to live with dignity and be free from fear and want. At the same time, new transnational threats emerged, and the traditional paradigm shifted to a more comprehensive notion of security. So, human security became relevant to address complex challenges to the survival, livelihood, and dignity of people. Human dignity (freedom from indignity) is understood here as the

> conditions where individuals and groups are assured of the protection of their fundamental rights and allowed to make choices and take advantage of opportunities in their everyday lives.
>
> *(United Nations Development Program, 2022, p. 36)*

The SR, addressing the threats of horizontal inequalities, posits that dignity lies at the heart of human rights, "based on the recognition that everyone has inherent worth, solely by virtue of being human" (*United Nations Development Program*, 2022, p. 93). However, we are still left with the question of what it truly means to be human. A possible answer is the explanation of Gómez and Gasper on the significance of the adjective "human" to "security"; they affirmed that it refers to the characteristic that makes humans human: vulnerability. Awareness of your own vulnerability is human, and this is a source of empathy for others (Gómez and Gasper, 2022, p. 40).

In the development of the concept of Human Security, especially, between the 2003 Ogata-Sen report and the UN General Assembly 2012, three elements are constant in the discussion: freedom from want, freedom from fear, and human dignity. But there is no mention of religious freedom as an element of the "vital core of all human lives" (Alkire, 2003).

The relationship between human security and religious freedom is what will be explored in the next section. It is proposed that dialogue with different religious perspectives could enrich the human security approach and contribute to deepening the exchange of the different practices and insights in promoting social cohesion, solidarity, human dignity, peace.

PART II

4 Religious Freedom and Human Security

The relationship between religious freedom and human security can be traced in three different ways, analyzing: 1) how religion can generate insecurity, conflict, and violence; 2) what religious actors and faith-based organizations (FBOs) do to contribute to human security locally and globally, such as humanitarian work, peacebuilding, reconciliation, and resilience; and 3) the normative dimension that refers to the teachings of religious traditions and their intersection with security issues. The analysis of the normative dimension will focus in this section on the reflections from the Catholic tradition and other ecumenical and interreligious documents, such as the Document on Human Fraternity for World Peace and Living Together.

5 Religions as Drivers of Insecurity, Conflict, and Violence

As mentioned previously, since the Second World War and especially after the Twin Towers attacks in 2001, the view of religion as a cause of terrorism, violence, and international instability has been reinforced. Amid the recent scholarship, Philpott identifies the diverse views on religion and security. While some scholars argue, first, that religion is inherently violent and can shape violence and religious fundamentalisms, others have identified religion as a rhetorical instrument for violence and that the limits to religious freedom could contribute to different kinds of violence (Philpott, 2018). Philpott affirms that if states guarantee religious freedom, societies are far less likely to suffer violence, so that "religious freedom can become an antidote to religious violence and intolerance" (Philpott, 2018, p. 9).

6 How Do Religious Actors Contribute to Human Security?

Religious actors and FBOs are usually the first responders and local providers of assistance. They are also key stakeholders in conflicts and humanitarian contexts due to their long-term trust relationship with local communities, and their ability to mobilize networks, resources, and community leaders.

As it was stated for the ninth Annual Symposium on the Role of Religion and Faith-Based Organizations in International Affairs "*Securing People's Wellbeing and Planetary Sustainability*," held in January 2023:

> Faith-based organizations have rich and diverse histories of discourse and practice demonstrating the nexus of human development, humanitarian work, peace, and human rights advocacy. Such discourses and practices affirm a people-centered, community-focused and human rights-based approach to peace and human security.
>
> *(Ecumenical Office to the United Nations, 2023)*

FBOs, as Barnett and Stein suggest, have reshaped the global humanitarian movement in recent times and have increased their role in the humanitarian space (Barnett and Stein, 2012). A significant milestone for the commitment of FBOs to humanitarian action was at the World Humanitarian Summit, in which more than 160 faith-based actors, representing major traditions, signed the Charter for Faith-Based Humanitarian Action. The Charter contains concrete commitments from religious leaders and other humanitarian actors to increase the impact of faith-based actors in reducing humanitarian needs and suffering and to call for their inclusion within policy and decision-making at all levels of humanitarian response (*Agenda for Humanity*, 2016).

It has also been acknowledged that religious communities have a relevant role to play in peacebuilding processes, preventing violent conflict and generating conditions for resilience and inclusive participation (Trotta and Wilkinson, 2019). Contrary to the voices that religions are drivers of violence and conflicts, the Institute for Economics and Peace's research has shown that, first, religion is not the main cause of conflict today; and, second, that religion through group membership, interfaith dialogue for conflict resolution, and other religiously motivated initiatives contributes to overcome conflicts and build strong social cohesion (*Institute for Economics and Peace*, 2014). For this reason, it is significant that in 2019, Religions for Peace, one of the most representative multi-religious coalitions, and the Institute for Economics and Peace (IEP) announced their commitment to strengthening their partnership, "to spread their shared vision of Positive Peace worldwide" (*Religions for Peace*, 2019).

The concept of "positive peace" is based on the Norwegian researcher Johan Galtung's concept of peace which distinguishes two types of peace: negative peace (absence of war and violent conflict) and positive peace, which is understood as "a transformational concept because it shifts the focus from the negative to the positive by describing the necessary conditions for peace and society to flourish" (*Institute for Economics and Peace*, 2022). Based on this, the IEP has created the positive peace index that measures the necessary conditions for peace and society to flourish, identifying its eight pillars: a well-functioning government; a sound business environment; an equitable distribution of resources; an acceptance of the rights of others; good relations with neighbors; free flow of information; a high level of human capital; and low levels of corruption (*Institute for Economics and Peace*, 2022).

Also, the Organization for Security and Co-operation in Europe (OSCE) Office for Democratic Institutions and Human Rights (ODIHR) launched its Freedom of Religion or Belief and Security: Policy Guidance to clarify the interrelationship between Freedom of Religion and Security in light of the comprehensive framework for Peace and Security (OSCE, 2019). It suggests to states seven guiding principles for the formulation and implementation of a variety of measures, policies, and laws to ensure both freedom of religion or belief and security. Among those principles, it is affirmed that interfaith and interreligious dialogue as well as engagement initiatives between States and religious communities are "essentials to develop a peaceful, secure and cohesive society" (OSCE, 2019, p. 23).

The Human Security approach highlights the added value of working with multiple stakeholders to respond with integrated solutions, improve operational efficiency, and generate more effective improvements in the life of people and communities (*United Nations Trust Fund for Human Security*, 2021a and 2021b). Based on this, "a new way of working" among UN agencies was proposed (*OCHA*, 2017) and new multi-stakeholder partnerships have been promoted between UN agencies, government entities, the private sector, civil society, local communities, and FBOs.

Within the UN system, the Interagency Task Force on Religion and Sustainable Development (UN-IATF-Religion), was created in 2010

> to provide policy guidance around engaging with faith-based actors, deepen UN system staff capacities on/around intersections of religion with the UN pillars of development, human rights, and peace and security dynamics, as well as provide strategic policy guidance on the above.
> *(The United Nations Interagency Task Force on Religion and Sustainable Development, 2020)*

In recent years, there has been an increased interest among UN agencies in engaging faith-related organizations. Today, 27 UN entities are members of the UN-IATF-Religion.

A few months after the UNDP released its 2022 Special Report on Human Security *New Threats to Human Security in the Anthropocene: Demanding Greater Solidarity* (*United Nations Development Program*, 2022), the United Nations Environment Programme (UNEP) celebrated the 50th anniversary of the 1972 UN Conference on the Human Environment, the first world conference to make the environment a major issue. Hosted by the government of Sweden, the international meeting Stockholm+50: A Healthy Planet for the Prosperity of All – Our Responsibility, Our Opportunity brought together leaders who made calls for bold environmental action. The event also recognized the central role of civil society engagement and multi-stakeholder collaboration in advancing environmental protection and governance. In this context, more than 100 religious representatives and FBOs acknowledged and committed to the care of people and the planet by signing the Stockholm+50 Interfaith Statement "Faith Values and Reach – Contribution to Environmental Policy,". They called for action from governments, UN entities, and civil society to commit to concrete ways such as divesting from fossil fuels and strengthening climate action to secure a better future on a healthy planet, as recommended by the United Nations Environment Program (2022).

7 The Normative Dimension of Religious Teachings

The analysis of the normative dimension proposed here is based on the capability approach of Nussbaum and Sen's work (Nussbaum and Sen, 1993), who understood it as a moral framework to find adequate criteria to assess the quality of life from the perspective of human freedom: "The focus here is on the freedom that a person actually has to do this or be that, things that he or she may value doing or being" (Sen, 2009, p. 232). Deneulin and Zampini point out that religion has been incorporated into the capability approach, first, by being aware that religious beliefs can underpin reasoning and serve as a basis for decisions and actions, influencing people's lives, choices, and what they value; and, second, through religious narratives that, considered "great art or classics," transcend their original religious context reaching an audience beyond the boundaries of a specific religion, whether or not one believes in the existence of God (Deneulin and Zampini-Davies, 2020; 2016). Because of this, it is affirmed that religious narratives could be a hermeneutic tool to open a space of dialogue, acknowledge the text from other perspectives, and understand it from the context of the reader. Religious narratives can help readers discover "a word of possibility," inspiring them to find new ways of "being" and "acting" (Zampini, n.d.), contributing to public reasoning and expansion of human capabilities.

The following analysis of the biblical parable known as "The Good Samaritan" focuses on the reflections from within the Catholic tradition and other ecumenical and interreligious documents, such as the Document on Human Fraternity for World Peace and Living Together.

PART III

8 Revisiting the Parable of the "Good Samaritan": A Religious Narrative of Human Insecurity?

The parable of the Good Samaritan can be framed in two scenes. In the first one, a lawyer asks Jesus what he must do to inherit eternal life. Jesus answered him with two questions: "What is written in the law?" and "How do you read it?" (Luke 10: 26). This first dialogue ends with Jesus affirming that the lawyer has answered correctly by saying that he must love God with all his soul, heart, and mind and love his neighbor as himself, and if he does this, he will live (Luke 10: 27–28).

The first question is about what must be done to inherit eternal life.

From the Jewish tradition, Rabbi Sacks suggests that eternal life or life after death was not central to the Torah as it was for other civilizations. In his commentary on Moses' last testament (Sacks, 2020a), he emphasizes that Torah's central teaching is choosing life instead of death, blessings over curses. A critical choice that would determine that "you and your children may live" (Deuteronomy 30: 19). Moses knows that he is about to die and, confronting his own mortality, asks each generation to confront theirs while affirming, as Sacks highlights, that immortality is not achieved in an afterlife, but is here "by being part of a covenant – a covenant with eternity itself, that is to say, a covenant with God" (Sacks, 2020a). The biblical conception of Jewish law is set within the dynamic of a covenant that draws the contours of the relationship between God and the Israelites by a divine commandment (mitzvah) (David, 2019, p. 23). By observing and living the "mitzvot" (commandments/obligations), the people walk with and in the presence and nearness of God (Shekinah) (Sievers, 2017, p. 31). If Israelites do not obey the commandments or violate it, biblical law requires ratifications and timely reaffirmations or they could earn expulsion, abandonment, and loss of power (David, 2019) and the "departure" of "Shekinah." This shows the unique bonds between "The Torah" and "Shekinah" characterized by ethical implications: the existence of sinful behavior (murder, idolatry, slander, adultery) causes its departure. As Sievers distinguishes, later in Rabbinic literature the "obligation to apply and reflect the 'words of Torah,' its values, its norms, and laws, in our everyday social and business world" implies a sharing in God's own activity, "a way to experience his nearness" (Sievers, 2017, p. 31), and, if the covenant is kept, "the gate to eternity is not death: it is life lived in a covenant endlessly renewed, in words engraved on our hearts and the hearts of our children" (Sacks, 2020a).

From a philosophical perspective, the lawyer's question about what must be done to inherit eternal life could be interpreted as asking what it means to live a meaningful and good life. This question is what Aristotle addresses in the Nicomachean Ethics, a moral philosophy work in which he states that happiness is the moral end of human beings. Happiness is not understood as maximizing pleasure or as a feeling or emotion, but as a fulfilled and flourishing life (Aristotle, 350 BCE[1925]). It is a way of being that could be achieved through the cultivation of virtues within a social and political community (polis). In this framework, justice is a moral virtue that orients human actions toward the common good (Aristotle, 350 BCE[1925]). But, it may not be possible to say what is just without arguing about the nature of the good life and the kind of society one wants to live in (Sandel, 2009, p. 207). This is why politics for Aristotle is essential to a good life (Aristotle, 350 BCE[1946]). Its purpose is to form good citizens and to cultivate good character; and law aims to cultivate the habits that lead to good character (Aristotle, 350 BCE[1946]). By living in a political community and participating in politics, human beings, first, realize and fulfill their distinctive human capacities and nature; second, they learn to deliberate with others about justice and injustice and the common good; and, third, they acquire practical judgment and practical wisdom (Sandel, 2009). "Reasoning together about the good life" (Sandel, 2009, p. 261) means exercising practical reasoning and political deliberation to make the best decision in a given context. Envisioning a wider vision of the common good and creating the conditions and attitudes to live a good human life with others is what makes a just political society.

As mentioned above, the Nussbaum and Sen capacity approach provides a moral framework to find adequate criteria to evaluate the quality of life from the perspective of human freedom (Nussbaum and Sen, 1993). However, since they proposed it and throughout the 30 years in which they have been advocating for it, there have been differences between them. As an economist, Sen provided alternative foundations to the economy, by affirming that well-being is best evaluated not in the space of utility but in the capability space. Nussbaum brought the idea of capability toward a more robust theory of justice, offering a stronger program for political action and constitutional guarantees. But, as Deneulin adverts, there are two different versions of the capability approach in Nussbaum's work. In her early work developed in the late 80s, she presented an Aristotelian account for the capability approach; and, later, in the mid-90s, she presented a political-liberal account for the capability approach, after Nussbaum shifted her political activism to political liberalism, concerned with pluralism in democratic societies and acknowledging that people have different perspectives about how they should live (Deneulin, 2013, 2011).

The move from an Aristotelian account to a political-liberalism account of the capability approach in Nussbuam's thought has concrete implications, first, by strengthening or weakening the relationships and social bonds in which the political community is built; and, second, on the notion of the human good. While the Aristotelian version of the capability approach is characterized by a comprehensive vision of the human good in which the individual's good is mutually related to the good of the relationships in which each person is part; the political-liberalism account focuses on the people's choice to live a life based on their own conceptions of the good. For this reason, rooted in relational anthropology, Deneulin calls to recover the Aristotelian roots of the capability approach because, as she argues, it is the best framework in which "the purpose of the capabilities approach is best fulfilled" (Deneulin, 2011, p. 35).

At the end of the first scene of the parable of the Good Samaritan, the lawyer answered Jesus as to what is written in the law, but he did not answer the other question: "How do you read it?" (Luke 10: 26–28). Jesus's question expresses his interest in knowing the reasoning and belief of the lawyer about the written law; and even more, it could suggest that the text has a texture open to interpretation from the reader's position to provoke new reasoning and expand the reader's imagination. Sen addressed this idea in his book *A Theory of Justice*. He affirms that the world is "read" and "reasoned" by people from their own positions: "The reach of public reasoning may be limited in practice by the way people read the world in which they live" (2009, p. 168). For this reason, Sen insists that to ensure that no one is excluded and to avoid parochialism, "assessment of justice demands engagement with the 'eyes of mankind'" (2009, p. 130).

This idea resonates to some extent with what Pope Francis understands as listening to the "peripheries," because "hidden there are ways of looking at the world that can give us all a fresh start" (Pope Francis and Ivereigh, 2020, p. 119). At the beginning of his pontificate, he proposed "the periphery" as a hermeneutical category to reconceptualize the world order that could now be looked at from the multiple and diverse faces and peripheries of the "polyhedric world" (Pope Francis, 2013a). In this sense, "It reveals to be a powerful rhetorical device, insofar as it suggests that it is possible to get a wider perspective of the current state of the world looking from the edge rather than from the center" (Ferrara, 2015, p. 42).

In the second part of the dialogue between Jesus and the lawyer, the story of the Good Samaritan begins. A lawyer asks Jesus, "Who is my neighbor?" (Luke 10: 29). Jesus did not answer a question of what we owe to each other, the source and foundations of obligations, or what an obligation is. He answers with a story of a Jewish man who was robbed and left lying half-dead on the road from Jerusalem to Jerichó. Three people, a Levite, a Priest, and a Samaritan, see him and show different attitudes toward the wounded man. The Levite and the Priest continue on their way without stopping (Luke 10: 31–32). The Samaritan "was moved with compassion" (Luke 10: 33) when he saw the strange man on the road. He stopped and bandaged the man's wounds, pouring oil and wine on them. He then lifted him onto his mount, took him to an inn, and looked after him. The next day, he took out two denarii and handed them to the innkeeper, and said, "Take care of him. If you spend more than what I have given you, I shall repay you on my way back" (Luke 10: 34–35). Jesus then asks the lawyer, "Which of these three, in your opinion, was neighbor to the robbers' victim? He answered, 'The one who treated him with mercy.' Jesus said to him, 'Go, and do the same yourself'" (Luke 10: 36–37).

This passage has inspired many humanitarian and charitable initiatives; provoked different questions, social experiments,[5] and reflections from a wide range of authors.

In *The Idea of Justice*, Sen uses this Christian narrative to introduce his argument about responsibility and universal concern for others. He tries to answer the following question: Who is our neighbor in our contemporary and interconnected world? (Sen, 2009, p. 170).

By revisiting the Good Samaritan parable, Sen highlights that the main issue of the discussion with the lawyer is not the duty to help others or see the story only as a moral for universal concern. Instead, Sen affirms that Jesus questioned and rejected the idea of thinking of people in terms of fixed communities of neighbors (Sen, 2009, p. 171).

The Samaritan is linked to the wounded Israelite through the event itself: he found the stricken man, saw the need to help, provided that help, and was now in a relationship with the injured person. It does not matter whether the Samaritan was moved by charity, or by a "sense of justice," or by some deeper "sense of fairness" in treating others as equals. Once he finds himself in this situation, he is in a new "neighborhood" (Sen, 2009, p. 172).

Therefore, Sen argues that today in our contemporary and globalized world there are few non-neighbors left; hence, the duty to neighbors is not confined only to those who live next door. As a result, he calls for attention to the importance that increased connections have in expanding the reach of our sense of justice. For this reason, an engagement with the "eyes of mankind" is needed in the pursuit of justice to overcome the limits and barriers of positionality perceptions.

With a slightly different emphasis, Jeremy Waldron in *Who Is My Neighbor? Humanity and Proximity* presents an interesting insight from which the parable could also be analyzed. He argues that the lawyer's question is about the scope of the commandment, not about the content (2003, p. 334). The first issue he explores is the question of whether there is a duty to help or a duty not to harm (Not Helping vs. Not Harming). Waldron affirms that it is taken for granted that the Good Samaritan acts correctly. This is a hard question about acts and omissions. However, this was not the central point of the dialogue between Jesus and the lawyer insofar that it was clear "on all sides that one's duty to one's neighbor is a duty to help as well as a duty not to harm" (2003, p. 335). So, for Waldron, the main issue of the discussion is the definition of "neighbor": where to draw the line that differentiates neighbors from non-neighbors in order to identify who is the beneficiary of the duty to help and not harm.

At this point, Waldron explores whether the duty to assist diminishes the further away one is from a human plight or what is understood by distance in this context. By concluding that it is possible to conceive the notion of distance in a quite literal and geographical sense, he affirms that the Good Samaritan parable turns on the argument of "actual proximity" (2003, p. 347). He understands that this parable could be approached as an instance of focused concern for a particular person in a particular circumstance of space and time. As a result, the immediacy and proximity of the Samaritan to the wounded Jewish man also distinguishes his response, as he was close enough to take care of him. Therefore, Waldron suggests that in order to identify who is a neighbor, one must take into consideration the notions of humanity and proximity.

Regarding "humanity," the Samaritan responds to a compelling urgent circumstance, a demand of necessity as he sees the wounded man on the road. No special relationship or ethnicity, community, nor traditional categories of neighborliness are considered here; he focuses on the fact of the wounded man's humanity. By echoing Peter Winch's thought, "I can't just leave him here to die," Waldron concludes that "in a case like this, where I am on the spot, and where help, if it is to come at all, can only come from me, the demands of morality are compelling. I have no choice" (2003, p. 345). "Proximity" is understood in a literal sense. Although Waldron affirms that it is not a condition for the existence of the duty to help, he infers that the further away one is from a human plight, the duty to help weakens, as it is less compelling:

> They (the Levite, the Priest and the Samaritan) are *there* and that makes them his neighbors. To pass by and do nothing to help a person whose need is so immediately present seems plainly wrong: even the lawyer in the original story sees this.
>
> *(2003, p. 348)*

There are three symbolic elements that complete the picture of the Good Samaritan parable: the road, the Samaritan, and the sight.

a **The road:** the whole story takes place on the road from Jerusalem to Jerichó. The encounter between the Samaritan and the wounded Jewish man takes place on the road. It is not a fixed place for a particular community or nation. It is a threshold and dynamic space in which strangers would meet each other, and, by the circumstances, become neighbors. The road is a place of transition and a channel that connects different cities and people and allows many encounters between strangers. As Waldron affirms, the road was an exception in times of the Good Samaritan parable, as most people used to live within the confines of a community, but "we do not live in such an era. Much of our life is lived 'on the road, among strangers'" (2003, p. 351).

b **The Samaritan:** Jesus acknowledged that there was antipathy between Jews and Samaritans and that they were despised, hated, and heretics to Jews. However, this could be understood as a deliberate attempt to overcome these divisions by broadening the scope of neighbor. As Collins explains, in the original biblical context, the imperative to love and care for others appears to have been limited to relationships between members of the same nation; love here was not a matter of feelings but practice, and it was applied only to Israelites and to the *ger* (foreigners) that lived among them. However, the application of the "neighbor" would be gradually extended to all people and grounded in the recognition of shared humanity (Collins, 2020). As Rabbi Sacks states, the commandment to "love your neighbor" is interrelated with the notion of "imago Dei": "The ethic of holiness is based on the vision of creation as God's work of love. This vision sees all human beings – ourselves, our neighbor, and the stranger – as in the image of God, and that is why we are to love our neighbor and the stranger as ourselves" (Sacks, 2020b).

Furthermore, in his last encyclical Fratelli Tutti, Pope Francis, recalling the Abu Dhabi Document on Human Fraternity, considers the universal scope of fraternal love that envisions the human family and the whole world as one great neighbor. In Chapter II, "A Stranger in the Road," he affirms that Jesus "asks us not to decide who is close enough to be our neighbor, but rather that we ourselves become neighbors to all" (Pope Francis, 2020).

c **Sight:** The Levite, the Priest, and the Samaritan all saw the wounded man on the road. But only the Samaritan who "came upon him was moved with compassion at the sight" (Luke 10: 33). The question here is what the Samaritan saw that neither the Levite nor the Priest saw. We might not know what the Samaritan saw, but we do know that it mobilized him, and he chose to act with compassion. Here we could recall what was said earlier about Sen's theory of positionality. Even more, after seeing him, the Samaritan recognizes the vulnerable situation of the wounded man, his humanity striving for survival, and chooses to act in consequence by taking care of him (Waldron, 2003, p. 350).

So, it could be affirmed that to some extent the parable of the Good Samaritan could be a religious narrative that addresses human insecurity. The wounded Jewish man certainly suffers insecurity and is striving for his life while lying on the road. The actions of the Good Samaritan are (1) see with compassion, (2) go to the encounter, (3) heal the wounds, (4) lift him onto his mount, (5) look after him, and (6) pay the innkeeper. These actions are evidence that in order to provide human security, an integrated system and a culture of care are needed.

The Catholic Social Teaching (CST) also sees the parable of the Good Samaritan as the main biblical grounds of the principle of solidarity, and the foundation of the CST methodology of "seeing-judging-acting." The Argentinian Catholic theologian Zampini highlights that the question is not "Who is my neighbor?" but "Who behaves in a neighborly way?" (Zampini, n.d.). In this sense, he continues arguing, the parable suggests that loving our neighbor requires the entire dimension of our being – all our heart, soul, strength, and mind – since the neighbor is somebody to whom one is essentially related and not an object of aid or charitable actions. Therefore, this love comprises a compassionate way of seeing, a sight that can deeply move us to express this love with appropriate external actions (Zampini, n.d.).

This is a new emphasis on the teaching of the Catholic Church that shifts the tone and style with pastoral, theological, and ecclesiological implications. Pope Francis envisions the church as "a hospital after the battle", with the mission to heal and care with openness and without boundaries of wounded humanity.

As the German-French Jesuit theologian Christoph Theobald points out, fraternity and dialogue are the new style of the Church. This "mystique of fraternity" is characterized by the experience of hospitality, which consists of welcoming and listening to one another, especially to those who are fragile and excluded. According to him, fraternity represents a new call for all Christians to live with the flavor of the Gospel and with the responsibility of addressing a central issue such as the cohesion of society and the way of treating others.

9 Human Fraternity and Solidarity: From the Document on Human Fraternity for World Peace and Living Together to the Encyclical Letter *Fratelli Tutti*

Even before freedom and equality became the founding principles of modernity and constitutive of the political order, fraternity had been lived in since ancient times and in different cultures. In Christianity, over the centuries, fraternity has not been confined to the family or within the religious communities. Living in a spirit of fraternity, the Christian communities acted in the public space, developed practices of hospitality, and brought to life institutions, centers, and hospices for the care of the poor, the elderly, the orphans, the vulnerable, the children, and the sick (Baggio, 2018, p. 110). With the French Revolution of 1789, the word "Fraternity" was taken up in its "Triptych." While "Liberty" and "Equality" saw an evolution that enabled them to become authentic political categories, capable of manifesting both as constitutional principles and as inspiring ideas of different political movements (Barroso, 2019), the word "Fraternity" was soon abandoned and faded by the violence of the post-revolutionary order, up to the point of its removal from the political lexicon.

Fraternity was the first theme Pope Francis referred to on the day of his election as Pope, ten years ago. On the same day that Bergoglio was elected and became Pope Francis, on the occasion of his first apostolic blessing "Urbi et Orbi" he said: "Let us pray for the whole world, that there may be a great spirit of fraternity" (Pope Francis, 2013b). Since then and throughout these years, fraternity has been the core of its reflection and pastoral mission of his pontificate.

Rooted and nourished by the evangelical witness of St. Francis and his school of thought and life, the meaning of fraternity has been preserved over the centuries till today, understood at the same time as the complement and the exaltation of the principle of solidarity (Pope Francis, 2017).

On the occasion of the Plenary Session of the Pontifical Academy of Social Sciences, entitled "Towards a Participatory Society: New Roads to Social and Cultural Integration," Pope Francis distinguishes

> Solidarity is the principle of social planning that allows the unequal to become equal; fraternity is what allows the equal to be different people. Fraternity allows people who are equal in their essence, dignity, freedom, and their fundamental rights to participate differently in the common good according to their abilities, their life plan, their vocation, their work, or their charism of service.
>
> *(Pope Francis, 2017)*

Saint Francis of Assisi has been a source of inspiration and guidance for Bergoglio and has motivated his Encyclical Letters "Laudato Si" and "Fratelli Tutti." In 2015, even before the adoption of the 2030 Agenda for Sustainable Development and the Paris Agreement on Climate Change, he wrote his second Encyclical Letter "Laudato Si," which is an appeal "for a new dialogue about how we are shaping the future of our planet" (Pope Francis, 2015, 14).

In 2020, Pope Francis presented "Fratelli Tutti" the Encyclical Letter written within the context of the first year of the Covid-19 pandemic and in a fragmented and fractured world by "a third world war in pieces" (Pope Francis, 2020). Because of this, the Italian professor Borghesi has called it the "New Pacem in Terris," re-echoing John XXIII's encyclical Pacem in Terris

(1963), launched in the context of the Cuban Missile Crisis and the menace of a nuclear war, and which message remains to our day: peace is a result of the consolidation of relations, between people, communities, and states, not solely an absence of war (Borghesi, 2020).

With the words "Fratelli Tutti," Saint Francis of Assisi addressed his brothers and sisters and proposed to them a new way of life that is characterized by a spirit of "fraternal openness that allows us to acknowledge, appreciate and love each person, regardless of physical proximity, regardless of where he or she was born or lives" (Pope Francis, 2020, p. 1).

Fraternity, dialogue, and friendship in society are the central axis of Fratelli Tutti. But fraternity is not naive, or utopic; it does not comprise an abstract or idealistic significance. On the contrary, Pope Francis is a realist that "in order to avoid crossing into cynicism, takes the risk of reaching out towards the ideal, and for this, it must be open to hope. Authentic realism is real idealism" (Borghesi, 2020). However, it must also be noted that Pope Francis characterizes "fraternity" with the adjective "human" to intentionally indicate that fraternity is not for him a new version of an abstract of universalism; instead, "Human Fraternity" is nourished by practicing 1) the courage of otherness, which involves the full recognition of the other; 2) dialogue and prayer, which are based on sincerity of intentions; 3) the promotion of education and justice, to form open identities in a relationship and in reciprocity and with sensitivity to injustices, decreasing hatred and growing civility; and 4) The fulfillment of flourished and dignified future, through an integral and cohesive development for every human person, everywhere. The cultivation of these four practices are, for pope Francis, the seeds for peace and a fraternal living together of the human family (Pope Francis, 2019).

At this point, it is important to acknowledge that fraternity could be referred to as: (a) solidarity among people and communities, (b) the social cohesion of a community, (c) the participation in the public discussion within a democratic society; and, (d) when applied to multilateral action is translated into a "diplomacy of mercy" (Spadaro, 2013), through which courage and generosity aim to

> freely establish certain common goals and to ensure their fulfillment of certain essential norms throughout the world while maintaining faith with legitimately manifested will and resolving disputes through means offered by diplomacy, to achieve a truly universal common good and the protection of weaker states.
>
> *(Mayakin, 2021)*

Fratelli Tutti was preceded by two documents: first, the *Document on Human Fraternity for World Peace and Living Together,* which in its introduction states that "Faith leads a believer to see in the other a brother or sister to be supported and loved" and that "believers are called to express this human fraternity by safeguarding creation and the entire universe and supporting all persons, especially the poorest and those most in need" (Pope Francis and al-Tayyib, 2019); and, second, the document *Serving a Wounded World: A Christian Call to Reflection and Action during COVID-19 and Beyond*, a joint document of the World Council of Churches (WCC) and the Pontifical Council for Interreligious Dialogue (PCID) that aims to encourage churches and Christian organizations to reflect on the importance of interreligious solidarity in a wounded world (*Pontifical Council for Interreligious Dialogue and World Council of Churches*, 2020). Both documents are respectively reshaping, on the one hand, the relations between Catholics and Muslims and interreligious relations; and, on the other hand, the relations between Christians from different Christian communities and denominations, revitalizing and strengthening ecumenical relations.

The *Document on Human Fraternity for World Peace and Living Together*, also called the Abu Dhabi Declaration, was jointly signed by Sheikh Ahmed Al-Tayeb and Pope Francis in 2019 to promote "a culture of tolerance, acceptance of others, and of living together peacefully" (Pope Francis and al-Tayyib, 2019). As a powerful and strategic historic symbol, the two main religious institutions, the Catholic Church and Al-Azahar, gathered to bring together a religious response to the challenge of pluralism and to raise awareness of diversity as a good rooted in religious freedom. They sought to reinforce the conviction that inciting war, hateful attitudes, hostility, and extremism are the consequence of a deviation from religious teachings, and have recognized that it is crucial to establish in our societies the concept of "full citizenship," based on the equality of rights and duties, under which all enjoy justice (Pope Francis and al-Tayyib, 2019).

This document is a centerpiece in the journey of Catholic-Muslim relationships, marked also by other encounters between Pope Francis with Muslim leaders and trips, to the Holy Land, Jordan, Turkey, Egypt, the United Arab Emirates, Morocco, Iraq, Azerbaijan, Macedonia, Bangladesh, and the most recent one to Bahrain, among others.

Furthermore, to assess the historic significance of the document it is relevant to note that it was signed and sealed on a timely and unique occasion, such as on the commemoration of the 800th Anniversary of the encounter between St. Francis of Assisi and the Sultan Malek el-Kamel in Damietta, Egypt during the Fifth Crusade (1213–1221). This encounter "has become an important part of the contemporary context for Muslim-Christian relations, Middle East politics, and international relations" (Thomas, 2018, p. 3). However, the relevance of going back to this Muslim-Christian encounter is not just to remember a historic fact but because of the need of the present time, as it has become a symbol of peace, reconciliation, and fraternity to overcome the logic of the "clash of civilizations."

The Abu Dhabi Declaration and Fratelli Tutti, as Borghessi suggests, are intrinsically connected by the promotion of the "culture of encounter" (Pope Francis, 202, p. 215). It implies a cultural revolution rooted in Assisi's spirit of fraternity that expands across peoples and nations, generating a profound movement of peace (Borghessi, 2020).

Catalano, an expert in interreligious and intercultural dialogue, highlights that this journey of Catholic-Muslim relationships is the consequence of the path of dialogue initiated since Vatican Council II, with the Conciliar Declarations *Nostra Aetate* on the relationship between the Church and believers of other religions and *Dignitatis Humanae* on religious freedom. The novelty that the Abu Dhabi Declaration represents in the two-millennia-long history of Catholic Church is that for the first time, a successor of Peter co-signed an official document with a leader of another religion; second, it was published by the *Libreria Vaticana* in the series, which comprises the official documents of the Holy See considered as the "magisterium" of the Catholic Church and part of its legacy. For these reasons, he suggests that this document is "paving the way to a new age of cooperation and common engagement in issues involving men and women of our times" (Catalano, 2021, p. 210).

Furthermore, another novelty that calls attention to the Abu Dhabi Declaration and Fratellit Tutti is the way that both documents embrace pluralism and diversity as religious goods. In the report *Human Fraternity and Inclusive Citizenship*, it is suggested that both categories of "human fraternity" and "inclusive citizenship" should be understood as "a way to embrace and engage cultures and communities in a public space of creative interculturality" (Petito et al., 2021) and as a "model of managing religious diversity through a strategy of legal pluralism" (Ferrari, 2021). These are innovative responses, drawn from substantive religious contributions and political proposals, to the challenges of pluralism and the management of diversity in our societies.

As was mentioned in Part I, the Special Report on Human Security (*United Nations Development Program*, 2022) mentions solidarity as a new human security strategy but, as Gómez and Gasper pointed out, it has not been theorized in-depth in the SR and thus provides an open door to subsequent work.

This section aimed to bring up the understanding of solidarity within the Catholic tradition. The CST sees the parable of the Good Samaritan as the main biblical grounds of the principle of solidarity.

However, it is "fraternity" and not "solidarity" that has been the core of Pope Francis's reflection and pastoral mission throughout his ten years of the pontificate. Fraternity is understood at the same time "as the complement and the exaltation of the principle of solidarity" (Pope Francis, 2017).

The notion of Human Fraternity brings a new style of relating, fostering, and encountering others with profound respect, trust, and with openness to learn from each other. It is a transformative encounter that enables the other "become ever more fully themselves" (Pope Francis, 2020, p. 4). The act of recognition of others enables the other to be and to participate in society from its unique identity; and as it becomes a culture, the "culture of encounter" makes possible the creation of a dynamic and sustainable social covenant.

10 Conclusion

The Human Security framework refocused the debate on security from territorial security to the security of people: to the survival, livelihood, and dignity of people. This approach does not mention religious freedom due to its "value-agnostic" background. Sen's capability approach is based on the pluralism of values, which implies taking into account the context dependence of values and the plurality of the source of values, and it could also include those coming from religious traditions (Deneulin, 2018, p. 14).

Both Human Security and Human Fraternity are two frameworks that could be complementary and mutually reinforced in two core dimensions to both: the understanding of human dignity (what it means to be human) and solidarity. Solidarity starts when someone takes care of the vulnerability of the other. The acknowledgment that people hold multiple identities at once and that much of our life is lived "on the road" among strangers provides for solidarity to be built across groups over shared values and goals, respecting each other's inherent human dignity and human rights.

Human Fraternity looks after the quality and harmony of the relationships that shape and permeate the "good living" of each group, and as they are mutually interdependent, thanks to the bonds of fraternity, together they contribute to envision and build the good of the human family.

By revisiting the parable of the Good Samaritan, what comes into evidence is, first, that religious narratives are a powerful hermeneutic methodology to generate a dialogic encounter between religious traditions and philosophical contributions, as Sen and Waldron's insights show. Second, religious teachings nourish and deepen their understanding in dialogue with their socio-historical context, as it happened with the notion of "neighbor" and the recognition of pluralism and diversity as religious goods in both documents *Fratelli Tutti* and the *Document on Human Fraternity for World Peace and Living Together*. This could be an antidote to those tendencies that either oversimplify religion or understand it only as a fixed doctrine. Third, it could be affirmed that many religious actors, inspired by their religious teachings, are redefining their public role in politics and civil society not as competitors to the government but as key stakeholders and catalysts of new relational dynamics in the joint search for strategies and policies "for living together in diversity" and "in a spirit of fraternity."

Notes

1 Both expressions, the "silent God" and "forsaken by God," refer here to the sense that God is often deaf to the cries of human suffering. See, for example, Schorsch, I.(2005) "Accounting for God's silence" [Online]. Available at http://www.jtsa.edu/accounting-for-gods-silence (Accessed 08 October 2023).

It is important to note that Psalm 22:2 is significant in the New Testament because Jesus recites it "as a dying prayer" in Mt. 27:46. Christian theologians have affirmed that Jesus experienced in that cry "the abyss of nothingness". Piero Coda, an Italian theologian, understands that the paschal mystery is intrinsically related to the mystery of the Trinity, which is fully revealed in a dynamic interplay between kenosis (self-emptying) and perichoresis (communion and mutual indwelling of the three divine persons). This has profound theological and social implications, as the relational dimension based on the Trinity can open human beings to interpersonal communion with those who are uniquely different from them but united by love. The theologian Hubertus Blaumeiser states that this cry offers an opportunity for the encounter between peoples, cultures, and religions in their diversity. To further understand these developments within Catholic theology, see Coda, P. (2007) Dio che dice Amore, Cittá Nuova.

2 For example, in Japan, the Rissho Kosei Kai movement (1938) and Soka Gakkai (1930), both lay Mahayana Buddhist movements, emerged. For the Jewish tradition, on the one hand, the post-Holocaust theology and philosophy have reshaped the dynamics of Jewish life, and, on the other hand, the creation of the State of Israel in 1948 marked a milestone in the configuration of Jewish identity. The Christian world was also being transformed by the war and by the different responses given to it, and this has shaped the emergence of new spiritual families. Between 1928 and 1969, for example, in the Catholic Church, the Opus Dei (1928); the Little Brothers of Jesus (1933); the Catholic Worker Movement (1933); the Catholic War Relief Service (1943–1950); Caritas Internationalis (1947–1950); the Focolare Movement (1943); Communion and Liberation (1954); Communitá Sant' Egidio (1969). All these new charismatic and communitarian realities, in some way, pushed the renewal of the Catholic Church toward the spirit of Vatican Council II in 1962–1966. And within the Reformed churches, there were also new realities founded and inspired in a spirit of ecumenism, diakonía, and interecclesiastical cooperation: the United Methodist Committee on Relief (1940); the Taizé Community (1940); the Lutheran World Federation (1947); the Church World Service (1945); the Bossey Ecumenical Institute (1946); the World Council of Churches (1948), among many others.

3 It is relevant to note that the American Declaration of the Rights and Duties of Man was adopted six months before the UDHR, and it has underlined the region's commitment to the international protection of human rights and laid the foundations for the adoption of the American Convention on Human Rights (Pact of San José de Costa Rica), which was approved in 1969 and entered into force in 1978. The Latin American contribution and influence on the idea and the drafting process of the UDHR has been retrieved by Paolo Carozza and Mary Ann Glendon (Carozza, 2003; Glendon, 2003).

4 The drafting of the UDHR marked a milestone achieved with the greatest effort at a time unpropitious and represented a kind of common denominator in the process of uniting a divided world (*United Nations General Assembly*, 1948a).

5 See, for example, Darley, J. M. and Batson, C. D. (1973) 'From Jerusalem to Jericho: A Study of Situational and Dispositional Variables in Helping Behavior', *Journal of Personality and Social Psychology*, vol. 27, no. 1, pp. 100–108. The study aimed to examine the influence of several situational and personality variables on helping behavior in an emergency situation suggested by the Good Samaritan parable. The

conclusion was that "*Thinking about the Good Samaritan did not increase helping behavior, but being in a hurry decreased it. It is difficult not to conclude from this that the frequently cited explanation that ethics becomes a luxury as the speed of our daily lives increases is at least an accurate description*" (1973, p. 107). Addressing the challenges that AI presents to our ideas about freedom, Israeli historian Yuval Harari in *21 Lessons for the 21st Century* (2018) refers to this study and argues that algorithms could make better moral decisions than human beings. As the experiment demonstrated, he states, human beings in times of crisis and emergency behave driven by their visceral emotions rather than be guided by their philosophical and religious beliefs. In a totally different tone, reflecting about leadership and how to create a safe environment and trusting teams, Simon Sinek in *The Infinite Game* (2019) cites the same psychology study to illustrates how an organizational culture of pressure, demands, and incentives gives room to ethical fading, that allows people – who are willing to do the right thing – to act in unethical ways to respond to demands placed upon them and meet the organizational goals.

References

Agenda for Humanity (2016) *Charter for Faith-Based Humanitarian Action*, New York, United Nations Office for the Coordination of Humanitarian Affairs [Online]. Available at https://agendaforhumanity.org/sites/default/files/CHARTER%20FOR%20FAITH-BASED%20HUMANITARIAN%20ACTION.pdf (Accessed 30 January 2022).

Alkire, S. (2003) *A Conceptual Framework for Human Security*, Oxford, Center for Research on Inequality, Human Security and Ethnicity [Online]. Available at https://ora.ox.ac.uk/objects/uuid:d2907237-2a9f-4ce5-a403-a6254020052d (Accessed 30 January 2022).

Appleby, R. S. (1999) *The Ambivalence of the Sacred: Religion, Violence, and Reconciliation*, Lanham, MD, Rowman & Littlefield.

Aristotle (350 BCE [1946]) *The Politics* [trans. Ernest Barker], New York, Univeristy Press.

Aristotle (350 BCE [1925]) *Nicomachean Ethics* [trans. David Ross], New York, Oxford University Press.

Baggio, A. (2018) 'La sfida della fraternità nella politica e nel diritto', *Inaugurazione* [Online]. Available at https://www.sophiauniversity.org/it/wp-content/uploads/2020/08/LiberAnnualis-2018-19_Lectio-Magistralis.pdf (Accessed 20 May 2022).

Baldwin, D. A. (1995) 'Security Studies and the End of the Cold War', *World Politics*, vol. 48, no. 1, pp. 117–141 [Online]. Available at https://dbaldwin.scholar.princeton.edu/sites/g/files/toruqf4596/files/dbaldwin/files/baldwin_1995_security_studies_and_the_end_of_the_cold_war.pdf (Accessed 30 January 2021).

Barnett, M. and Stein, J. (2012) *Sacred Aid: Faith and Humanitarianism*, Oxford, Oxford University Press.

Barroso, I. M. (2019) 'In Spirit of Brotherhood: The Principle of Fraternity between Rights and Duties. A Reflection since the Universal Declaration of Human Rights', *Cross-cultural Human Rights Review*, vol. 1, no. 1, pp. 81–104 [Online]. Available at https://storage.googleapis.com/jnl-up-j-chrr-files/journals/1/articles/29/submission/proof/29-1-55-1-10-20210405.pdf (Accessed 20 November 2022).

Borghesi, M. (2020) 'A New Pacem in Terris', *MassimoBorghesi.com* [Blog], 19 October. Available at http://www.massimoborghesi.com/a-new-pacem-in-terris/ (Accessed 3 February 2022).

Bottoni, R., Cristofori, R. and Ferrari, S. (eds) (2016) *Religious Rules, State Law, and Normative Pluralism - A Comparative Overview*, New York, Springer Publishing.

Buber, M. (2016) *Eclipse of God: Studies in the Relation between Religion and Philosophy*, Princeton, NJ, Princeton University Press.

Calo, Z. (2009) 'The Internationalization of Church-state Issues', in Duncan, A. W. and Jones, S. L. (eds) *Church and State Issues in America Today: Religion and Government*, Westport, CT, Praeger Publishing, pp. 135–164.

Carozza, P. G. (2003) 'From Conquest to Constitutions: Retrieving a Latin American Tradition of the Idea of Human Rights,' *Human Rights Quarterly*, vol. 25, pp. 281–314 [Online]. Available at https://scholarship.law.nd.edu/law_faculty_scholarship/581 (Accessed 30 January 2022).

Casanova, J. (2014) 'Secularisation, Religion and Multicultural Citizenship', in Weisse, W., Amirpur, K., Koers, A. and Vieregge, D. (eds) *Religions and Dialogue: International Approaches*, Münster, Waxmann Verlag, pp. 21–32.

Catalano, R. (2021) 'Is Interreligious Dialogue Changing the Church? The Significance of the Document on Human Fraternity', in Chapman, M. D. and Latinovic, V. (eds) *Changing the Church: Transformations of Christian Belief, Practice, and Life*, London, Palgrave Macmillan, pp. 209–215 [Online]. Available at https://doi.org/10.1007/978-3-030-53425-7_24 (Accessed 2 February 2022).

Collins, J. J. (2020) 'Love Your Neighbor: How It Became the Golden Rule', *TheTorah.com* [Blog]. Available at https://thetorah.com/article/love-your-neighbor-how-it-became-the-golden-rule (Accessed 3 February 2022).

Darley, J. M. and Batson, C. D. (1973) 'From Jerusalem to Jericho: A Study of Situational and Dispositional Variables in Helping Behavior', *Journal of Personality and Social Psychology*, vol. 27, no. 1, pp. 100–108.

David, J. (2019) 'The Jewish Tradition. A History', in Ferrari, S. and Bottoni, R. (eds) *Routledge Handbook of Religious Laws*, London, Routledge, pp. 21–34.

Deneulin, S. (2018) 'Integral Human Development through the Lens of Sen's Capability Approach and the Life of a Faith Community at the Latin American Urban Margins', *Kellogg Institute for International Studies*, April [Online]. Available at https://kellogg.nd.edu/sites/default/files/working_papers/427.pdf (Accessed 30 January 2023).

Deneulin, S. (2011) 'Recovering Nussbaum's Aristotelian Roots', *Revista Cultura Económica*, vol. 29, no. 81/82, pp. 31–37 [Online]. Available at https://erevistas.uca.edu.ar/index.php/CECON/article/view/2465/2295 (Accessed 23 May 2023).

Deneulin, S. and Rakodi, C. (2011) 'Revisiting Religion: Development Studies Thirty Years On,' *World Development*, vol. 39, no. 1, pp. 45–54 [Online]. Available at http://www.povertystudies.org/TeachingPages/EDS_PDFs4WEB/Deneulin_Revisiting%20Religion:%20Development%20Studies%2030%20Yrs%20On.pdf (Accessed 30 May 2023).

Deneulin, S. and Zampini-Davies, A. (2020) 'Religion and the Capability Approach', in Chiappero-Martinetti, E., Osmani, S. and Qizilbash, M. (eds) *The Cambridge Handbook of the Capability Approach*, Cambridge, Cambridge University Press, pp. 686–705.

Deneulin, S. and Zampini Davies, A. (2016) 'Theology and Development as Capability Expansion', *HTS Teologiese Studies/Theological Studies*, vol. 72, no. 4 [Online]. Available at https://hts.org.za/index.php/HTS/article/view/3230 (Accessed 30 January 2023).

Deuteoronomy 29: 9, 30: 20, New American Bible (Revised Edition).
Doe, N. (2018) *Comparative Religious Law: Judaism, Christianity, Islam*, 1st edn, Cambridge, Cambridge University Press.
Ecumenical Office to the United Nations (2023) *9th Annual Symposium on the Role of Religion and Faith-Based Organizations in International Affairs* [Online]. Available at https://www.oikoumene.org/programme-activity/euno#annual-symposium (Accessed 24 January 2023).
Ferrara, P. (2015) 'The Concept of Periphery in Pope Francis' Discourse: A Religious Alternative to Globalization?', *Religions*, vol. 6, no. 1, pp. 42–57 [Online]. Available at http://hdl.handle.net/1814/34302 (Accessed 3 February 2022).
Ferrari, S. (2021) 'Overcoming the "Same Rights for All Special Rights for Minorities Dichotomy', in Petito, F., Daou, F. and Driessen, M. (eds) *Human Fraternity and Inclusive Citizenship: Interreligious Engagement in the Mediterranean*, Milan, Italian Institute for International Political Studies pp. 133-143 [Online]. Available at https://www.ispionline.it/sites/default/files/ispi_report_human_fraternity_web.pdf (Accessed 30 January 2021).
Fukuyama, F. (2018) *Identity: Contemporary Identity Politics and the Struggle for Recognition*, 1st edn, London, Profile Books Ltd.
Gilles, K. (1994 [1991]) *The Revenge of God: The Resurgence of Islam, Christianity and Judaism in the Modern World* [trans. Alan Braley], Cambridge, Polity.
Glendon, M. A. (2011) 'The First Lady and the philosopher Eleanor Roosevelt, Charles Malik, and the Human Rights Project', in Glendon, M. (ed) *The Forum and the Tower: How Scholars and Politicians Have Imagined the World, from Plato to Eleanor Roosevelt*, Oxford, Oxford University Press, pp. 199–220.
Glendon, M. A. (2003) 'The Forgotten Crucible: The Latin American Influence on the Universal Human Rights Idea', *Harvard Human Rights Journal*, vol. 16, pp. 27–39.
Glendon, M. A. (2002) *A World Made New: Eleanor Roosevelt and the Universal Declaration of Human Rights*, New York, Random House Trade.
Gómez, O. A. and Gasper, D. (2023) 'Solidarity and Human Insecurity: Interpreting and Extending the HDRO's 2022 Special Report on Human Security', *Journal of Human Development and Capabilities* [Online]. Available at https://www.tandfonline.com/doi/full/10.1080/19452829.2022.2161491 (Accessed 24 April 2023).
Gómez, O. A. and Gasper, D. (2022) *The Position of Crisis in Human Development Processes and Thinking: Using the Human Security Perspective in an Era of Transitions*, New York, United Nations Development Program [Online]. Available at https://hdr.undp.org/system/files/documents/background-paper-document/2022hsrgomezgasperpdf.pdf (Accessed 30 January 2023).
Habermas, J. (2006). Religion in the Public Sphere. En *European Journal of Philosophy*14:1 pp. 1– 25. https://doi.org/10.1111/j.1468-0378.2006.00241.x
Harari, Y. N. (2018) *21 Lessons for the 21st Century*, New York, Spiegel & Grau.
Hathaway, O. A. and Shapiro, S. (2017) *The Internationalists and their Plan to Outlaw War*, 1st edn, London, Allen Lane.
Hatzopoulos, P. and Petito, F. (2003) *Religion in International Relations: The Return from Exile*, London, Palgrave MacMillan.
Heschel, A. (1965) *Who Is Man?*, 1st edn, Redwood City, Stanford University Press.
Huntington, S. (1993) 'The Clash of Civilizations?', *Foreign Affairs*, vol. 72, no. 3, pp. 22–49.

Institute for Economics and Peace (2022) *Positive Peace 2023 Briefing* [Online]. Available at https://www.visionofhumanity.org/wp-content/uploads/2023/05/Positive-Peace-2023-briefing.pdf (Accessed 25 November 2022).

Institute for Economics and Peace (2014) Peace and Religion. A global statistical analysis on the empirical link between peace and religion. [Online]. Available at: https://www.economicsandpeace.org/wp-content/uploads/2015/06/Peace-and-Religion-Report.pdf (Accessed: 09 October 2023).

Koskenniemi, M. (2017) 'International Law and Religion: No Stable Ground', in Koskenniemi, M., García Salmones, N. and Amorosa, P. (eds) *International Law and Religion: Historical and Contemporary Perspectives*, 1st edn, Oxford, Oxford University Press, pp. 3–21.

Kulbálková, V. (2009) 'A "turn to religion" in International Relations?', *Perspectives Review of International Affairs*, vol. 17, no. 2, pp. 13–41.

Luke 10, New American Bible (Revised Edition).

Mayakin, B. (2021) 'Cardinal Parolin: Multilateralism, Fraternity Needed on Path toward Better Society', *Vatican News* [Online]. Available at https://www.vaticannews.va/en/vatican-city/news/2021-04/parolin-fratelli-tutti-fraternity-online-meeting-discourse.html (Accessed 1 February 2022).

McCrudden, C. (2018) *Litigating Religions: An Essay on Human Rights, Courts, and Beliefs*, 1st edn, Oxford, Oxford University Press.

Neo, J. and Scharffs, B. (2020) 'Law and Politics of Freedom of Religion in Comparative Perspective', *The University of Western Australia Law Review*, vol. 47, no. 1, pp. 1–14 [Online]. Available at https://www.able.uwa.edu.au/centres/uwalr/issues/2020-volume-47,-issue-1 (Accessed 30 January 2022).

Nussbaum, M.C. and Sen, A. (eds.) (1993) *The Quality of Life*, 1st edn, Oxford, Oxford University Press.

OSCE (2019) *Freedom of Religion or Belief and Security: Policy Guidance to Clarify the Interrelationship Between Freedom of Religion and Security*, Warsaw, OSCE Office for Democratic Institutions and Human Rights [Online]. Available at https://www.osce.org/files/f/documents/e/2/429389.pdf (Accessed 1 February 2022).

Petito, F. (2016) 'Dialogue of Civilizations in a Multipolar World: Toward a Multicivilizational-Multiplex World Order', *International Studies Review*, vol. 18, no. 1, pp. 78–91.

Petito, F., Daou F. and Driessen, M. (2021) (eds) *Human Fraternity and Inclusive Citizenship: Interreligious Engagement in the Mediterranean*, Milan, Italian Institute for International Political Studies [Online]. Available at https://www.ispionline.it/sites/default/files/ispi_report_human_fraternity_web.pdf (Accessed 30 January 2021).

Philpott, D. (2018) 'Religion and International Security', in Gheciu, A. and Wohlforth W. C. (eds) *The Oxford Handbook of International Security* [Online]. Available at https://danielphilpott.info/wp-content/uploads/2019/10/Philpott-Religion-and-International-Security.pdf (Accessed 10 November 2022).

Pontifical Council for Interreligious Dialogue and World Council of Churches (2020) *Serving a Wounded World in Interreligious Solidarity: A Christian Call to Reflection and Action During COVID-19 and Beyond*, Vatican City, Libreria Editrice Vaticana [Online]. Available at https://press.vatican.va/content/dam/salastampa/it/bollettino/documentazione-linkata/ServingWoundedWorld_.pdf (Accessed 1 February 2022).

Pope Francis (2020) *Encyclical Letter Fratelli Tutti of the Holy Father Francis: On Fraternity and Social Friendship*, Vatican City, Libreria Editrice Vaticana [Online]. Available at https://www.vatican.va/content/francesco/en/encyclicals/documents/papa-francesco_20201003_enciclica-fratelli-tutti.html (Accessed 2 February 2022).

Pope Francis (2019) *General Audience: 28 August 2019*, Vatican City, Libreria Editrice Vaticana [Online]. Available at https://www.vatican.va/content/francesco/en/audiences/2019/documents/papa-francesco_20190828_udienza-generale.html (Accessed 2 February 2022).

Pope Francis (2017) *Message of His Holiness Pope Francis to Prof. Margaret Archer, President of the Pontifical Academy of Social Sciences*, Vatican City, Libreria Editrice Vaticana [Online]. Available at https://www.vatican.va/content/francesco/en/messages/pont-messages/2017/documents/papa-francesco_20170424_messaggio-accademia-scienzesociali.html (Accessed 2 February 2022).

Pope Francis (2015) *Meeting with Young People on the Caracciolo Seafront: Address of the Holy Father*, Vatican City, Libreria Editrice Vaticana [Online]. Available at https://www.vatican.va/content/francesco/en/speeches/2015/march/documents/papa-francesco_20150321_napoli-pompei-giovani.html (Accessed 2 February 2022).

Pope Francis (2013a) *Apostolic Exhortation Evangelii Gaudium of the Holy Father Francis to the Bishops, Clergy, Consecrated Persons and the Lay Faithful: On the Proclamation of the Gospel in Today's World*, Vatican City, Libreria Editrice Vaticana [Online]. Available at https://www.vatican.va/content/francesco/en/apost_exhortations/documents/papa-francesco_esortazione-ap_20131124_evangelii-gaudium.html (Accessed 3 February 2022).

Pope Francis (2013b) *Apostolic Blessing "Urbi et Orbi": First Greeting of the Holy Father Pope Francis*, Central Loggia of St. Peter's Basilica [Online]. Available at https://www.vatican.va/content/francesco/en/speeches/2013/march/documents/papa-francesco_20130313_benedizione-urbi-et-orbi.html (Accessed 20 May 2023).

Pope Francis and al-Tayyib, A. (2019) *A Document on Human Fraternity for World Peace and Living Together*, Vatican City, Libreria Editrice Vaticana [Online]. Available at https://www.vatican.va/content/francesco/en/travels/2019/outside/documents/papa-francesco_20190204_documento-fratellanza-umana.html (Accessed 2 February 2022).

Pope Francis (2019) *Apostolic Journey of His Holiness Pope Francis to the United Arab Emirates, Interreligious Meeting at the Founder's Memorial (Abu Dhabi): Address of His Holiness,* Vatican City, Libreria Editrice Vaticana [Online]. Available at https://www.vatican.va/content/francesco/en/speeches/2019/february/documents/papa-francesco_20190204_emiratiarabi-incontrointerreligioso.html (Accessed 08 October 2023).

Pope Francis and Ivereigh, A. (2020) *Let Us Dream: The Path to a Better Future*, London, Simon & Schuster.

Psalm 22: 1, New American Bible (Revised Edition).

Religions for Peace (2019) *Religions for Peace and Institute for Economics and Peace Launch New Positive Peace Partnership for Communities of Faith* [Online]. Available at https://www.rfp.org/religions-for-peace-and-institute-for-economics-and-peace-launch-new-positive-peace-partnership-for-communities-of-faith/#:~:text=Religions%20for%20 Peace%20is%20the,societies%20and%20protect%20the%20earth (Accessed 1 February 2022).

Roosevelt, F. D. (1941) *Annual Message to Congress*, College Park, National Archives [Online]. Available at https://www.archives.gov/milestone-documents/president-franklin-roosevelts-annual-message-to-congress (Accessed 30 January 2022).

Sachedina, A. (2007) 'The Clash of Universalisms: Religious and Secular in Human Rights', *The Hedgehog Review*, vol. 9, no. 3, pp. 49–62.

Sacks, J. (2020a) 'Defeating Death', *RabbiSacks.org* [Blog]. Available at https://www.rabbisacks.org/covenant-conversation/nitzavim/defeating-death/ (Accessed 30 May 2023).

Sacks, J. (2020b) 'Made with Love', *RabbiSacks.org* [Blog]. Available at https://www.rabbisacks.org/covenant-conversation/acharei-mot/made-with-love/ (Accessed 3rd February 2022).

Sandel, M. (2009) *Justice: What's the Right Thing to Do?*, New York, Farrar, Strauss and Giroux.

Schorsch, I. (2005) 'Accounting for God's Silence', *The Jewish Theological Seminary*, 22 January [Online]. Available at http://www.jtsa.edu/accounting-for-gods-silence (Accessed 30 January 2022).

Sen, A. (2009) *The Idea of Justice*, Cambridge, Harvard University Press.

Sievers, J. (2017) '"Where Two or Three …": Shekhinah and Matthew 18:20: Foundations for Jewish-Christian Dialogue and Beyond?', *Claritas: Journal of Dialogue and Culture*, vol. 6, no. 1 [Online]. Available at https://docs.lib.purdue.edu/claritas/vol6/iss1/4.

Sinek, S. (2019) *The Infinite Game*, New York, Portfolio.

Spadaro, A. (2013) *Interview with Pope Francis* [Online]. Available at https://www.vatican.va/content/francesco/en/speeches/2013/september/documents/papa-francesco_20130921_intervista-spadaro.html (Accessed 1 February 2022).

Theobald, C. (2015) 'Mistica della fraternità: Lo stile nuovo della Chiesa e della teología nei documenti programmatici del pontificato', *Il Regno Attualità*, no. 9. [Online] Available at https://www.religionandtransformation.at/fileadmin/user_upload/p_religions_transformation/Veranstaltungen_2._Laufzeit/Franziskuskongress/Il_Regno.pdf (Accessed 30 May 2023).

Thomas, S. (2018) 'St. Francis and Islam: A Critical Appraisal for Contemporary Muslim-Christian Relations, Middle East Politics, and International Relations', *The Downside Review*, vol. 136, no. 1, pp. 3–28.

Thomas, S. (2010) 'Religious and Global Security', *Quaderni di Relazioni Internazionale*, vol. 12, pp. 4–21.

Thomas, S. (2005) *The Global Resurgence of Religion and the Transformation of International Relations: The Struggle for the Soul of the Twenty-First Century*, London, Palgrave Macmillan.

Trotta, S. and Wilkinson, O. (2019) *Partnering with Local Faith Actors to Support Peaceful and Inclusive Societies*, Washington, DC, Joint Learning Initiative on Faith and Local Communities and the International Partnership on Religion and Sustainable Development [Online]. Available at https://jliflc.com/wp-content/uploads/2019/07/PaRD_SDG16_Scoping-Study.pdf (Accessed 1 February 2023).

United Nations (2016) *Agenda for Humanity: Annex to the Report of the Secretary-General for the World Humanitarian Summit*, New York, United Nations [Online]. Available at https://agendaforhumanity.org/sites/default/files/AgendaforHumanity.pdf (Accessed 30 January 2022).

United Nations (1945) *Charter of the United Nations*, New York, United Nations [Online]. Available at https://www.un.org/en/about-us/un-charter/full-text (Accessed 30 January 2022).

United Nations Commission on Human Security (2003) *Human security now: protecting and empowering people,* New York, The Commission [Online]. Available at: https://digitallibrary.un.org/record/503749?ln=es (Accesed: 13 October 2023).

United Nations Development Program (2022) *New Threats to Human Security in the Anthropocene: Demanding Greater Solidarity*, New York, United Nations [Online]. Available at https://hs.hdr.undp.org/pdf/srhs2022.pdf (Accessed 30 January 2022).

United Nations Development Program (1994) *Human Development Report 1994: New Dimensions of Human Security*, New York, United Nations [Online]. Available at http://www.hdr.undp.org/en/content/human-development-report-1994 (Accessed 30 January 2022).

United Nations Environment Program (2022) *Stockholm+50 Interfaith Statement: Faith Values and Reach - Contribution to Environmental Policy*, New York, United Nations [Online]. Available at https://wedocs.unep.org/handle/20.500.11822/40048 (Accessed 24 January 2023).

United Nations General Assembly (2015a) *Sendai Framework for Disaster Risk Reduction 2015–2030*, New York, United Nations [Online]. Available at https://digitallibrary.un.org/record/793460?ln=en#record-files-collapse-header (Accessed 30 January 2021).

United Nations General Assembly (2015b) *Transforming Our World: The 2030 Agenda for Sustainable Development*, New York, United Nations [Online]. Available at: https://www.un.org/en/development/desa/population/migration/generalassembly/docs/globalcompact/A_RES_70_1_E.pdf (Accessed 30 January 2022).

United Nations General Assembly (2012) *A/RES/66/290*, New York, United Nations [Online]. Available at https://www.un.org/humansecurity/wp-content/uploads/2022/06/N1147622.pdf (Accessed 30 January 2022).

United Nations General Assembly (1948a) *Hundred and Eightieth Plenary Meeting, Held at the Palais de Chaillot, Paris, on Thursday, 9 December 1948*, Paris, United Nations [Online]. Available at https://digitallibrary.un.org/record/617875?ln=en (Accessed 30 January 2021).

United Nations General Assembly (1948b) *Universal Declaration of Human Rights*, Paris, United Nations [Online]. Available at https://www.un.org/en/universal-declaration-human-rights/ (Accessed 30 January 2022).

United Nations Interagency Task Force on Religion and Sustainable Development (2020) *Annual Report of the United Nations Interagency Task Force on Religion and Sustainable Development: Engaging with Religion and Faith-based Actors on the 2030 Sustainable Development Agenda*, New York, United Nations Environment Program [Online]. Available at https://www.unep.org/resources/annual-report/2020-annual-report-united-nations-interagency-task-force-religion-and (Accessed 1 February 2022).

United Nations Office for the Coordination of Humanitarian Affairs (OCHA) Policy Development and Studies Branch (PDSB) (2017), *A New Way of Working* [Online]. Available at: https://agendaforhumanity.org/sites/default/files/20170228%20NWoW%2013%20high%20res.pdf (Accessed 9 October 2022).

United Nations Trust Fund for Human Security (2021a) *Leave No One Behind: Harnessing Lessons Learned from Implementing the Human Security Approach*, New York, United Nations [Online]. Available at https://www.un.org/humansecurity/wp-content/uploads/2022/03/FINAL-LNOB-Guidance-Note-for-web_compressed.pdf (Accessed 31 January 2022).

United Nations Trust Fund for Human Security (2021b) *Realizing the Triple Nexus: Experiences from Implementing the Human Security Approach*, New York, United

Nations [Online]. Available at https://www.un.org/humansecurity/wp-content/uploads/2022/03/FINAL-Triple-Nexus-Guidance-Note-for-web_compressed.pdf (Accessed 31 January 2022)

United Nations Trust Fund for Human Security (2016) *Human Security Handbook: An Integrated Approach for the Realization of the Sustainable Development Goals and the Priority Areas of the International Community and the United Nations System*, New York, United Nations [Online]. Available at https://www.un.org/humansecurity/wp-content/uploads/2017/10/h2.pdf (Accessed 30 January 2022).

Waldron, J. (2006) 'Safety and Security', *Nebraska Law Review*, vol. 85, no. 2, pp. 454–507.

Waldron, J. (2003) 'Who Is My Neighbor? Humanity and Proximity', *The Monist*, vol. 86, no. 3, pp. 333–354.

Wellman, J. K. and Lombardi, C. (2012) 'Introduction: Religion and Human Security: An Understudied Relationship', in Wellman, J. K. and Lombardi, C. (eds) *Religion and Human Security: A Global Perspective*, Oxford, Oxford University Press, pp. 1–17.)

Zampini, D. A. (n.d.) 'Loving God's Creation: Biblical Stories for CAFOD's One Climate One World Campaign' [Online]. Available at https://assets.ctfassets.net/vy3axnuecuwj/529b55dad81e097bad3e6817ff236962a3d3bf3780677607abf32f21260562e2/aa853c7ee6408c2077db64b09c5f1fed/Prayer_climate_Genesis-and-Good-Samaritan.pdf (Accessed 3 February 2022).

PART II

Religion, Security, and Geopolitics

3

THE INTERNATIONAL PROTECTION OF FREEDOM OF RELIGION OR BELIEF IN THE CONTEXT OF COUNTER-TERRORISM[1]

Rodrigo Vitorino Souza Alves

1 Counter-Terrorism in the United Nations System

Within the framework of the United Nations, different counter-terrorism initiatives have been developed either by creating institutional structures specifically geared to this end or by forming a regulatory framework to support and guide the actions of the organization and the member states.[2]

In organizational terms, the United Nations has acted in recent decades, culminating in the creation of the United Nations Counter-Terrorism Office on June 15, 2017[3]. Its purposes are to lead the actions within the United Nations system to combat terrorism; to strengthen coordination and coherence between the 38 entities of the Counter-Terrorism Implementation Task Force to ensure a balanced implementation of the four pillars of the Global Strategy (see below); to strengthen the assistance provided by the United Nations to member states in the fight against terrorism[4]; to improve visibility, advocacy, and resource mobilization for United Nations efforts against terrorism; and to ensure that the appropriate priority is given to counter-terrorism throughout the United Nations system and that the actions to prevent violent extremism are firmly rooted in the Global Strategy (Guterres, 2017a, Art. 64).

The new office has brought together the Counter-Terrorism Implementation Task Force[5] and the United Nations Counter-Terrorism Center[6] and should work in collaboration with other offices and departments, especially the United Nations Office on Drugs and Crime, the Counter-Terrorism Committee of the Security Council, and the United Nations Office of the High Commissioner for Human Rights, under which the Special Rapporteur on the Promotion and Protection of Human Rights and Fundamental Freedoms while Countering Terrorism was established in 2005, preventing violations and promoting best practices.[7]

DOI: 10.4324/9781003453086-6

The regulatory framework consists mainly of international conventions and resolutions of the General Assembly and the Security Council. The relevant international conventions deal with issues related to crimes in civil aviation[8] and maritime shipping,[9] protection of internationally protected persons,[10] hostage-taking,[11] explosive materials,[12] nuclear materials,[13] nuclear terrorism,[14] bomb attacks,[15] and terrorist financing.[16]

In its resolutions, the General Assembly has addressed problems related to terrorist activities as a threat to international relations,[17] prevention[18] and elimination[19] of international terrorism, prevention of the risk of radiological terrorism,[20] prevention of the acquisition by terrorists of radioactive materials and sources,[21] and weapons of mass destruction.[22] The body has also dealt with other issues, including technical assistance for the implementation of international conventions and protocols relating to terrorism,[23] the inadmissibility of policies that constitute official or state terrorism, and of any actions by states aimed at undermining the socio-political system of other sovereign states,[24] hostage-taking,[25] and terrorist attacks on internationally protected persons.[26] The terrorist attacks on the United States of America were also condemned through a resolution.[27] Regarding human rights, there is a significant body of resolutions dealing with the relationship between human rights and terrorist activities,[28] the protection of human rights in the fight against terrorism,[29] and the problem of intolerance, stigmatization, and violence motivated by religion.[30]

The most comprehensive resolution and Plan of Action has been called the "United Nations Global Counter-Terrorism Strategy."[31] Resulting from the negotiations at the 2005 World Summit,[32] the document was adopted unanimously by the General Assembly and establishes a common strategy for combating and preventing terrorism in all its forms and manifestations, which is submitted to review every two years when surveys, reports, and recommendations are presented.[33] The Plan of Action, consisting of four pillars, has been attached to the Global Strategy: (1) "Measures to address the conditions conducive to the spread of terrorism," (2) "Measures to prevent and combat terrorism," (3) "Measures to build States' capacity to prevent and combat terrorism and to strengthen the role of the United Nations system in this regard," and (4) "Measures to ensure respect for human rights for all and the rule of law as the fundamental basis of the fight against terrorism". For each pillar, there is a set of guidelines, recommendations, and strategies related to counter-terrorism.

Within the Security Council, resolutions address problems related to the prevention and fight against terrorism and terrorist organizations,[34] condemnation of actions and establishment of sanction regimes for Al-Qaeda, Taliban, the Islamic State, and associated groups,[35] exceptions for humanitarian reasons,[36] human trafficking,[37] protection of critical infrastructure,[38] protection of cultural heritage,[39] hostage-taking,[40] civil aviation,[41] non-payment of ransom to kidnapping terrorists,[42] travel and arms embargo,[43] establishment and arrangement of monitoring and supervision bodies,[44] international judicial cooperation,[45] and the condemnation of terrorist attacks.[46]

It is important to note that Resolution No. 1373[47] sets out the general framework for counter-terrorism within the Security Council. The document was adopted unanimously (by 15 votes) on September 28, 2001, and inaugurated the exercise of legislative competence by the body, marking a significant and controversial transformation in international law.[48] In reaction to the attacks on the Twin Towers and showing deep concern "by the increase, in various regions of the world, of acts of terrorism motivated by intolerance or extremism" (*United Nations Security Council*, 2001a), the Council defined a series of measures to be adopted by states, which relates to the prevention and suppression of funding, planning, support, facilitation, preparation, and execution of terrorist acts, including the freezing of funds, values, and other financial resources; blocking the recruitment of members and arms supply; the refusal of entry, shelter, and refuge; the development of preventive alert mechanisms; effective enforcement of justice; criminalization of terrorism; assistance and international cooperation in administrative, judicial, investigative, and operational matters; strict control at borders and in procedures for issuing travel and identification documents; and adoption and implementation of relevant international instruments.

2 Protecting Human Rights while Countering Terrorism Motivated by Religious Extremism

The normative and organizational architecture presented above expresses the United Nations' concern with the problem of terrorism. However, the same documents that reinforce the importance of implementing counter-terrorism measures require compliance with human rights standards.[49] Although they may be considered popular or consistent with public opinion, any limitations imposed by states that are not supported by the grounds for limitation or suspension provided in international instruments are characterized as violations of human rights.[50] The occurrence of terrorist acts, although violent and frequent, does not justify or allow states to disregard human rights. Indeed, this seems to be one of the goals of religious extremism: that states and collectivities succumb to fear, become similar to those that promote it, favor the creation of a highly polarized environment, and thus contribute to the radicalization of victims from the abuse of power.

Themes related to the protection of human rights in counter-terrorism, as well as the intersection of these issues with religion or belief, are dealt with by the General Assembly in the Global Strategy, Plan of Action, and resolutions on the protection of human rights when fighting against terrorism and religious intolerance, as well as by the Security Council and the

Human Rights Council.[51] In addition, international declarations and treaties set out fundamental guidelines, such as the Charter of the United Nations, the Universal Declaration of Human Rights, the International Covenant on Civil and Political Rights, the 1949 Geneva Conventions and their additional 1977 Protocols, the 1951 Convention Relating to the Status of Refugees and its 1967 Protocol, the 1981 Declaration on the Elimination of All Forms of Intolerance and Discrimination Based on Religion or Belief, and the 1993 Vienna Declaration and Programme of Action.

The United Nations Global Counter-Terrorism Strategy recalls respect for human rights, in particular, equality and non-discrimination on grounds of race, sex, language, and religion. In this sense, and in a manner consistent with the Universal Declaration and the International Covenant, religion cannot operate as a basis for any kind of unfavorable state treatment. Furthermore, it is stated that terrorism cannot and must not be associated with any religion, nationality, civilization, or ethnic group, so it must not be assumed, presupposed, or inferred that there is a connection or identification between a particular religion, national origin or ethnicity, and extremism, violence, or terrorism.[52] It is also recognized that development, peace and security, and human rights are interconnected and mutually reinforcing. The document also declares that member states will continue to promote human rights for all, the rule of law, intercultural understanding, and respect for all religions, religious values, beliefs, or cultures.

As for the Plan of Action, the first pillar aims to tackle the conditions that favor the spread of terrorism. Although they are neither excuses nor justifications for the practice of terrorism, the following situations are recognized as some of the conditions that favor it: the existence of prolonged conflicts, the dehumanization of victims, the absence of the rule of law, the violation of human rights, ethnic, national and religious discrimination, political exclusion, socioeconomic marginalization, and the absence of good governance. To cope with these situations, the Plan of Action recommends different measures, which include the development of initiatives and programs to promote dialogue, tolerance, and understanding between civilizations, cultures, peoples, and religions, and to promote mutual respect and prevent defamation of religions, religious values, beliefs, and cultures (measure 2)[53]; the establishment and encouragement of education and awareness programs aimed at promoting a culture of peace, justice, and human development, ethnic, national and religious tolerance, and respect for all religions, religious values, beliefs, or cultures (measure 3).

Especially relevant for this discussion, the fourth pillar of the Plan of Action brings together measures aimed at ensuring respect for human rights for all people and the rule of law as the fundamental basis of the fight against terrorism. Essentially, the document encourages states to observe international human rights protection instruments, highlights the interrelationship between the rule of law, respect for human rights and criminal justice, values the effectiveness of criminal justice, recommends that terrorist acts should be prohibited by law as serious criminal offenses, and reaffirms the importance of the United Nations system and international collaboration in the fight against terrorism. In addition to these measures, the document refers to the resolution on the protection of human rights in the fight against terrorism (see below for the latest version of the resolution, adopted in 2013).

Through the review at the end of the first decade of implementing the Global Strategy and Plan of Action in 2016,[54] the General Assembly reinforces its concern about acts of intolerance, violent extremism leading to terrorism, violence in general, sectarian violence, and terrorism in various parts of the world, which have claimed innocent lives, caused destruction and population displacement, condemning them in all their forms and manifestations, including in incitements to commit acts of terrorism. Furthermore, it recognizes the commitment of all religions to peace and reaffirms that terrorism, even when motivated by violent extremism, cannot and must not be associated with any religion, nationality, civilization, or ethnic group, and notes that respect for all religions, religious values, beliefs, and cultures must be ensured. Like the Plan of Action, while recognizing the conditions conducive to the spread of terrorism, it reaffirms that none of them can dig into or justify acts of terrorism. As regards preventive strategies, the resolution encourages states to establish mechanisms for engaging young people in the promotion of a culture of peace, tolerance, and intercultural and interreligious dialogue; recommends states to promote understanding of respect for human dignity and diversity through educational programs that discourage participation in acts of terrorism, violent extremism conducive to terrorism, violence, xenophobia and all forms of discrimination; empowers young people by promoting media and information literacy and inclusion in decision-making processes; and calls on states, regional organizations, non-governmental organizations, religious communities, and the media to contribute to the promotion of tolerance, mutual understanding, dialogue, and respect for cultural and religious diversity and for human rights. The document adds that states should prevent abuse or misuse of the status of non-governmental, non-profit, and philanthropic organizations by terrorists, without violating the freedoms of expression, association, and religion or belief of all persons, freedoms that must be fully respected. It is also affirmed that terrorists have produced distorted narratives based on a misinterpretation of religion to justify violence, which is used to recruit foreign supporters and combatants, to mobilize resources and gain support from sympathizers, especially through the Internet and social media, a situation that requires international mobilization to combat such activities. Finally, the document recognizes the continuity, severity, and breadth of the risks posed by the Islamic State, Al-Qaeda, and individuals, groups, or entities affiliated with them, while encouraging states to observe the sanctions established by the Security Council and to implement measures to combat terrorism through transparent and fair procedures.

Resolution 178 of 2013,[55] which dealt with the protection of human rights in counter-terrorism, stands out. The document reaffirms the importance of respect for human rights in reaction to terrorism and fear of terrorism, the obligation of states to protect human rights, and that any anti-terrorism measure must be consistent with international human rights law, refugee law, and humanitarian law. Specifically, it is stated that terrorism cannot and must not be associated with any religion, nationality, civilization, or ethnic group; counter-terrorism measures must be applied taking into account the human rights of all, including persons belonging to national, ethnic, religious, and linguistic minorities, in order to avoid discrimination based on race, color, sex, language, social origin, or religion[56]; even in the case of terrorism, the sending of persons by means of deportation, extradition, or expulsion procedures to the state of origin or a third party should be avoided in the event of danger to life, physical integrity, or freedom on grounds of race, nationality, participation in a particular social group, political opinion, or religion, although the state must abide by the duty to apply the legislation to the subject that has not been sent; and, furthermore, no use must be made of profiles created from stereotypes based on discrimination prohibited by international law, such as discrimination on racial, ethnic, and/or religious grounds.

Resolution 157 of 2015[57] dealt with the fight against intolerance, the creation of negative stereotypes, stigmatization, discrimination, incitement to violence, and violence against people based on religion or belief, an approach taken by the General Assembly since the body replaced the resolution that used to deal with the ban on "defamation of religions," in 2012 (see note above). As in previous documents, the resolution reaffirms that terrorism cannot and must not be associated with any religion, nationality, civilization, or ethnic group, while it condemns the criminal acts committed by extremist groups on the grounds of religion or belief and deplores the attempts to associate these acts with a particular religion or belief. Moreover, it is stated that violence cannot be an acceptable response to acts of intolerance motivated by religion or belief, demonstrating concern about the increase in incidents involving religious intolerance and hatred, and the creation of negative stereotypes and stigmatization based on religion or belief. The document also condemns the spread of religious hatred to incite discrimination, hostility, or violence, whether through printed, audiovisual, electronic, or other media. Recognizing the need for public debate of ideas and intercultural, interreligious, and inter-faith dialogue for the elimination of prejudice alongside the need to promote awareness of the gravity of these crimes and the importance of tolerance toward cultural and religious diversity, the document calls upon states to implement a series of measures based on the proposal of the Organization for Islamic Cooperation, which aimed to promote a domestic environment of religious tolerance, peace, and respect, including the creation of collaborative networks for mutual understanding and dialogue; establishment of government mechanisms for identifying sources of inter-religious tension and conflict prevention; capacity building for public actors; encouragement of community leaders to identify causes of discrimination and develop prevention strategies; development of campaigns against intolerance; criminalization of incitement to imminent violence based on religion or belief; education and awareness of the problem of negative religious stereotypes and incitement to religious hatred; and recognition of the importance of dialogue. Finally, it calls on states to ensure that public officials avoid the promotion of discrimination, protect religious freedom and plurality by guaranteeing the free manifestation of religion, encourage the effective representation and participation of individuals in all sectors of society regardless of their religion or belief, and combat the creation of religious profiles, i.e. the offensive and unfair use of religion as a criterion in the conduct of questions, searches, and other legal investigation procedures.[58]

The Security Council has expressed similar concerns, emphasizing the importance of intercultural dialogue to prevent the indiscriminate segregation of religions and cultures. The Council underlines the role of various sectors of society (including communities and religious organizations) in the promotion of tolerance and coexistence, and calls on states to take the necessary measures to contain incitement to terrorism motivated by extremism and intolerance and to prevent the subversion of educational, cultural, and religious institutions by terrorists and their supporters.[59] The Council has also stressed that countering the threat posed by foreign terrorist combatants requires the confrontation of the underlying factors, which can be done by promoting political and religious tolerance, economic development, cohesion, and social inclusion. Furthermore, states are encouraged to face the conditions that facilitate the spread of violent extremism through the empowerment of young people, families, women, and leaders in the religious, cultural, and educational sectors, as well as involve local communities and non-governmental actors in the development of strategies to combat extremist narratives.[60]

On the last point, a comprehensive international framework for combating terrorist narratives or discourses has been established.[61] In condemning the incitement to terrorism and repudiating attempts to justify or glorify terrorist acts, the Security Council calls on states and international organizations to cooperate in a comprehensive approach to prevent and disable the terrorist threat and calls on the media, civil society, religious communities, the business sector, and educational institutions to engage in promoting tolerance and fighting terrorist narratives. With the new framework, guidelines are established for actions aimed at preventing the Islamic State, Al-Qaeda, and associates from using narratives to encourage, motivate, and recruit others to practice acts of terrorism. On the one hand, counter-narrative campaigns must refute the terrorist message and operate as instruments for countering incitement to hatred; on the other, they must amplify positive narratives, provide viable alternatives, and address issues of concern to vulnerable groups that may be affected by terrorist discourse.

Finally, the reports presented by the Special Rapporteur on the Promotion and Protection of Human Rights and Fundamental Freedoms while Countering Terrorism of the Human Rights Council are also relevant to this legal framework. In the document prepared by the then-Special Rapporteur Martin Scheinin in 2010,[62] he proposes a set of ten best practices for the better implementation of the Global Strategy by states, addressing some of the main problems related to anti-terrorist measures, namely: (1) consistency of anti-terrorist legislation with human rights, refugee law, and humanitarian law; (2) consistency of anti-terrorist practices with human rights, refugee law, and humanitarian law; (3) the exceptional nature of regimes and emergency measures; (4) independent mechanism for reviewing counter-terrorism laws and practices; (5) provision of remedies and guarantees against human rights violations; (6) reparation and assistance to victims of terrorism; (7) definition of terrorism consistent with international legal instruments; (8) prohibition of incitement to terrorism and protection of freedom of expression; (9) listing of entities and persons associated with terrorism; and (10) arrest and interrogation of persons suspected of terrorism.

In turn, in the document drawn up by then-Special Rapporteur Ben Emmerson in 2016, recommendations were presented for the prevention of and the fight against violent extremism from the perspective of human rights.[63] While the report considers that the concept of violent extremism is broader than that of terrorism (because not all forms of violence are motivated by religious or ideological extremism are acts of terrorism), extremism can lead to acts of terrorism (as those perpetrated by the Islamic State, Al-Qaeda, and Boko Haram, mentioned above), so that countering extremism is intrinsically linked to counter-terrorism. According to the report, in order to prevent abuses and violations of human rights, it is necessary that further research on the phenomenon of violent extremism, and especially on the factors leading to radicalization, be promoted; states strive to implement pillars I and IV of the Global Strategy, as this is the only holistic, effective, and sustainable approach to counter-terrorism; strategies and policies adopted by states be firmly based on international human rights law, so that, in the application of restrictions, the potential impact on women, children, ethnic and religious communities, and other specific groups is considered; all restrictive measures be subject to parliamentary and judicial control; particular attention be paid to the impact of the measures on freedom of expression and freedom of thought, conscience, and religion; the measures be non-discriminatory; and states promote the human rights of all people, of all ages, genders, and ethnic and religious affiliations, without discrimination and without making this protection conditional on some other agenda.[64]

3 International Parameters for Restricting Freedom of Manifestation of Religion or Belief in the Context of Counter-Terrorism

Freedom of religion or belief provides comprehensive protection related to the internal or subjective aspects of belief and conscience, as well as to the external manifestation of religion and beliefs, including these rights:

1. to adopt, change, or renounce a religion or belief, without coercion;
2. not to reveal religious affiliation;
3. to be gathered together in private or public worship;
4. to observe religious rites and practices;
5. to carry out the teaching, proselytizing, and dissemination of religious materials and publications[65];
6. to not fulfill an obligation imposed on everyone on the grounds of conscience, without prejudice to an alternative obligation (conscientious objection);
7. to create, acquire, and use religious symbols;
8. to observe religious holidays and days of rest;
9. to train, appoint, and elect religious leaders;
10. of parents to promote and ensure the religious and moral education of their children;
11. of communication between individuals and communities in the field of religion, including in the international sphere; and
12. to establish religious, humanitarian, and charitable institutions (cf. Bielefeldt et al., 2016, pp. 55–306).[66]

These rights and freedoms are reinforced by equality and non-discrimination, which protects individuals and collectivities from undue demands of registration for religious organizations, from discriminatory treatment by public bodies, and from discriminatory treatment against women, among others. In addition, the right to the protection of places of worship imposes a duty of respect on people in general and the duties of protection and promotion on the state. In the case of religious minorities, special protections have been affirmed to ensure that members of religious minority groups can effectively exercise their human rights.

Concerning restrictions on freedom of religion or belief, the two dimensions of their exercise must be considered. The rights and freedoms that make up the *forum internum* (i.e. the internal dimension), which includes adherence to a belief or religion, the freedom to maintain, renounce, or change a belief or religion, as well as the freedom not to reveal one's belief or religion (items 1 and 2) are absolute freedoms; the state is not allowed to impose any restrictions on their exercise or scope.[67] On the other hand, the rights and freedoms associated with the *forum externum* (i.e. the externalization of belief or religion) cannot be protected in an absolute way, as their exercise can interfere in relevant and legally protected assets or interests (Joseph et al., 2005, p. 506) (for a discussion on the problems of the distinction between *forum internum* and *forum externum*, see Ghanea (2008)).[68] The manifestation of religion (items 3–12) will be subject to the limitations provided for in Article 18.3 of the International Covenant.

Thus, the International Covenant, while protecting the *forum externum* in a strengthened or qualified manner, does so only relatively, because restrictions on freedom of religion or belief in that dimension are allowed. Article 18.3 presents as the legitimate grounds for restriction (or permissible limitations) the protection of public safety, order,[69] health, and[70] morals,[71] as well as the protection of the rights and freedoms of other persons. Besides, the principle of legality must be observed and the need for restriction shall be demonstrated.

To this end, the imposition of restrictions must be provided for in the law and must not be carried out in such a way as to vitiate the freedoms guaranteed in Article 18 together with the other rights and principles contained in the International Covenant, in particular equality and non-discrimination. Since the list is exhaustive, only the restrictions specifically provided for in Article 18.3 are authorized, and the means to achieve the intended purpose should be applied in a less restrictive manner, respecting the proportionality between means and aims, considering whether the impact of the restrictive measures on freedom of religion or belief does not exceed the interest or asset they sought to protect.[72]

Because of the above, the following test must be observed for the identification of the conformity of a restrictive intervention with international law:

1 Does the restriction on the manifestation of religion or belief pursue a legitimate aim?
2 Is the restriction on the manifestation of religion or belief provided for in the law?
3 Is the restriction on the manifestation of religion or belief necessary?

If such questions are answered positively in the context of a democratic society, the restriction on freedom of religion or belief may be considered appropriate to the international standards agreed by the 173 states that are parties to the International Covenant.

Regarding the issue of terrorism, since the International Covenant on Civil and Political Rights does not authorize the suspension of freedom of thought, conscience, and religion in exceptional situations of threat to the existence of the nation,[73] and considering that the freedom to adopt, change, or renounce a religion or belief is not subject to limitations, any restriction may be applied only to the manifestation of religion or belief under Article 18.3. In this sense, it is essential that actions to combat terrorism are designed to fulfill a legitimate purpose, are provided for in the law, and are necessary.[74]

Concerning legitimate grounds, only those provided for in the International Covenant are permitted to justify a restriction, namely, the promotion of public safety, order, health, or morals, or the protection of the rights and freedoms of other persons. In this sense, it is reasonable to conclude that any form of terrorist act (as defined in this study) may be viewed as a legitimate ground for the imposition of restrictions since terrorism (by its nature) seriously endangers public order, safety, and health, as well as the rights to life, physical integrity, freedom, and property of others. It is worth pointing out that the manifestation of religion or belief cannot be restricted in the name of national security,[75] understood as the protection of the nation's existence, territorial integrity, or political independence.[76]

As for the provision in the law, it is essential that the restriction of freedom of religion or belief on the grounds of terrorism is adequately described in legislation, especially supported by an accessible and precise criminal offense rule that does not promote discrimination and is not retroactive, which penalty is proportional to the seriousness of the act and is consistent with international law, including human rights.[77] These characteristics must also be present in the legal provision of other judicial and administrative measures, including those applied to legal persons.

Finally, the analysis of the necessity of the measure should assess at least:

1 The effectiveness of the measure for the attainment of the desired end;
2 The absence of a viable alternative capable of achieving the same intended purpose in a less invasive or harmful manner;
3 The existence of a founded suspicion or demonstration of participation in terrorist activity (because religion or belief *per se* cannot operate as a basis for any kind of unfavorable treatment by the state);
4 Respect for equality and non-discrimination (with special care to avoid the creation of stigmatizing effects or the establishment of negative stereotypes on a religious community);
5 The impact of the measure on the freedoms it restricts (so that it is considered whether the interest in imposing the measure overcomes interest in the good it seeks to protect);
6 The potential impact of the measures adopted on women, children, ethnic or religious communities, and any other specific groups, especially minority groups or vulnerable groups;

7 The impact of the measures on freedom of expression and freedom of thought, conscience, and religion, so that there is no excess fueled by the state of fear or alarm;
8 The differentiation between a religious denomination and the terrorist agent (while the religious element in terrorist activity – the violent extremism – is identifiable, a religion should not be associated with terrorism, to prevent a criminal act perpetrated by an individual or group from being attributed to the religious community in general or to prevent restrictive measures from being applied in a generalized and indiscriminate manner); and
9 The existence or absence of abuse or misuse of the status of non-governmental, non-profit, philanthropic, or religious entities by terrorists for the practice of illicit acts.

In applying these considerations to the limitation of the rights and freedoms related to religion or belief, it can be concluded that it may be considered legitimate and necessary, for example, the interference in the autonomy of religious organizations, freedom of association for religious purposes, freedom of assembly for religious purposes and the protection of places of worship (by entering into a religious building or interrupting religious acts) for the repression or prevention of terrorism, as well as interference in the freedoms of teaching religion and disseminating religious material (digital or printed) to contain incitement or apology to terrorism.[78]

On the other hand, limitations on entry or residence in the national territory, access to public places, registration of religious organizations, training of religious leaders, the use of religious symbols and garments when founded on the requirement of a particular religious doctrine are excessive, as well as discrimination in the recognition of conscientious objections. However, it must be acknowledged that, in the case of an organization or movement clearly associated with violent religious extremism, interference becomes legitimate, since the ideology itself turns into a violation of human rights when it promotes hatred that constitutes incitement to discrimination, hostility, or violence.

4 Conclusion

In a context of insecurity and violent extremism, measures imposed by states aiming to prevent and counter terrorism might be converted into an interference offensive to international human rights law. Restricting freedom of religion or belief on the grounds of security and terrorism, accordingly, shall contain a series of inherent qualities and shall be scrutinized under a strict necessity test to shield that human right from abuses and violation.

In order to ensure consistency between counter-terrorism measures and protection of freedom of religion or belief, the chapter formulates a set of nine standards or conditions, in addition to the tripartite test of limitations (focusing on the necessity prong), that can guide the assessment of the necessity of a restriction imposed on freedom of religion or belief.

Notes

1 An earlier version of this chapter was published in Portuguese at Rodrigo Vitorino Souza Alves, "A Proteção Internacional Da Liberdade de Crença e Religião No Contexto Do Combate Ao Terrorismo," in *Novos Estudos Sobre Liberdade Religiosa, Risco e Segurança No Século XXI*, ed. Davide Argiolas (Lisboa: Petrony, 2018), 181–223.

2 The oldest document available in the United Nations electronic archive on the subject of terrorism and counter-terrorism is a letter sent to the Secretary-General and Security Council by the Israeli Interim Government, which presents a summary of the emergency rules adopted for the prevention of terrorism (Law 5708), which consists of the definition of terrorist crimes and applicable sanctions (Bunche, 1948).

3 Resolution of General Assembly No. A/RES/71/291 of June 15, 2017 (*United Nations General Assembly,* 2017).

4 In addition to the Global Strategy and Plan of Action, a report of the Secretary-General aimed to provide concrete suggestions to the General Assembly for their implementation, which are outlined in the document "Capability of the United Nations system to assist Member States in implementing the United Nations Global Counter-Terrorism Strategy" (Guterres, 2017a).

5 Institutionalized by Resolution No. A/RES/64/235 of December 24, 2009 (*United Nations General Assembly*, 2009a). Here and in what follows, all United Nations documents may be accessed at https://undocs.org.

6 Created by Resolution No. A/RES/66/10 of November 18, 2011 (*United Nations General Assembly*, 2011a).

7 Resolution of the Commission on Human Rights No. 2005/80 of April 21, 2005 (*United Nations Commission on Human Rights*, 2005), and General Assembly Resolution No. A/RES/60/251 of March 15, 2006 (*United Nations General Assembly*, 2006a). For the annual reports submitted to the Human Rights Council and the General Assembly of the United Nations, see http://www.ohchr.org/EN/Issues/Terrorism/Pages/Annual.aspx.

8 See Convention on Offences and Certain Other Acts Committed on Board Aircraft (*United Nations*, 1963), Convention for the Suppression of Unlawful Seizure of Aircraft (*United Nations*, 1970), Convention for the Suppression of Unlawful Acts against the Safety of Civil Aviation (*United Nations*, 1971), Protocol on the Suppression of Unlawful Acts of Violence at Airports Serving International Civil Aviation (*United Nations*, 1988a), Convention on the Suppression of Unlawful Acts Relating to International Civil Aviation (*United Nations*, 2010a), Protocol Supplementary to the Convention for the Suppression of Unlawful Seizure of Aircraft (*United Nations*, 2010b), and Protocol to Amend the Convention on Offences and Certain Other Acts Committed on Board Aircraft (*United Nations*, 2014).

9 See Convention for the Suppression of Unlawful Acts against the Safety of Maritime Navigation (*United Nations*, 1988b), Protocol for the Suppression of Unlawful Acts against the Safety of Fixed Platforms Located on the Continental Shelf

(*United Nations*, 1988c), and Protocol to the Convention for the Suppression of Unlawful Acts against the Safety of Maritime Navigation (*United Nations*, 2005a).

10 See Convention on the Prevention and Punishment of Crimes against Internationally Protected Persons, Including Diplomatic Agents (*United Nations*, 1973). Internationally protected persons include Heads of State, Ministers of Foreign Affairs, representatives or officers of a state or international organization, and their relatives.

11 See International Convention against the Taking of Hostages (*United Nations*, 1979a).

12 See Convention on the Marking of Plastic Explosives for the Purpose of Detection (*United Nations*, 1991).

13 See Convention on the Physical Protection of Nuclear Material (*United Nations*, 1979b) and Amendments to the Convention on the Physical Protection of Nuclear Material (*United Nations*, 2005b).

14 See International Convention for the Suppression of Acts of Nuclear Terrorism (*United Nations*, 2005c).

15 See International Convention for the Suppression of Terrorist Bombing (*United Nations*, 1997).

16 See International Convention for the Suppression of the Financing of Terrorism (*United Nations*, 1999).

17 In the Declaration on Principles of International Law concerning Friendly Relations and Co-operation among States in accordance with the Charter of the United Nations (*United Nations General Assembly*, 1970), the issue is addressed in the context of two principles. Regarding the principle that prohibits states "from the threat or use of force against the territorial integrity or political independence of any State, or in any other manner inconsistent with the purposes of the United Nations," it is affirmed that

> Every State has the duty to refrain from organizing, instigating, assisting or participating in acts of civil strife or terrorist acts in another State or acquiescing in organized activities within its territory directed towards the commission of such acts, when the acts referred to in the present paragraph involve a threat or use of force.
>
> *(United Nations General Assembly, 1970)*

In turn, in relation to the principle "concerning the duty not to intervene in matters within the domestic jurisdiction of any State, in accordance with the Charter," it is affirmed that

> No State may use or encourage the use of economic, political or any other type of measures to coerce another State in order to obtain from it the subordination of the exercise of its sovereign rights and to secure from It advantages of any kind. Also, no State shall organize, assist, foment, finance, incite or tolerate subversive, terrorist or armed activities directed towards the violent overthrow of the regime of another State, or interfere in civil strife in another State.
>
> *(United Nations General Assembly, 1970)*

18 See Resolutions No. A/RES/44/29 of December 4, 1989 (*United Nations General Assembly*, 1989), A/RES/42/159 of December 7, 1987 (*United Nations General Assembly*, 1987), A/RES/40/61 of December 9, 1985 (*United Nations General Assembly*, 1985), A/RES/38/130 of December 19, 1983 (*United Nations General Assembly*, 1983), A/RES/36/109 of December 10, 1981 (*United Nations General Assembly*, 1981a), A/RES/34/145 of December 17, 1979 (*United*

Nations General Assembly, 1979), A/RES/32/147 of December 16, 1977 (*United Nations General Assembly*, 1977), A/RES/31/102 of December 15, 1976 (*United Nations General Assembly*, 1976), and A/RES/3034(XXVII) of December 18, 1972 (*United Nations General Assembly*, 1972).

19 See Resolutions No. A/RES/71/151 of December 13, 2016 (*United Nations General Assembly*, 2016a), A/RES/68/119 of December 16, 2013 (*United Nations General Assembly*, 2013a), A/RES/67/99 of December 14, 2012 (*United Nations General Assembly*, 2012a), A/RES/66/105 of December 9, 2011 (*United Nations General Assembly*, 2011b), A/RES/65/34 of December 6, 2010 (*United Nations General Assembly*, 2010a), A/RES/64/118 of December 16, 2009 (*United Nations General Assembly*, 2009b), A/RES/63/129 of December 11, 2008 (*United Nations General Assembly*, 2008a), A/RES/62/71 of December 6, 2007 (*United Nations General Assembly*, 2007a), A/RES/61/40 of December 4, 2006 (*United Nations General Assembly*, 2006b), A/RES/60/43 of December 8, 2005 (*United Nations General Assembly*, 2005a), A/RES/59/46 of December 2, 2004 (*United Nations General Assembly*, 2004a), A/RES/58/81 of December 9, 2003 (*United Nations General Assembly*, 2003a), A/RES/57/27 of November 19, 2002 (*United Nations General Assembly*, 2002a), A/RES/56/88 of December 12, 2001 (*United Nations General Assembly*, 2001a), A/RES/55/158 of December 12, 2000 (*United Nations General Assembly*, 2000), A/RES/54/110 of December 9, 1999 (*United Nations General Assembly*, 1999a), A/RES/53/108 of December 8, 1998 (*United Nations General Assembly*, 1998), A/RES/52/165 of December 15, 1997 (*United Nations General Assembly*, 1997a), A/RES/51/210 of December 17, 1996 (*United Nations General Assembly*, 1996), A/RES/50/53 of December 11, 1995 (*United Nations General Assembly*, 1995a), A/RES/49/60 of December 9, 1994 (*United Nations General Assembly*, 1994a), and A/RES/46/51 of December 9, 1991 (*United Nations General Assembly*, 1991). For a report by the General Assembly on the role of states in relation to measures to eliminate international terrorism, see U.N. Doc. No. A/72/111 of June 21, 2017 (Guterres, 2017b).

20 See Resolution No. A/RES/60/73 of December 8, 2005 (*United Nations General Assembly*, 2005b).

21 See Resolutions No. A/RES/65/74 of December 8, 2010 (*United Nations General Assembly*, 2010b) and A/RES/62/46 of December 5, 2007 (*United Nations General Assembly*, 2007b).

22 See Resolutions No. A/RES/66/50 of December 2, 2011 (*United Nations General Assembly*, 2011c), A/RES/65/62 of December 8, 2010 (*United Nations General Assembly*, 2010c), A/RES/64/38 of December 2, 2009 (*United Nations General Assembly*, 2009c), A/RES/63/60 of December 2, 2008 (*United Nations General Assembly*, 2008b), A/RES/62/33 of December 5, 2007 (*United Nations General Assembly*, 2007c), A/RES/61/86 of December 6, 2006 (*United Nations General Assembly*, 2006c), A/RES/60/78 of December 8, 2005 (*United Nations General Assembly*, 2005c), A/RES/59/80 of December 3, 2004 (*United Nations General Assembly*, 2004b), A/RES/58/48 of December 8, 2003 (*United Nations General Assembly*, 2003b), and A/RES/57/83 of November 22, 2002 (*United Nations General Assembly*, 2002b).

23 See Resolutions No. A/RES/68/187 of December 18, 2013 (*United Nations General Assembly*, 2013b), A/RES/66/178 of December 19, 2011 (*United Nations General Assembly*, 2011d), A/RES/64/177 of December 18, 2009 (*United Nations General Assembly*, 2009d), and A/RES/62/172 of December 18, 2007 (*United Nations General Assembly*, 2007d).

24 See Resolution No. A/RES/39/159 of Monday, December 17, 1984 (*United Nations General Assembly*, 1984).

25 See Resolutions No. A/RES/61/172 of December 19, 2006 (*United Nations General Assembly*, 2006d), and A/RES/57/220 of December 18, 2002 (*United Nations General Assembly*, 2002c).

26 See Resolution No. A/RES/66/12 of Friday, November 18, 2011 (*United Nations General Assembly*, 2011e).

27 See Resolution No. A/RES/56/1 of Wednesday, September 12, 2001 (*United Nations General Assembly*, 2001b).

28 See Resolutions No. A/RES/59/195 of December 20, 2004 (*United Nations General Assembly*, 2004c), A/RES/58/174 of December 22, 2003 (*United Nations General Assembly*, 2003c), A/RES/56/160 of December 19, 2001 (*United Nations General Assembly*, 2001c), A/RES/54/164 of December 17, 1999 (*United Nations General Assembly*, 1999b), A/RES/52/133 of December 12, 1997 (*United Nations General Assembly*, 1997b), A/RES/50/186 of December 22, 1995 (*United Nations General Assembly*, 1995b), A/RES/49/185 of December 23, 1994 (*United Nations General Assembly*, 1994b), and A/RES/48/122 of December 20, 1993 (*United Nations General Assembly*, 1993).

29 See Resolutions No. A/RES/68/178 of December 18, 2013 (*United Nations General Assembly*, 2013c), A/RES/66/171 of December 19, 2011 (*United Nations General Assembly*, 2011f), A/RES/65/221 of December 21, 2010 (*United Nations General Assembly*, 2010d), A/RES/64/168 of December 18, 2009 (*United Nations General Assembly*, 2009e), A/RES/63/185 of December 18, 2008 (*United Nations General Assembly*, 2008c), A/RES/62/159 of December 18, 2007 (*United Nations General Assembly*, 2007e), A/RES/61/171 of December 19, 2006 (*United Nations General Assembly*, 2006e), A/RES/60/158 of December 16, 2005 (*United Nations General Assembly*, 2005d), A/RES/59/191 of December 20, 2004 (*United Nations General Assembly*, 2004d), A/RES/58/187 of December 22, 2003 (*United Nations General Assembly*, 2003d), A/RES/57/219 of December 18, 2002 (*United Nations General Assembly*, 2002d).

30 See Resolutions No. A/RES/70/157 of December 17, 2015 (*United Nations General Assembly*, 2015), and A/RES/69/174 of December 18, 2014 (*United Nations General Assembly*, 2014a).

31 See Resolution No. A/RES/60/288 of September 8, 2006 (*United Nations General Assembly*, 2006f).

32 At the summit of world leaders, issues related to development, security, and human rights were discussed. For the results of the meeting, see General Assembly Resolution No. A/RES/60/1 of September 16, 2005 (*United Nations General Assembly*, 2005e).

33 See Resolutions No. A/RES/72/284 of June 26, 2018 (*United Nations General Assembly*, 2018), A/70/L.55 of July 1, 2016 (*United Nations General Assembly*, 2016b), A/RES/68/276 of June 13, 2014 (*United Nations General Assembly*, 2014b), A/RES/66/282 of June 29, 2012 (*United Nations General Assembly*, 2012b), A/RES/64/297 of September 8, 2010 (*United Nations General Assembly*, 2010e), and A/RES/62/272 of September 5, 2008 (*United Nations General Assembly*, 2008d).

34 Resolutions No. S/RES/1269 of October 19, 1999 (*United Nations Security Council*, 1999a), S/RES/1373 of September 28, 2001 (*United Nations Security Council*, 2001a), S/RES/1377 of November 12, 2001 (*United Nations Security Council*, 2001b), S/RES/1624 of September 14, 2005 (*United Nations Security Council*, 2005a), S/RES/1887 of September 25, 2009 (*United Nations Security Council*, 2009), S/RES/2178 of September 24, 2014 (*United Nations Security Council*, 2014a), S/RES/2195 of September 24, 2014 (*United Nations Security Council*, 2014b), S/RES/2250 of December 9, 2015 (*United Nations Security Council*, 2015a), S/RES/2354 of May 24, 2017 (*United Nations Security Council*,

2017a) (complemented by document No. S/2017/375 of April 26, 2017(Aboulatta, 2017)).

35 See Resolutions No. S/RES/1267 of October 15, 1999 (*United Nations Security Council*, 1999b), S/RES/1333 of December 19, 2000 (*United Nations Security Council*, 2000), S/RES/1388 of January 15, 2002 (*United Nations Security Council*, 2002a), S/RES/1456 of January 20, 2003 (*United Nations Security Council*, 2003a), S/RES/1526 of January 30, 2004 (*United Nations Security Council*, 2004a), S/RES/1988 of June 17, 2011 (*United Nations Security Council*, 2011a), S/RES/1989 of June 17, 2011 (*United Nations Security Council*, 2011b), S/RES/2082 of December 17, 2012 (*United Nations Security Council*, 2012a), S/RES/2160 of June 17, 2014 (*United Nations Security Council*, 2014c), S/RES/2161 of June 17, 2014 (*United Nations Security Council*, 2014d), S/RES/2170 of August 15, 2014 (*United Nations Security Council*, 2014e), S/RES/2199 of February 12, 2015 (*United Nations Security Council*, 2015b), S/RES/2249 of November 20, 2015 (*United Nations Security Council*, 2015c), S/RES/2253 of December 17, 2015 (*United Nations Security Council*, 2015d), and S/RES/2368 of July 20, 2017 (*United Nations Security Council*, 2017b).

36 See Resolution No. S/RES/1452 of December 20, 2002 (*United Nations Security Council*, 2002b).

37 See Resolution No. S/RES/2331 of Tuesday, December 20, 2016 (*United Nations Security Council*, 2016a).

38 See Resolution No. S/RES/2341 of Monday, February 13, 2017 (*United Nations Security Council*, 2017c).

39 See Resolution No. S/RES/2347 of Friday, March 24, 2017 (*United Nations Security Council*, 2017d).

40 See Resolution No. S/RES/579 of Wednesday, December 18, 1985 (*United Nations Security Council*, 1985).

41 See Resolutions No. S/RES/286 of September 9, 1970 (*United Nations Security Council*, 1970), and S/RES/2309 of September 22, 2016 (*United Nations Security Council*, 2016b).

42 See Resolution No. S/RES/2133 of Monday, January 27, 2014 (*United Nations Security Council*, 2014f).

43 See Resolution No. S/RES/1390 of Monday, January 28, 2002 (*United Nations Security Council*, 2002c).

44 See Resolutions No. S/RES/1363 of July 30, 2001 (*United Nations Security Council*, 2001c), S/RES/1455 of January 17, 2003 (*United Nations Security Council*, 2003b), S/RES/1535 of March 26, 2004 (*United Nations Security Council*, 2004b), S/RES/1540 of April 28, 2004 (*United Nations Security Council*, 2004c), S/RES/1566 of October 8, 2004 (*United Nations Security Council*, 2004d), S/RES/1617 of July 29, 2005 (*United Nations Security Council*, 2005b), S/RES/1730 of December 19, 2006 (*United Nations Security Council*, 2006a), S/RES/1735 of December 22, 2006 (*United Nations Security Council*, 2006b), S/RES/1787 of December 10, 2007 (*United Nations Security Council*, 2007), S/RES/1805 of March 20, 2008 (*United Nations Security Council*, 2008a), S/RES/1810 of April 25, 2008 (*United Nations Security Council*, 2008b), S/RES/1822 of June 30, 2008 (*United Nations Security Council*, 2008c), S/RES/1963 of December 20, 2010 (*United Nations Security Council*, 2010), S/RES/1977, April 20, 2011 (*United Nations Security Council*, 2011c), S/RES/1989, June 17, 2011 (*United Nations Security Council*, 2011b), S/RES/2055, June 29, 2012 (*United Nations Security Council*, 2012b), S/RES/2082, December 17, 2012 (*United Nations Security Council*, 2012a), S/RES/2083, December 17, 2012 (*United Nations Security Council*, 2012c), S/RES/2129, December 17, 2013 (*United Nations Security*

Council, 2013), and S/RES/2161, June 17, 2014 (*United Nations Security Council*, 2014d).

45 Resolution No. S/RES/2322 of Monday, December 12, 2016 (*United Nations Security Council*, 2016c).

46 For all, see Resolution No. S/RES/1189 of August 13, 1998 (Kenya and Tanzania) (*United Nations Security Council*, 1998), and S/RES/1368 of September 12, 2001 (United States of America) (*United Nations Security Council*, 2001d).

47 The above-mentioned Resolution No. S/RES/1373 of September 28, 2001 (*United Nations Security Council*, 2001a).

48 For a discussion on the problem of the legitimacy of the Security Council and the limits of competence laid down in Chapter VII of the Charter of the United Nations, see Rosand (2004), Talmon (2005), Grodin (2012), and Popovski and Frase (2014).

49 This is reinforced by the Security Council, initially through Resolution No. S/RES/1456 of January 20, 2003 (*United Nations Security Council*, 2003a), and later in Resolutions S/RES/1624 of September 14, 2005 (*United Nations Security Council*, 2005a), and S/RES/2178 of September 24, 2014 (*United Nations Security Council*, 2014a). These resolutions affirm that states must ensure that anti-terrorism measures are in accordance with international human rights law, refugee law, and humanitarian law.

50 On the subject, see Williams (2015), Marian (2012), Smith (2002), and Shor (2016).

51 As for the analysis, it is important to clarify that the documents considered most current and/or relevant have been selected and that special attention has been paid to the intersection between terrorism, human rights, and religion. The analysis therefore does not comprise the whole counter-terrorism approach of the United Nations and does not exhaust the content of the documents mentioned.

52 In this same sense, see Security Council Resolution No. S/RES/2178 of September 24, 2014, Preamble (*United Nations Security Council*, 2014a).

53 Within the framework of the United Nations, the problem of "religious defamation" was repeatedly discussed between 1999 and 2010. On the one hand, the Organization for Islamic Cooperation sought to ban speeches that were offensive to religion. On the other hand, religious groups, human rights organizations, and other sectors argued that such a ban would mean international recognition of so-called "blasphemy laws." Different resolutions were approved in this period with the aim of combating religious defamation, until the adoption by the Human Rights Council, in 2011, of the Resolution No. A/HRS/RES/16/18 of April 12, 2011 (*United Nations Human Rights Council*, 2011), which changed the focus of protecting religion to the protection of people who profess religion (see also Resolution No. A/HRC/RES/19/8 of April 03, 2012 (*United Nations Human Rights Council*, 2012)). In this same sense, the Human Rights Committee adopted an amendment to the General Comment No. 34 (U.N. CCPR/C/GC/34 of September 12, 2011, para. 48), that "blasphemy laws" shall be considered incompatible with the International Covenant:

> Prohibitions of displays of lack of respect for a religion or other belief system, including blasphemy laws, are incompatible with the Covenant, except in the specific circumstances envisaged in article 20, paragraph 2, of the Covenant. Such prohibitions must also comply with the strict requirements of article 19, paragraph 3, as well as such articles as 2, 5, 17, 18 and 26. Thus, for instance, it would be impermissible for any such laws to discriminate in favor of or against one or certain religions or belief systems, or their adherents over another, or religious believers over non-believers. Nor would it be permissible for

such prohibitions to be used to prevent or punish criticism of religious leaders or commentary on religious doctrine and tenets of Faith.

(United Nations Human Rights Committee, 2011, paragraph 48)

Within the General Assembly, the paradigm shift was initially made through Resolution No. A/RES/67/178 of December 20, 2012 (*United Nations General Assembly*, 2012c), which dealt with the fight against intolerance, the creation of negative stereotypes, stigmatization, discrimination, incitement to violence, and violence against people based on religion or belief, the approach that has been adopted since then. Certainly, the new approach is safer and more appropriate to the human rights perspective, since the prohibition of defamation of religions created a high risk to human rights in general, especially freedom of expression, and was subject to be illegitimately and abusively used to justify the persecution of religious minorities (e.g. prohibition of registration of religious organization, prohibition of worship or assembly in places open to the public) and the excessive limitation of freedom (e.g. prohibition of proselytism, criminalization of conversion to another religion, apostasy, and blasphemy). It should be noted that "blasphemy," "apostasy," and the like are theological or religious concepts that are not supported in the normative framework of human rights. Furthermore, religions, beliefs, ideologies, and ideas are not holders of rights, so that the restriction of human rights to the protection of those against criticism, ridicule, and offense cannot be allowed. About the problem, see Scharffs (2013) and Temperman (2017).

54 Resolution No. A/RES/70/291 of July 1, 2016 (*United Nations General Assembly*, 2016c).

55 Resolution No. A/RES/68/178 of December 18, 2013 (*United Nations General Assembly*, 2013c). For previous resolutions on the same subject, see note above.

56 On this point, see Declaration on the Rights of Persons Belonging to National or Ethnic, Religious and Linguistic Minorities of 1992 (*United Nations General Assembly*, 1992) and Declaration on the Elimination of All Forms of Intolerance and of Discrimination Based on Religion or Belief of 1981 (*United Nations General Assembly*, 1981b).

57 Resolution No. A/RES/70/157 of December 17, 2015 (*United Nations General Assembly*, 2015).

58 On the subject, see Human Rights Council Resolution No. A/HRC/RES/31/26 of March 24, 2016 (*United Nations Human Rights Council*, 2016), and Report of the High Commissioner for Human Rights U.N. Doc. No. A/HRC/34/35 of March 8, 2017 (Hussein, 2017).

59 Resolution No. S/RES/1624 of September 14, 2005 (*United Nations Security Council*, 2005a).

60 Resolution No. S/RES/2178 of Wednesday, September 24, 2014 (*United Nations Security Council*, 2014a).

61 Resolution No. S/RES/2354 of May 24, 2017 (*United Nations Security Council*, 2017a) in conjunction with document No. S/2017/375 of April 26, 2017 (Aboulatta, 2017).

62 U.N. Doc. A/HRC/16/51 of December 22, 2010 (Scheinin, 2010).

63 U.N. Doc. No. A/HRC/31/65 of April 29, 2016 (Emmerson, 2016).

64 Emmerson (2016, paragraphs 54–56). On the subject, see also Security Council Resolution No. S/RES/2178 of September 24, 2014 (*United Nations Security Council*, 2014a); Human Rights Council Resolution No. A/HRC/RES/30/15 of October 2, 2015 (*United Nations Human Rights Council*, 2015); Plan of Action to Prevent Violent Extremism – Report of the Secretary-General of the United Nations (U.N. Doc. No. A/70/674 of December 24, 2015) (Ki-Moon, 2015).

65 Not every kind of religious discourse is guaranteed by religious freedom. The International Covenant expressly excludes from its scope discourse commonly referred to as "hate speech," when determining in Article 20 that "1. Any propaganda for war shall be prohibited by law. 2. Any advocacy of national, racial or religious hatred that constitutes incitement to discrimination, hostility or violence shall be prohibited by law" (*United Nations General Assembly*, 1966). In this regard, see "Rabat Plan of Action on the prohibition of advocacy of national, racial or religious hatred that constitutes an invitation to discrimination, hostility or violence" (Pillay, 2013). After several seminars organized by the United Nations High Commissioner for Human Rights in 2011 and 2012, the Rabat Plan of Action was published in 2012, mainly with the aim of making recommendations on legislation, judicialization, and public policies, for the best implementation of that prohibition.

66 See also the Office of the High Commissioner for Human Rights "International Standards on Freedom of Religion or Belief," available at http://www.ohchr.org/EN/Issues/FreedomReligion/Pages/Standards.aspx.

67 GeneralCommentNo. 22 (U.N.CCPR/C/ 21 /Rev. 1 /Add. 4 ofJuly 30, 1993, para. 5).In this regard, Joseph et al. (2005, p. 504) state that the Human Rights Committee has reinforced in several General Comments that the absolute right to change religion is guaranteed, contrary to the policies of numerous Islamic States.

68 The distinction between *forum internum* and *forum externum*, although it is didactically relevant and contributes to the better systematization and understanding of religious freedom, is not without problems. In this regard, Ghanea (2008, p. 305) considers that the duality of the protection of religious identity and its expression is closer to a legal myth than to a concept with practical relevance. While the right to have or change religion is absolute, excessive limitations to the manifestation of religion may indicate to individuals and communities that the fact that "having" a particular religion or belief is also limited. Diversely, if there is an environment in which the free manifestation of religion or belief is allowed, the right to have or change religion is more effectively guaranteed. About the problems that involve this distinction, see McCrea (2010, p. 121) and Petkoff (2012).

69 In the case of *Coeriel et al. v the Netherlands* (Communication No. 453/1991, U.N. Doc. CCPR/C/52/D/453/1991–1994, para. 6.1), the Human Rights Committee considered that the Dutch government's refusal to meet the requests for changes in names made by individuals who intended to become Hindu masters, based on the requirement of their religious doctrine, did not violate the International Covenant (*United Nations Human Rights Committee*, 1994). According to the Committee, the regulation of the change of names, as provided for in Dutch legislation, is a matter of public order, which authorizes the restriction of religious freedom.

70 In *Karnel Singh Bhinder v Canada* (Communication 208/1986, U.N. Doc. CCPR/C/37/D/208/1986–1989, para. 6.2), the Committee acknowledged that the existence of legislation obliging federal government employees to wear a helmet for protection against damage and electric shock is considered reasonable and directed to objective purposes that are compatible with the Convention, even if they involve restricting the freedom to use a turban, which is mandatory for members of the Sikh religion (*United Nations Human Rights Committee*, 1989).

71 The United Nations Human Rights Committee has recognized that the concept of morality derives from many social, philosophical, and religious traditions. In this way, limitations on the freedom to manifest religion or belief for the purpose of protecting morality should be based on principles that do not derive exclusively

from a single tradition (cf. *United Nations Human Rights Committee*, 1993, paragraph 8).

72 For a discussion on the principle of proportionality, and the relation between adequacy, necessity, weighting, and reasonableness in the context of the globalization of human rights and the internationalization of the protection of these rights through international courts, see Silva (2013).

73 Article 4 of the International Covenant on Civil and Political Rights. "2. No derogation from articles 6, 7, 8 (paragraphs I and 2), 11, 15, 16 and 18 may be made under this provision" (*United Nations General Assembly*, 1966).

74 In his report, Martin Scheinin (2010) discusses the problem in the context of counter-terrorism:

> In the application and exercise of all functions under the law relating to terrorism, it is unlawful for any person to act in any way that is incompatible with the purposes and provisions of international human rights and refugee law that are binding upon the State in this regard: 1. The exercise of functions and powers shall be based on clear provisions of law that exhaustively enumerate the powers in question. 2. The exercise of such functions and powers may never violate peremptory or non-derogable norms of international law, nor impair the essence of any human right. 3. Where the exercise of functions and powers involves a restriction upon a human right that is capable of limitation, any such restriction should be to the least intrusive means possible and shall: (a) Be necessary in a democratic society to pursue a defined legitimate aim, as permitted by international law; and (b) Be proportionate to the benefit obtained in achieving the legitimate aim in question. 4. If the State is involved, as a party, in an ongoing armed conflict, the above provisions shall apply also to securing compliance with principles and provisions of international humanitarian law, without prejudice to the obligation to comply with international human rights and refugee law.

75 Which is provided for, for example, in relation to freedom of expression in Article 19 of the International Covenant:

> 1. Everyone shall have the right to hold opinions without interference. 2. Everyone shall have the right to freedom of expression; this right shall include freedom to seek, receive and impart information and ideas of all kinds, regardless of frontiers, either orally, in writing or in print, in the form of art, or through any other media of his choice. 3. The exercise of the rights provided for in paragraph 2 of this article carries with it special duties and responsibilities. It may therefore be subject to certain restrictions, but these shall only be such as are provided by law and are necessary: (a) For respect of the rights or reputations of others; (b) For the protection of national security or of public order (*ordre public*), or of public health or morals.
>
> *(United Nations General Assembly, 1966)*

National security is also envisaged as a legitimate ground for restriction in Articles 12, 13, 14, 21, and 22 of the International Covenant.

76 Cf. The Siracusa Principles on the Limitation and Derogation Provisions in the International Covenant on Civil and Political Rights, U.N. Doc. No. E/CN.4/1985/ Annex of September 28, 1984, para. 29–32 (*United Nations Economic and Social Council*, 1984).

77 Resolution of General Assembly No. A/RES/68/178 of December 18, 2013, item "m" (*United Nations General Assembly*, 2013c).

78 The legal basis for prohibiting is found in Article 20 of the International Covenant on Civil and Political Rights, when determining that:

> 2. Any advocacy of national, racial or religious hatred that constitutes incitement to discrimination, hostility or violence shall be prohibited by law. It is important, however, that its implementation consider the Human Rights Committee's manifestation in General Comment No. 34, so that abuses are avoided.... 46. States parties should ensure that counter-terrorism measures are compatible with paragraph 3 [of Article 19]. Such offences as "encouragement of terrorism" and "extremist activity" as well as offences of "praising," "glorifying," or "justifying" terrorism, should be clearly defined to ensure that they do not lead to unnecessary or disproportionate interference with freedom of expression. Excessive restrictions on access to information must also be avoided. The media plays a crucial role in informing the public about acts of terrorism and its capacity to operate should not be unduly restricted. In this regard, journalists should not be penalized for carrying out their legitimate activities.
>
> *(United Nations General Assembly, 1966)*

On this subject, see the Rabat Plan of Action (Pillay, 2013). An adequate definition of incitement to terrorism was offered by the Special Rapporteur on the Promotion and Protection of Human Rights and Fundamental Freedoms while Countering Terrorism: "It is an offence to intentionally and unlawfully distribute or otherwise make available a message to the public with the intent to incite the commission of a terrorist offence, where such conduct, whether or not expressly advocating terrorist offences, causes a danger that one or more such offences may be committed" (Scheinin, 2010, paragraph 32). For a discussion on religious extremism and interference in the freedoms of expression and assembly, see Guiora (2013, pp. 35–76).

References

Aboulatta, A. A. (2017) *Letter Dated 26 April 2017 from the Chair of the Security Council Committee Established Pursuant to Resolution 1373 (2001) Concerning Counter-Terrorism Addressed to the President of the Security Council*, New York, United Nations Security Council, Document S/2017/375 [Online]. Available at https://undocs.org/Home/Mobile?FinalSymbol=S%2F2017%2F375&Language=E&DeviceType=Desktop&LangRequested=False (Accessed 15 January 2023).

Bielefeldt, H., Ghanea, N., and Wiener, M. (2016) *Freedom of Religion or Belief: An International Law Commentary*, Oxford, Oxford University Press.

Bunche, R. (1948) *Israel Ordinance on Prevention of Terrorism/Assassination of UN Mediator – Cablegram from Acting Mediator*, New York, United Nations Security Council, Document S/1008 [Online]. Available at https://www.un.org/unispal/document/auto-insert-210629/ (Accessed 15 January 2023).

Emmerson, B. (2016) *Report of the Special Rapporteur on the Promotion and Protection of Human Rights and Fundamental Freedoms while Countering Terrorism*, New York, United Nations, Document A/HRC/31/65 [Online]. Available at https://undocs.org/Home/Mobile?FinalSymbol=A%2FHRC%2F31%2F65&Language=E&DeviceType=Desktop&LangRequested=False (Accessed 15 January 2023).

Ghanea, N. (2008) 'Religious or Minority? Examining the Realisation of International Standards in Relation to Religious Minorities in the Middle East', *Religion, State & Society*, vol. 36, no. 3, pp. 305–325.

Grodin, E. (2012) '"Making the World Safe for Democracy": UN Security Council Resolution 1373, the International Imposition of Counterterrorism Policies, and the "Arenas of Power" Model', *The Cornell Policy Review*, vol. 2, no. 1, https://blogs.cornell.edu/policyreview/2012/03/15/making-the-world-safe-for-democracy-un-security-council-resolution-1373-the-international-imposition-of-counterterrorism-policies-and-the-arenas-of-power-model/.

Guiora, A. G. (2013) *Freedom from Religion: Rights and National Security*, Oxford, Oxford University Press.

Guterres, A. (2017a) *Capability of the United Nations System to Assist Member States in Implementing the United Nations Global Counter-Terrorism Strategy*, New York, United Nations, Document A/71/858 [Online]. Available at https://undocs.org/Home/Mobile?FinalSymbol=A%2F71%2F858&Language=E&DeviceType=Desktop&LangRequested=False (Accessed 15 January 2023).

Guterres, A. (2017b) *Measures to Eliminate International Terrorism*, New York, United Nations, Document A/72/111 [Online]. Available at https://undocs.org/Home/Mobile?FinalSymbol=A%2F72%2F111&Language=E&DeviceType=Desktop&LangRequested=False (Accessed 15 January 2023).

Hussein, Z. R. (2017) *Combating Intolerance, Negative Stereotyping and Stigmatization of, and Discrimination, Incitement to Violence and Violence Against, Persons Based on Religion or Belief: Report of the United Nations High Commissioner for Human Rights*, New York, United Nations Human Rights Council, Document A/HRC/34/35 [Online]. Available at https://undocs.org/Home/Mobile?FinalSymbol=a%2Fhrc%2Fres%2F34%2F35&Language=E&DeviceType=Desktop&LangRequested=False (Accessed 15 January 2023).

Joseph, S., Schultz, J., and Castan, M. (2005) *The International Covenant on Civil and Political Rights: Cases, Materials, and Commentary*, 2nd edn, Oxford, Oxford University Press.

Ki-Moon, B. (2015) *Plan of Action to Prevent Violent Extremism: Report of the Secretary-General*, New York, United Nations, Document A/70/674 [Online]. Available at https://undocs.org/Home/Mobile?FinalSymbol=A%2F70%2F674&Language=E&DeviceType=Desktop&LangRequested=False (Accessed 15 January 2023).

Marian, I. (2012) 'Protecting Human Rights and International Humanitarian Law in the Fight against Terrorism', *Contemporary Readings in Law and Social Justice*, vol. 4, no. 1, pp. 174–179.

McCrea, R. (2010) *Religion and the Public Order of the European Union*, Oxford, Oxford University Press.

Petkoff, P. (2012) 'Forum Internum and Forum Externum in Canon Law and Public International Law with a Particular Reference to the Jurisprudence of the European Court of Human Rights', *Religion & Human Rights*, vol. 7, no. 3, pp. 183–214.

Pillay, N. (2013) *Report of the United Nations High Commissioner for Human Rights on the Expert Workshops on the Prohibition of Incitement to National, Racial or Religious Hatred*, New York, United Nations, Document A/HRC/22/17/Add.4 [Online]. Available at https://www.ohchr.org/sites/default/files/Rabat_draft_outcome.pdf (Accessed 15 January 2023).

Popovski, V., and Frase, T. (eds) (2014) *The Security Council as Global Legislator*, London, Routledge.

Rosand, E. (2004) 'The Security Council as Global Legislator: Ultra Vires or Ultra Innovative?', *Fordham International Law Journal*, vol. 28, no. 3, pp. 542–590.

Scharffs, B. G. (2013) 'International Law and the Defamation of Religion Conundrum,' *The Review of Faith & International Affairs*, vol. 11, no. 1, pp. 66–75.

Scheinin, M. (2010) *Report of the Special Rapporteur on the Promotion and Protection of Human Rights and Fundamental Freedoms while Countering Terrorism*, New York, United Nations Human Rights Council, Document A/HRC/16/51 [Online]. Available at https://undocs.org/Home/Mobile?FinalSymbol=A%2FHRC%2F16%2F51&Language=E&DeviceType=Desktop&LangRequested=False (Accessed 15 January 2023).

Shor, E., et al. (2016) 'Does Counterterrorist Legislation Hurt Human Rights Practices? A Longitudinal Cross-national Analysis', *Social Science Research*, vol. 58, pp. 104–121 [Online]. Available at http://dx.doi.org/10.1016/j.ssresearch.2015.12.007 (Accessed 15 January 2023).

Silva, S. T. (2013) 'O tetralemma do controlo judicial da proporcionalidade no contexto da universalização do princípio: Adequação, necessidade, ponderação e razoabilidade', *Boletim Da Faculdade de Direito Da Universidade de Coimbra*, vol. 88, no. 2, pp. 639–678.

Smith, G. H. (2002) 'Religious Freedom and the Challenge of Terrorism', *BYU Law Review*, vol. 2002, no. 2, pp. 205–215.

Talmon, S. (2005) 'The Security Council as World Legislature', *The American Journal of International Law*, vol. 99, no. 1, pp. 175–193.

Temperman, J. (2017) 'Blasphemy, Defamation of Religions and Human Rights Law,' *Netherlands Quarterly of Human Rights*, vol. 26, no. 4, pp. 517–545.

Williams, G. (2015) 'Anti-terrorism Laws and Human Rights', *Review of Constitutional Studies*, vol. 19, no. 2, pp. 127–145.

4

RELIGION AS A MATTER OF U.S. NATIONAL (IN)SECURITY?

Michelle Flynn

1 Introduction

As early as 2004 it was observed that

> Although religion has long been recognized as one factor, among many, relevant to discussions of security and war making (for example, the *jus ad bellum* and *jus in bello* criteria of just war theory), it is now emerging (or rather, re-emerging) as the single most important political-ideological default mechanism in global conflict.
>
> *(Otis, 2004, p. 11)*

The role of religion in the context of U.S. national security was first acknowledged in the National Security Strategy Report ("the NSS Report") in 1997. The NSS Report sets out the ambit of national security policy goals and the strategies to be employed. The importance of religious freedom in reducing religiously inspired violence and terrorism cannot be overestimated and its inclusion within the NSS Reports is to be welcomed. Since 1997 a total of nine NSS Reports have been issued by four presidents. Within the 20-year period between 1997 and 2017, President Bill Clinton issued four NSS Reports (1997, 1998, 1999, and 2000), President George W. Bush issued two NSS Reports (2002 and 2006), President Barack Obama also issued two NSS Reports (2010 and 2015), and President Donald J. Trump issued one NSS Report (2017). Most recently, in March 2021, President Joseph R. Biden issued the Interim National Security Strategic Guidance, which outlines the aims and priorities in respect of the forthcoming NSS of the Biden administration.

DOI: 10.4324/9781003453086-7

Examining the provisions that deal specifically with issues concerning religion within these NSS Reports and the latest Interim National Security Strategic Guidance document is instructive in tracing the development of the role of religion in the context of national security policy in the U.S.

2 Relationship between Government and Religion in the U.S.

The First Amendment of the U.S. Constitution guarantees religious liberty through the dual provisions of (i) the Establishment Clause, and (ii) the Free Exercise Clause. This constitutional provision emerged as a result of a shared experience across a diverse group of immigrants as many of the early settlers had left Europe to escape religious persecution. The First Amendment provides that

> Congress shall make no law respecting an establishment of religion, or prohibiting the free exercise thereof; or abridging the freedom of speech, or of the press; or the right of the people peaceably to assemble, and to petition the Government for a redress of grievances.

The First Amendment of the U.S. Constitution prohibits an "established religion" in this new polity and expressly provides for the free exercise of religious belief. Whilst the provision is set out in absolute terms, judicial interpretation has placed some limits on the exercise of religion; thus, the freedom to believe is absolute, but the outward manifestation of those beliefs is a qualified right. This reflects the Western philosophical conception of the *forum internum* and the *forum externum*. The *forum internum* is described as the internal dimension to freedom of religion concerning matters of personal conscience and it attracts absolute protection. The *forum externum* refers to the external dimension to religion or belief, such as its manifestation, and it is a qualified right. The commitment to uphold the clauses of the First Amendment continues to be at the forefront of legislative and policy debates, in addition to being the subject of judicial scrutiny in the U.S. courts. Curiously, the relationship between these two clauses remains unclear: whether each clause is to reinforce the other or whether each is entirely separate remains to be clarified. Nevertheless, there is considerable clarity concerning the ambit of the Establishment Clause as it serves to provide protection to the institutions of the state from the influence of religion. As a result of this constitutional commitment, a constitutional culture has developed which is focused on the dangers of religious heteronomy in the political sphere. Yet, despite the text of the First Amendment, it is questionable whether such a strict separation exists between government and religion in the U.S. Indeed, the prevalence of public religiosity in the U.S. stands in contradistinction to other countries which emphasize a strict separation between religion and the state such as France with its constitutional principle of *laïcité*. It should also be noted that Article 1 of the French Constitution affirms that France is a secular republic. In contradistinction, examples of public religiosity in the U.S. include the official motto "In God We Trust," which appears on monetary bills (*U.S. Department of the Treasury*, 2011), and the use of the phrase "one nation under God" in the Pledge of Allegiance (Siegel, 2018). As Lester (2010) aptly observed, "This would explain the often remarked paradox that the United States is one of the most religious countries in the world but also one of the strongest enforcers of a separation between Church and State." Interestingly, the U.S. has been identified as a Western liberal democracy in which the "secularization theory" does not apply due in part to the "long and positive experience of integration through religious identities" for immigrant populations resulting in high levels of religious pluralism (Taylor, 2007, p. 524). Thus, the language of neutrality and separation may be viewed as an attempt to purport a bifurcation of the religious and political realms, which does not entirely reflect the *de facto* situation.

3 Overview of NSS Reports

The Goldwater-Nichols Department of Defense Reorganization Act of 1986 requires the President to submit an NSS Report to Congress on an annual basis. However, there has been a total of 17 NSS Reports (out of a potential total of 34) delivered in the period between 1987 and 2020. Indeed, a tendency has emerged amongst the previous three presidents (George W. Bush, Barack Obama, and Donald J. Trump) to issue one NSS Report within a four-year presidential term. As DuMont (2019) observed, the NSS Report offers the President the opportunity to express national security priorities and is "specifically understood to be an accurate reflection of the President's intent and guidance." This unclassified NSS Report is intended for a diverse audience stretching beyond the executive branch and Congress, to include foreign governments, supranational organizations, and individuals both in the U.S. and globally (Dale, 2008). Each NSS Report must contain a discussion of U.S. international interests, commitments, policies, objectives, and defense capabilities to protect national security.

Despite criticism of the NSS Reports serving a public affairs role but doing "little to guide U.S. national security policymaking and resource allocation" (Murdock et al., 2005, p. 28), the NSS Report provides valuable insight into the viewpoints of the President and the National Security Council of the perceived threats to national security and the strategies required to meet such challenges. The NSS Reports reveal key areas of focus for an administration and point to the relevance of issues in the context of U.S. national security, whilst also indicating emerging security threats in a broader geopolitical context. Of interest, therefore, is the role of religion in the context of these strategic documents. The relationship between religion and security is one that clearly dominated the minds of the framers of the U.S. Constitution in the late 18th century. However, within a modern-day context, the role of religion as a matter of national security did not feature in the NSS Reports until 1997.

4 Religion as a National Security Concern

Since 1986, the NSS Reports have been mandated to address specific issues in addition to being delivered on an annual basis. The identification of religion as a matter of national security in the context of the NSS Reports first arose during the presidency of Bill Clinton. Over the next 20 years between 1997 and 2017, encompassing the presidential terms of Bill Clinton, George W. Bush, Barack Obama, and Donald J. Trump, there were nine NSS Reports issued. Each of these NSS Reports mentioned religious freedom and/or the threat of religious extremism albeit to varying degrees of importance. Consideration must also be given to the Interim National Security Strategic Guidance issued by President Biden in March 2021 as it seeks to outline the policies to be adopted with the aim of providing guidance for departments and agencies to align their actions before the issuing of its NSS Report.

In 1997, President Clinton's NSS Report did not list religious freedom as one of the six priorities identified but rather in the context of continuing to work with international organizations to prevent religious persecution more generally (Clinton, 1997). In the NSS Report of 1998, the issue of religious freedom arose in the context of terrorism as an identified transnational threat. It was noted that "The groups associated with bin Laden come from diverse places, but share a hatred for democracy, a fanatical glorification of violence and a horrible distortion of their religion to justify the murder of innocents" (Clinton, 1998, p. 16). A more general endorsement of the commitment to improve international human rights organizations and mechanisms to combat religious persecution was also reiterated (Clinton, 1998, p. 34). Of interest, however, is the explicit reference to Islam within the NSS Report of 1998 wherein it is noted that:

> U.S. policies in the Middle East and Southwest Asia are not anti-Islamic – an allegation made by some opponents of our efforts to help bring lasting peace and stability to the region. Islam is the fastest growing religious faith in the United States. We respect deeply its moral teachings and its role as a source of inspiration and instruction for hundreds of millions of people around the world. U.S. policy in the region is directed at the actions of governments and terrorist groups, not peoples or faiths. The standards we would like all the nations in the region to observe are not merely Western, but universal.
>
> *(Clinton, 1998, p. 54)*

Indeed, this claim is reiterated almost verbatim in the subsequent NSS Reports of President Clinton's administration in 1999 and 2000.

In the NSS Report of 1999 the importance of religious freedom within the context of "Adherence to Universal Human Rights and Democratic Principles" was reiterated and expressed as follows:

> Promotion of religious freedom is one of the highest concerns in our foreign policy. Freedom of thought, conscience and religion is a bedrock issue for the American people. To that end, the President signed the International Religious Freedom Act of 1998, which provides the flexibility needed to advance religious freedom and to counter religious persecution. In September 1999, we completed the first phase outlined in the Act with publication of the first annual report on the status of religious freedom worldwide, and in October, we designated the most severe violators of religious freedom. The United States is active throughout the world assisting those who are persecuted because of their religion and promoting freedom of religious belief and practice. We will continue to work with individual nations and with international institutions to combat religious persecution and promote religious freedom.
>
> *(Clinton, 1999, p. 27)*

The passing of the International Religious Freedom Act of 1998 placed the promotion of religious freedom and the combating of religious persecution as aims of U.S. foreign policy (Gunn, 2000). The publication of the first annual report on the status of religious freedom worldwide was a 1,100-page document covering 194 countries. The report highlighted several countries as being of particular concern for having perpetrated or permitted severe violations of religious freedom. Annicchino (2016, p. 282) has also observed that the International Religious Freedom Act of 1998 influenced similar legislation in some European countries, such as Italy, the U.K., France, Norway, the Netherlands, and also at the supranational level of the European Union. Crucially the Act established four fundamental institutions to advance religious freedom as a matter of foreign policy: the Ambassador-at-Large for International Religious Freedom; the U.S. Commission on International Religious Freedom; the Office of International Religious Freedom within the Department of State; and, of particular importance within the context of this analysis, a special advisor on international religious freedom at the National Security Council. However, whilst the International Religious Freedom Act of 1998 created this position it remained vacant until 2020 when the Trump administration appointed Sarah Makin as the first-ever Senior Director for International Religious Freedom on the National Security Council. Since the

Biden administration took over in January 2021, that position has become vacant (*United States Commission on International Religious Freedom*, 2020, p. 5). Blitt (2019) has noted that the Frank R. Wolf International Religious Freedom Act of 2016 has made certain amendments to the International Religious Freedom Act of 1998 including the enhanced role of the Ambassador-at-Large for International Religious Freedom to report directly to the Secretary of State.

Returning to the NSS Reports, the Report issued in 2000 was more detailed and had a wider ambit than the previous NSS Reports delivered by President Clinton (Clinton, 2000). It reiterated the importance of religious freedom in the context of U.S. foreign policy. The Middle East and South Asia were specifically mentioned, and a request was made to end violence against minority religious groups and repeal blasphemy laws that were used to discriminate against minorities. Thus, from the NSS Reports of 1997, 1998, 1999, and 2000, whilst religious freedom was an issue that was coming into focus as a matter of national security, it was not to any significant degree. Indeed, Haley (2006, p. 110) has opined that President Clinton's strategy failed to adequately handle Islamic terrorism and ethnic or religious conflict.

The role of religion as a threat to national security emerged as a major issue following the terrorist attacks of 11 September 2001. The 9/11 attacks were carried out as an act of *jihad* by Islamist terrorists and brought the issue of religion as a matter of national security front and center in U.S. public discourse. The terrorist attacks of 9/11 prompted a paradigmatic shift in U.S. national security policy with the effects of that shift being experienced across much of the globe. This marked an epoch in the history of the inclusion of religion as a matter of importance to the stability of the U.S. George W. Bush was president at the time of the attacks and the NSS Report of 2002, which was the first NSS Report to be issued by George W. Bush during his presidency, remarkably did not identify religion as a significant issue (Bush, 2002). The Report refers to religious freedom in general terms and notes that the U.S. government will make "special efforts to promote freedom of religion and conscience and defend it from encroachment by repressive governments" (Bush, 2002, p. 4). In respect of the threat of terrorism, the Report noted that "The enemy is not a single political regime or person or religion or ideology. The enemy is terrorism – premeditated, politically motivated violence perpetrated against innocents" (Bush, 2002, p. 5).

It was not until the NSS Report of 2006 that the link between religion and security appears in definite terms. President George W. Bush commenced his introductory letter in the Report as follows:

> My fellow Americans, America is at war. This is a wartime national security strategy required by the grave challenge we face – the rise of terrorism fueled by an aggressive ideology of hatred and murder, fully revealed to

> the American people on September 11, 2001. This strategy reflects our most solemn obligation: to protect the security of the American people.
> *(Bush, 2006)*

The Report commences with an "Overview of America's National Security Strategy" in which the "triumph of freedom over the threats of fascism and communism" in the 21st century are lauded. However, it warns that

> a new totalitarian ideology now threatens, an ideology grounded not in secular philosophy but in the perversion of a proud religion. Its content may be different from the ideologies of the last century, but its means are similar: intolerance, murder, terror, enslavement, and repression.
> *(Bush, 2006, p. 1)*

In setting out the goals and the means to achieve these goals, religious freedom is explicitly noted wherein it is stated that

> Against a terrorist enemy that is defined by religious intolerance, we defend the First Freedom: the right of people to believe and worship according to the dictates of their own conscience, free from the coercion of the state, the coercion of the majority, or the coercion of a minority that wants to dictate what others must believe.
> *(Bush, 2006, p. 7)*

It is further noted that:

> While the War on Terror is a battle of ideas, it is not a battle of religions. The transnational terrorists confronting us today exploit the proud religion of Islam to serve a violent political vision: the establishment, by terrorism and subversion, of a totalitarian empire that denies all political and religious freedom. These terrorists distort the idea of jihad into a call for murder against those they regard as apostates or unbelievers – including Christians, Jews, Hindus, other religious traditions, and all Muslims who disagree with them. Indeed, most of the terrorist attacks since September 11 have occurred in Muslim countries – and most of the victims have been Muslims.
> *(Bush, 2006, p. 9)*

Later on, it is stated that "A proud religion – the religion of Islam – has been twisted and made to serve an evil end, as in other times and places other religions have been similarly abused" (Bush, 2006, p. 10). In terms of a strategic response, the Report notes that

> The strategy to counter the lies behind the terrorists' ideology is to empower the very people the terrorists most want to exploit: the faithful

> followers of Islam. We will continue to support political reforms that empower peaceful Muslims to practice and interpret their faith.
>
> *(Bush, 2006, p. 11)*

During President Barack Obama's two presidential terms, two NSS Reports were issued: the first in 2010 and the second in 2015. The NSS Report of 2010 opens with an acknowledgment that "Wars over ideology have given way to wars over religious, ethnic, and tribal identity" (Obama, 2010, p. 1). Under the heading of "Disrupt, Dismantle, and Defeat Al-Qa'ida and Its Violent Extremist Affiliates in Afghanistan, Pakistan, and around the World," the Report notes that the approach of the U.S. includes efforts to "build positive partnerships with Muslim communities around the world" (Obama, 2010, p. 19). There is an express rejection that al-Qa'ida represents any religious authority with the unequivocal statement that "They are not religious leaders, they are killers; and neither Islam nor any other religion condones the slaughter of innocents" (Obama, 2010, p. 22). This is furthered by an acknowledgment that "fissures between America and certain regions or religions will undercut our leadership and make us less safe" (Obama, 2010, p. 22). This NSS Report also attributes the strength of the U.S. to its diversity and acknowledges the specific threat by extremists to radicalize or recruit individuals noting that

> Within our own communities, those who seek to recruit and radicalize individuals will often try to prey upon isolation and alienation. Our own commitment to extending the promise of America will both draw a contrast with those who try to drive people apart, while countering attempts to enlist individuals in ideological, religious, or ethnic extremism.
>
> *(Obama, 2010, p. 37)*

Five years later, in February 2015, President Obama issued his second NSS Report. This Report noted the ongoing conflicts in the Middle East and North Africa and the difficulties arising in societies where "religious extremists take root, or rulers reject democratic reforms, exploit their economies, and crush civil society" (Obama, 2015, p. 5). This is followed by an unambiguous statement specifying that counter-terrorism efforts are not an attack on the religion of Islam but rather aimed at terrorists. However, apart from a mention of the need to work with religious leaders as one of many entities to promote universal values and a need to ensure equality for religious minorities, religion is not further mentioned within the Report (Obama, 2015, p. 9). Clearly, the increasing emphasis on religion as a matter of national security escalated from the first NSS Report of President George W. Bush in 2002 to become a definitive issue of concern in the NSS Report of 2006. With President Obama's Reports in both 2010 and 2015, a retreat from that escalation can be observed as religion is mentioned in limited terms. Nevertheless, Lucius (2013, p. 70) has aptly observed that "President Obama approaches religion as a freedom and as a unifying factor that serves to address U.S. national security interests and is in keeping with the American belief in civil liberties." This, however, is set to change as religion is elevated to a strategic priority within the context of the NSS Report of 2017 issued by the administration of President Donald J. Trump.

5 The NSS Report of 2017

The most recent NSS Report was issued in December 2017 by President Donald J. Trump. In his introduction, President Trump noted that "During my first year in office, you have witnessed my America First foreign policy in action. We are prioritizing the interests of our citizens and protecting our sovereign rights as a nation." The letter concludes with "This National Security Strategy puts America First" (Trump, 2017, pp. i–ii). This foreign policy marked a significant departure from recent U.S. foreign policy strategies and directly impacted the identification of national security goals and the formation of strategies to achieve those goals.

Whilst it received criticism for its lack of specific strategies to overcome certain identified threats, Cordesman (2017) has observed that the Report is nevertheless relevant in so far as it identifies religious freedom as a matter of strategic importance in terms of national security. The NSS Report of 2017 identifies four broad aims contained in "pillars" which include the following: (1) Protect the American People, the Homeland, and the American Way of Life; (2) Promote American Prosperity; (3) Preserve Peace through Strength; and (4) Advance American Influence. Religious freedom issues and/or the threats posed by religious extremists are expressly noted in three of the four pillars.

Within pillar 1, it is specified that

> Jihadist terrorist organizations present the most dangerous terrorist threat to the Nation. America, alongside our allies and partners, is fighting a long war against these fanatics who advance a totalitarian vision for a global Islamist caliphate that justifies murder and slavery, promotes repression, and seeks to undermine the American way of life. Jihadist terrorists use virtual and physical networks around the world to radicalize isolated individuals, exploit vulnerable populations, and inspire and direct plots.
>
> *(Trump, 2017, p. 10)*

In respect of this category of threat, the priority actions include disrupting terror plots, taking direct action against terrorist networks that threaten the homeland and U.S. citizens, eliminating safe havens, and disrupting financial, material, and personnel supply chains of terrorist organizations. There is also a specific action of encouraging shared responsibility for partners to work independently of U.S. assistance in fighting terrorism. Of particular interest, however, is the priority action to "Combat radicalization and recruitment in communities" and specifies that "U.S. intelligence and homeland security experts will work with law enforcement and civic leaders on terrorism prevention and provide accurate and actionable information about radicalization in their communities" (Trump, 2017, p. 11).

Within pillar 3, the Report notes that the U.S.

> continues to wage a long war against jihadist terrorist groups such as ISIS and al-Qa'ida. These groups are linked by a common radical Islamist ideology that encourages violence against the United States and our partners and produces misery for those under their control.
>
> *(Trump, 2017, p. 26)*

The Report notes that it will "craft and direct coherent communications campaigns to advance American influence and counter challenges from the ideological threats that emanate from radical Islamist groups and competitor nations" (Trump, 2017, p. 35). Within pillar 4, the Report notes that "Through our words and deeds, America demonstrates a positive alternative to political and religious despotism" (Trump, 2017, p. 38). A commitment is expressed to continue to promote "American Values" noting freedom of religion as one of those values. The NSS Report of 2017 confirmed its position in unequivocal terms with the assertion that

> The United States also remains committed to supporting and advancing religious freedom – America's first freedom. Our Founders understood religious freedom not as the state's creation, but as the gift of God to every person and a fundamental right for our flourishing society.
>
> *(Trump, 2017, p. 41)*

Within the specific priority actions noted were the aims of defeating *jihadist* terrorists and other groups that "foment hatred and use violence to advance their supremacist Islamist ideologies. We will continue to join with other states to defeat this scourge of all civilized peoples" (Trump, 2017, p. 42). Of particular importance is the listing of the protection of religious freedom and religious minorities as a strategic priority within the context of the national security policy of the U.S. It is, however, questionable whether the Biden administration will attribute a similar level of importance to the role of religious freedom in the context of protecting national security interests.

6 The Interim National Security Strategic Guidance 2021

On 3 March 2021, President Biden issued the Interim National Security Strategic Guidance. This is the first time that an administration has issued interim guidance in respect of a forthcoming NSS Report. The Interim National Security Strategic Guidance outlines the policies to be adopted with the aim of providing guidance for departments and agencies to align their actions prior to the administration issuing its NSS. This document, therefore, provides a strong indication of what can be anticipated in the NSS Report to be issued by the Biden administration. The Guidance is a short document comprising 24 pages in total and it asserts throughout that the security strategy to be adopted will be one based on international cooperation as it notes,

> Recent events show all too clearly that many of the biggest threats we face respect no borders or walls, and must be met with collective action. Pandemics and other biological risks, the escalating climate crisis, cyber and digital threats, international economic disruptions, protracted humanitarian crises, violent extremism and terrorism, and the proliferation of nuclear weapons and other weapons of mass destruction all pose profound and, in some cases, existential dangers. None can be effectively addressed by one nation acting alone. And none can be effectively addressed with the United States on the sidelines.
>
> *(Biden, 2021, p. 7)*

This approach is a complete departure from the isolationist foreign policy adopted by the former Trump administration in this respect.

A dominant theme within the document is the goal of reinvigorating a commitment to democracy in terms of domestic and foreign policy and a focus on rebuilding the domestic economy as a way to strengthen national security. However, the mention of religious freedom is quite limited in the Interim National Security Strategic Guidance. In his introductory letter, President Biden affirms a general goal of defending equal rights and includes within a list "people of every ethnic background and religion" (2021, p. 4). The next reference to religion is in the concluding paragraph of "Our National Security Priorities" which notes that the administration will ensure that "state, municipal, tribal, civil society, non-profit, diaspora, faith-based, and private sector actors are better integrated into policy deliberations" (Biden, 2021, p. 22). Other than these references, that of achieving the aim of equal rights for all including those of every religion, and the reference to the inclusion of faith-based actors in policy deliberations, religion is not otherwise explicitly referenced. There is a commitment to ensuring that U.S. companies uphold American values in conducting business in China and to the upholding of "democracy, human rights, and human dignity, including in Hong Kong, Xinjiang, and Tibet" (Biden, 2021, p. 21). It can be understood that the reference to the province of Xinjiang in China emerges in the context of the reported treatment of the Muslim Uighur community in that region. Thus, the commitment to protect religious freedom is not explicitly described; rather, it is encompassed within general human rights commitments. Pérez (2021) has pointed out that the treatment of the Uighurs was linked to other foreign policy objectives yet is silent on the objective of protecting religious freedom. It is also notable that a more generic and encompassing term of "terrorism and violent extremism" has been adopted without any specific reference to the threat of religiously motivated violence which has been evident in the previous NSS Reports discussed above.

The Interim National Security Strategic Guidance of course only signals areas of priority for the Biden administration in the development of a NSS. However, the limited reference to religion as a matter of national security is cause for concern. It is anticipated that the NSS Report will be released in late 2021 or early 2022 (McInnis, 2021).

7 Conclusion

Given the importance of religious freedom in reducing religiously inspired violence and terrorism, its inclusion within the NSS Reports is welcomed. In examining the nine NSS Reports issued by the previous four presidents between 1997 and 2017, it is clear that the role of religion within the context of developing a NSS is determined by the individual approaches of each administration. The four NSS Reports issued by President Clinton in 1997, 1998, 1999, and 2000 introduced the issue of religious freedom within the context of national security. Of course, the passing of the International Religious Freedom Act of 1998 contributed to affirming the role of religious freedom in U.S. foreign policy. Within the two NSS Reports issued by President George W. Bush, one in 2002 and the next in 2006, it was the latter that firmly linked religion and national security in definite terms. The two NSS Reports issued by President Barack Obama in 2010 and 2015 marked a retreat from the emphasis placed on religion within the context of national security in the latter NSS Report of 2006. It should be noted, however, that the Frank R. Wolf International Religious Freedom Act of 2016, which amended and (in many respects) strengthened provisions in the International Religious Freedom Act of 1998, was introduced during the Obama administration. Nevertheless, it was not until the NSS Report in 2017 issued by President Donald J. Trump that the protection of religious freedom and religious minorities was listed as a strategic priority within the context of the national security policy of the U.S. Furthermore, despite the creation of the role of special advisor on international religious freedom at the National Security Council by the International Religious Freedom Act of 1998, that role had remained vacant until 2020 and has once again become vacant with the commencement of the Biden administration. President Biden's Interim National Security Strategic Guidance outlines the aims and priorities in respect of the forthcoming NSS. Whilst, unsurprisingly, the Biden administration has focused on the challenges presented by the Covid-19 pandemic and climate change, in addition to indicating that the approach to be adopted will be one of international co-operation, the limited reference to matters of religious freedom is concerning. Whether the Biden administration will maintain the positioning of religious freedom as a matter of strategic importance in terms of national security is unknown at this juncture; however, it would be regrettable if the distinctive nature of religiously motivated violence was not specifically addressed or indeed the need for the protection of religious freedom as a matter of national security. As Pérez (2021) has astutely noted,

> Biden championed his Catholic faith as the core of his political ambition. He can and should use this as his starting point to build a bipartisan coalition for international religious freedom. Artful statecraft is, at its core, the use of the moral imagination to find creative solutions to seemingly intractable political problems. If the Biden administration can draw on Trump, Obama, Bush, and other previous administrations creatively, it will be able to strengthen international religious freedom for years after its tenure at the helm ends.

The first NSS Report of the Biden administration will undoubtedly clarify whether religious freedom will remain a strategic priority in the context of the NSS.

References

Annicchino, P. (2016) 'A Transatlantic Partnership for International Religious Freedom? The United States, Europe, and the Challenge of Religious Persecution', *Oxford Journal of Law and Religion*, vol. 5, no. 2, pp. 280–297.

Biden, J. R. (2021) *Interim National Security Strategic Guidance*, Washington, DC, The White House [Online]. Available at https://nssarchive.us/white-house-publishes-interim-national-security-strategic-guidance/ (Accessed 26 September 2022).

Blitt, R. C. (2019) 'The Wolf Act Amendments to the U.S. International Religious Freedom Act: Breakthrough or Breakdown?', *University of Pennsylvania Journal of Law and Public Affairs*, vol. 4, no. 2, pp. 151–202.

Bush, G. W. (2006) *The National Security Strategy of the United States of America*, Washington, DC, The White House [Online]. Available at http://nssarchive.us/national-security-strategy-2006/ (Accessed 26 September 2022).

Bush, G. W. (2002) *The National Security Strategy of the United States of America*, Washington, DC, The White House [Online]. Available at http://nssarchive.us/national-security-strategy-2002/ (Accessed 26 September 2022).

Clinton, W. J. (2000) *A National Security Strategy for a Global Age*, Washington, DC, The White House [Online]. Available at http://nssarchive.us/national-security-strategy-2000/ (Accessed 26 September 2022).

Clinton, W. J. (1999) *A National Security Strategy for A New Century*, Washington, DC, The White House [Online]. Available at https://nssarchive.us/national-security-strategy-2000-2/ (Accessed 26 September 2022).

Clinton, W. J. (1998) *A National Security Strategy for A New Century*, Washington, DC, The White House [Online]. Available at https://nssarchive.us/national-security-strategy-1998/ (Accessed 26 September 2022).

Clinton, W. J. (1997) *A National Security Strategy for A New Century*, Washington, DC, The White House [Online]. Available at https://nssarchive.us/national-security-strategy-1997/ (Accessed 26 September 2022).

Cordesman, A. H. (2017) *President Trump's New National Security Strategy*, Washington, DC, Center for Strategic and International Studies [Online]. Available at https://www.csis.org/analysis/president-trumps-new-national-security-strategy (Accessed 26 September 2022).

Dale, C. (2008) *National Security Strategy: Legislative Mandates, Execution to Date, and Considerations for Congress*, Washington, DC, Congressional Research Service [Online]. Available at https://fas.org/sgp/crs/natsec/RL34505.pdf (Accessed 26 September 2022).

DuMont, M. (2019) *Elements of National Security Strategy*, Washington, DC, Atlantic Council [Online]. Available at https://www.atlanticcouncil.org/content-series/strategy-consortium/elements-of-national-security-strategy/ (Accessed 26 September 2022).

Gunn, T. J. (2000) 'A Preliminary Response to Criticisms of the International Religious Freedom Act of 1998', *Brigham Young University Law Review*, vol. 2000, no. 3, pp. 841–865.

Haley, P. E. (2006) *Strategies of Dominance: The Misdirection of U.S. Foreign Policy*, Baltimore, MD, John Hopkins University Press.

Lester, T. (2010) 'Oh, Gods! Atlantic Monthly, February 2002', in Nafziger, J. A. R., Paterson, R. K., and Renteln, A. D. (eds) *Cultural Law: International, Comparative, and Indigenous*, New York, Cambridge University Press, p. 831.

Lucius, C. (2013) 'Religion and the National Security Strategy', *Journal of Church and State*, vol. 55, no. 1, pp. 50–70.

McInnis, K. J. (2021) *The Interim National Security Strategic Guidance*, Washington, DC, Congressional Research Service [Online]. Available at https://crsreports.congress.gov/product/pdf/IF/IF11798 (Accessed 26 September 2022).

Murdock, C. A., Flournoy, M. A., Campbell, K. M., Chao, P. A., Smith, J., Witkowsky, A. A., and Wormuth, C. E. (2005) *Beyond Goldwater-Nichols: U.S. Government and Defense Reform for a New Strategic Era, Phase 2 Report*, Washington, DC, Center for Strategic and International Studies [Online]. Available at https://www.csis.org/analysis/beyond-goldwater-nichols-phase-ii-report (Accessed 26 September 2022).

Obama, B. H. (2015) *National Security Strategy*, Washington, DC, The White House [Online]. Available at http://nssarchive.us/national-security-strategy-2015/ (Accessed 26 September 2022).

Obama, B. H. (2010) *National Security Strategy*, Washington, DC, The White House [Online]. Available at http://nssarchive.us/national-security-strategy-2010/ (Accessed 26 September 2022).

Otis, P. (2004) 'Religion and War in the Twenty-First Century', in Seiple, R. A., and Hoover, D. R. (eds) *Religion and Security: The New Nexus in International Relations*, Lanham, MD, Rowman and Littlefield Publishers, p. 11.

Pérez, L. M. (2021) *International Religious Freedom in the Biden Administration*, Washington, DC, Berkley Center for Religion, Peace & World Affairs [Online]. Available at https://berkleycenter.georgetown.edu/responses/international-religious-freedom-in-the-biden-administration (Accessed 26 September 2022).

Siegel, R. (2018) 'The Gripping Sermon that Got 'under God' Added to the Pledge of Allegiance on Flag Day', *The Washington Post*, 14 June [Online]. Available at https://www.washingtonpost.com/news/retropolis/wp/2018/06/14/the-gripping-sermon-that-got-under-god-added-to-the-pledge-of-allegiance-on-flag-day/.

Taylor, C. (2007) *A Secular Age*, Cambridge, MA, Harvard University Press.

Trump, D. J. (2017) *National Security Strategy of the United States of America*, Washington, DC, The White House [Online]. Available at http://nssarchive.us/national-security-strategy-2017/ (Accessed 26 September 2022).

United States Commission on International Religious Freedom (2020) *United States Commission on International Religious Freedom Annual Report 2020*, Washington, DC [Online]. Available at https://www.uscirf.gov/publications/2020-annual-report (Accessed 26 September 2022).

U.S. Department of the Treasury (2011) 'History of "In God We Trust"' [Online]. Available at https://web.archive.org/web/20110310163407/https://www.treasury.gov/about/education/pages/in-god-we-trust.aspx (Accessed 26 September 2022).

5

NEW RELIGIOUS LEGISLATION IN UKRAINE AS A RESPONSE TO RUSSIAN AGGRESSION

Maksym Vasin

1 Introduction

Unlike in other post-Soviet countries, Ukrainian law guarantees a high level of religious freedom; however, because of national security, the amendments of 2018–2019 and the new governmental draft law of January 2023 raise concerns in terms of both their content and the way they are implemented. While in previous years national security was not a decisive motive for amending religious legislation, now, because of Russian aggression beginning in 2014 and followed by the full-scale invasion in 2022, the Ukrainian government tried to reduce the effects of Russia weaponizing religion in Ukraine. One of the changes in the passage of new laws requires parishes of the Ukrainian Orthodox Church of the Moscow Patriarchate (UOC-MP) to change their names and simplify canonical severance with the Russian Orthodox Church (ROC) for all local Orthodox parishes. Government officials explained the change by pointing to the necessity of protecting national security, particularly in the field of religious affairs. Given the Kremlin's use of religious propaganda to justify its colossal destruction of civilian infrastructure in Ukraine due to massive missile attacks, the occupation of new Ukrainian territories, and atrocities of the Russian military against civilians, Ukrainian society is now debating draft laws that would permanently sever ties with Russian religious centers.

While not underestimating the importance of religious independence for Ukraine as a sovereign state, it is appropriate to analyze whether such measures by the Ukrainian authorities are in line with international obligations for freedom of religion or belief and whether these legislative measures may have the opposite effect by leading to a reduction of religious freedom, increasing

DOI: 10.4324/9781003453086-8

tensions on religious grounds. This chapter will delineate the limits of permissible state intervention in the internal affairs of religious organizations in situations that have developed in Ukraine due to external geopolitical factors.

2 Historical Background

Ukraine has been in de facto martial law over Russian aggression since February 2014, when Russian troops, wearing unmarked green uniforms, invaded the Ukrainian peninsula of Crimea and conducted a military operation to secure further annexation of the Crimea. For years, the international community has not recognized the pseudo-referendum of 16 March 2014, joining Russia with Crimea, which took place on the peninsula under the barrels of Russian machine guns and ignoring Ukraine's Constitution. Russia's aggression spread to the Donetsk and Luhansk regions in the eastern part of Ukraine, where Russian heavy military equipment, disguised soldiers, and volunteer Russian militants arrived to support a small group of local separatists. Russia's presence in Crimea and the eastern regions of Ukraine has made for a long-lasting military conflict and a permanent threat to the security of the entire European continent.

Since March 2021, a significant part of Russian military equipment and its regular army are now in the borders of Ukraine: from the east – closer to the non-controlled territories of the Donetsk and Luhansk regions, from the south – in the occupied Crimea and Transnistria, from the north – closer to Belarus, which is in a supranational union with Russia (Schwirtz and Reinhard, 2022). Finally, on 24 February 2022, Russia started a full-scale war against Ukraine by land offensives from different directions under cover of mass air and missile attacks. The Russian invasion was intended to eliminate Ukrainian leadership, take over Kyiv as a capital city, demolish Ukraine as a sovereign democratic state, and destroy Ukrainian historical and cultural heritage and religious pluralism to implement its imperialistic policy, based on the geopolitical ideology of the "Russkiy Mir" (Vasin et al., 2022).[1]

However, Russia's aggression against Ukraine is not limited to the use of military force. Since 2014, in the occupied territories of Crimea, Donetsk, and Luhansk regions, the Russian-backed authorities are systematically repressing religious minorities to consolidate their power, asserting baseless accusations of extremism and arbitrary imprisonment. Freedoms of speech, expression, and peaceful assembly are subject to the most severe restrictions (Novitchkova et al., 2015). While the Orthodox parishes of the Moscow Patriarchate enjoy a privileged status and loyalty from the occupying authorities, many believers fear for their safety. This is especially true in the Donetsk and Luhansk regions, where there are no legitimate judiciaries and legal mechanisms to avoid the arbitrariness and repressions committed by people with power and weapons (Vasin et al., 2018). Also, human rights organizations and international monitors can't document and verify human rights violations because this activity would be unsafe for them. The Russian full-scale invasion in 2022 only worsened the situation with religious freedom, especially in the newly occupied Ukrainian regions of Zaporizhzhia and Kherson. The ideological basis for the occupying authorities is the "Russian World" ideology, promoted by Patriarch Kirill of Moscow, the Primate of the ROC (Vasin et al., 2022).

As the President of Russia, Vladimir Putin (2018), explained:

> The Russian world has never been built exclusively and only along ethnic, national, or religious lines. It has gathered and united everyone who is spiritually connected with Russia, who feels this spiritual connection with our homeland, who considers themselves to be bearers of the Russian language, culture, and Russian history.

Based on the ideology of the Russian World, Putin explains his geopolitical claims to Ukraine; denies the historical emergence and development of the Ukrainian people and its independent state; imposes the idea of the brotherhood of Russia, Ukraine, and Belarus; and uses the Russian language and the Russian Orthodox Church (Moscow Patriarchate) as an excuse to intervene in the internal affairs of other independent states (*BBC News*, 2014).[2] As a consequence of the Russian policy of expansion, on 1 March 2014, at the request of President Putin, the Federation Council of the Federal Assembly of the Russian Federation (2014) approved the intervention of the Russian Armed Forces on the territory of Ukraine, citing the need to protect "Russian citizens, our compatriots," primarily in the Ukrainian peninsula of Crimea (Putin, 2021). These narratives are continuously promoted and are based on fake historical facts to expand Russian influence upon Ukraine as an independent state:

> Russians, Ukrainians, and Belarusians are all descendants of Ancient Rus. ... Modern Ukraine is entirely the product of the Soviet era. ... True sovereignty of Ukraine is possible only in partnership with Russia. Our spiritual, human, and civilizational ties formed for centuries. ... We are one people.
>
> *(Putin, 2021)*

In essence, the Russian World concept presupposes the loss of the Ukrainian people's identity, sovereignty, and statehood in favor of the imperial interests of Russia, which seeks to restore Soviet-era influence. And one of the key leaders of this geopolitical ideology is the ROC, which has recently become particularly close to the Russian state apparatus and relays the Kremlin's interests among Orthodox believers. For example, Moscow Patriarch Kirill called Russia's aggression against Ukraine a "civil conflict,"[3] and, in an interview with the Russian propaganda media, said: "For me, Ukraine is the same as Russia" (*Radio Free Europe/Radio Liberty*, 2018b; *RBC-Ukraine*, 2016).[4] As Casanova (2019, p. 329) noted: "Russia is … a union of the secular imperial and authoritarian state with the ROC, which – in the person of the Moscow Patriarchate – puts forward canonical-territorial claims to many post-Soviet states."

Because the UOC-MP is a part of the ROC with certain rights of autonomy, several Ukrainian politicians and experts have warned about Russian influence on Ukrainian society through the UOC-MP (*National Institute for Strategic Studies*, 2017). As an example, on 8 May 2015, the Primate of the UOC-MP, Metropolitan Onuphry, and other UOC-MP bishops refused to stand up during the ceremony at the Ukrainian Parliament in honor of fallen Ukrainian soldiers, who were posthumously awarded the title of "Hero of Ukraine for courageous protection of the homeland from Russian aggression" (*Radio Free Europe/Radio Liberty*, 2015).[5] They later explained their gesture as a call to end the war, as if the Ukrainian Army was not defending its people but fighting against them. This position of the UOC-MP leadership echoes the propaganda of the Kremlin and Vladimir Putin, about the alleged "civil war" in Ukraine, hiding the real presence of Russian troops and Russian heavy artillery in eastern Ukraine (*TASS*, 2015). The Kremlin using the church structure as a tool for spreading propaganda looks especially threatening, considering that the UOC-MP is the largest religious association in Ukraine, which has more than 12,000 parishes and other legal entities, a third of all religious organizations in the state (*State Service of Ukraine for Ethnopolitics and Freedom of Conscience*, 2021).

Furthermore, the actions of certain UOC-MP priests who aided the armed separatists in the occupied Crimea and eastern regions of Ukraine, and who subsequently continued to engage in activities such as directing fire against the Ukrainian Army and collaborating with Russian occupation authorities, represent the most significant national security breach for the state. For example, in 2014, according to the testimony of residents of the Sviatohirsk Lavra, the UOC-MP in the Donetsk region provided its housing for use by groups of Russian-backed militants at the beginning of the warfare (Novitchkova et al., 2015). Also, human rights activists have documented the participation of two Russian Cossack battalions among illegal armed groups in eastern Ukraine, which associate themselves with Russian Orthodoxy, fight against the Ukrainian Army under religious flags, call themselves defenders of the Russian World, terrorize the religious communities, torture and kill the believers of other denominations, and confiscate their cathedrals (Vasin et al., 2018). Among them was an illegal military battalion called the Russian Orthodox Army, which seized the city of Slovyansk in the Donetsk region and kept it under control until June 2014, carrying out systematic repressions against religious figures of other denominations and pro-Ukrainian public activists. Open sources and eyewitnesses have confirmed that these armed groups received support from the local UOC-MP parishes and some ROC clergymen, although the church leadership does not approve of the activities of Orthodox paramilitary groups (Novitchkova et al., 2015).

According to Slovyansk residents and confirmed by photo evidence, the rector of the Holy Resurrection parish of the UOC-MP, priest Oleg Khyzhnyakov, not only consecrated the battle flags of the illegal military battalion led by Russian officer Igor Girkin (Strelkov) but also provided the Russian-backed militants with food (*Censor.net*, 2014). Another illustrative case was when the archpriest of the UOC-MP, Volodymyr Maretskyi, was sentenced to six years in prison for organizing riots to block the movement of the Ukrainian Army in the Luhansk region and assisting the Russian-backed separatists in April–May of 2014 (*Ukrainian News*, 2018).

Igor Girkin confirmed publicly in the interview for media the engagement of the UOC-MP representatives in his military operations (*Religious Information Service of Ukraine*, 2018):

> My personal guard consisted of spiritual sons, monks, hieromonks of the Sviatohirsk Lavra. … [t]o the last man. It was not very large, but they were there … We had one of the units in the Slovyansk brigade commanded by the novice of the Sviatohirsk Lavra. And the novice held a rather serious position in the Lavra … a provisor.

Later he was sentenced by the Hague District Court to life in prison for the downing of the MH17 flight over Ukraine in 2014, and the killing of all 298 people on board (van den Berg and Sterling, 2022). Other facts documented by human rights activists indicate that the activities of individual priests of the UOC-MP working in the interests of Russia were not uncommon.[6]

At the same time, it cannot be said that every bishop, every priest, and every believer of each UOC-MP parish supports Russian aggression against Ukraine and poses a threat to national security. However, the leadership of the Ukrainian state has had to respond to the following:

- Russia uses religion as an instrument for increasing its influence worldwide, especially in Ukraine.
- Russia uses the Ukrainian Orthodox Church (affiliated with the Moscow Patriarchate) to hold Ukraine in its conception of the Russian World and to justify its interference in the internal affairs of Ukraine, followed by the full-scale military invasion since 24 February 2022.
- UOC-MP doesn't publicly respect the Ukrainian Army, using phrases to describe the conflict like "civil war," "fratricidal conflict," etc., according to the Kremlin's narratives. There are facts about rejecting funeral rituals

for the killed Ukrainian soldiers by certain UOC-MP clergy (*Ukrinform*, 2018).

- The facts uncovered of certain priests and bishops of the UOC-MP collaborating with representatives of the Russian authorities, including the occupation administration, which is a criminal offense of treason.[7]

3 New Religious Legislation in 2018–2019 as a Response to Threats in the Field of Religion

The Ukrainian state authorities acted on these blatant threats to national security. This chapter will analyze the measures taken and assess their legitimate aim, proportionality, and necessity in a democratic society, considering the context of Russia's ongoing aggression against Ukraine, which became much more brutal after 24 February 2022.

In the interests of national security, the Parliament of Ukraine during December 2018–January 2019 passed two laws that would:

- Ban all UOC-MP priests from serving in the Ukrainian Army and other military forces of Ukraine as chaplains.
- Force all UOC-MP parishes to change their names adding their affiliation with the ROC. The law doesn't mention the UOC-MP directly but states that any religious organization affiliated with the religious center in Russia as an aggressor state[8] to mark such affiliation in their names.[9]
- Introduce a simpler procedure of changing local parish affiliation with a religious center (denomination), primarily in favor of transitions from the Moscow Patriarchate to the newly established autocephalous Orthodox Church of Ukraine (OCU).[10]

The initiators of Law #2662-VIII of 20 December 2018 argued the proposed changes by affirming that "there is a direct threat of spreading destructive propaganda using a religious factor by the aggressor state, which will have real consequences for national interests, territorial integrity, and national security of Ukraine" (*Parliament of Ukraine*, 2016).

In balancing these state interference measures with the basic right of freedom of religion, it is appropriate to apply the test questions used by the European Court of Human Rights when examining complaints of violations of religious freedoms. According to Article 9(2) of the European Convention on Human Rights, religious freedoms shall be subject only to "limitations prescribed by law and necessary in a democratic society" and according to the ruling of the European Court of Human Rights established in 1983 that restrictions on human rights must be motivated by a "pressing social need," and be "proportionate to the legitimate aim pursued" (*Svyato-Mykhaylivska Parafiya v Ukraine* [2007]).

First, neither Article 9 of the European Convention on Human Rights nor Article 35 of the Constitution of Ukraine provides such a ground for restricting religious freedom as national security. The exception could only apply to a declaration of martial law or public emergency, which should be preceded by the adoption of a relevant bill indicating the specific duration of such restrictions. Article 4(2) of the ICCPR provides that countries may not in any way restrict the right to freedom of religion or belief, including in cases of public emergency (*United Nations*, 1966). In this regard, "the right to freedom of religion or belief is accorded even higher priority than freedom of expression or freedom of association" (*OSCE/ODIHR*, 2004, p. 19).

3.1 Denial of Access for Chaplains of the UOC-MP to the Ukrainian Army

Denial of access for chaplains of the UOC-MP to the Ukrainian Army can be considered as certain discrimination against clergy and limiting the ability of the UOC-MP soldiers to meet their religious needs during military service. Orthodox soldiers belonging to the Moscow Patriarchate have found themselves in a more awkward position than believers of other denominations, who may invite a priest of their denomination to visit them at the military unit's location. Nevertheless, for the UOC-MP believers in the Ukrainian Army remains the option to make an independent trip during a day off to their denomination's parish or to ask the commander of the military unit to invite a priest to provide pastoral care on a volunteer basis. In some cases, they may agree to use the services of a regular or guest chaplain of another denomination. However, it is unlikely that military leadership will agree to invite the Orthodox priest affiliated with the Moscow Patriarchate as a church that has a religious center in the aggressor state, especially after the outbreak of a full-scale invasion of Ukraine. In the case of *Kalaç v Turkey* [1997], the European Court of Human Rights noted that

> In choosing to pursue a military career [applicant] was accepting of his own accord a system of military discipline that by its very nature implied the possibility of placing on certain of the rights and freedoms of members of the armed forces limitations incapable of being imposed on civilians.

Recalling the above examples of UOC-MP priests working in the interests of Russian propaganda or even in active support of Russian-backed, armed separatists and occupational authorities, it is evident that the Ukrainian authorities had sound reasons for restricting their access to the army and other military formations in the capacity of staff chaplains while active warfare in Ukraine continued. Moreover, after Russia initiated a full-scale unprovoked war against Ukraine, it became clear that the Russian Orthodox Church is heavily dependent on the Kremlin, as demonstrated by Moscow

Patriarch Kirill's support for Russian aggression and encouragement of the Russian military's continued invasion of Ukraine (Smith, 2022). Kirill has even likened the conflict to a holy war, claiming that the sacrifice of Russian servicemen washes them of all their sins and brings them to Paradise (Shumylo, 2022).

In light of the evidence of high treason and collaboration among members of the UOC-MP and their ties to the Russian occupation authorities (Roshchyna, 2023), the measures taken by the Ukrainian authorities to restrict the presence of chaplains affiliated with the Moscow Patriarchate in the Ukrainian Army seem both reasonable and proportionate to the legitimate aim. Furthermore, the UOC-MP leadership has failed to condemn or take any disciplinary action against collaborators within the church, which has deepened distrust among Ukrainian society, including the Armed Forces of Ukraine.

3.2 Forcing All UOC-MP Parishes to Change their Names Adding the Affiliation with the Russian Orthodox Church

Forcing all UOC-MP parishes to change their names adding the affiliation with the Russian Orthodox Church is a more sensitive issue for Orthodox believers of the Moscow Patriarchate because it affects all local parishes and structural units of the UOC-MP. According to authors of Law #2662-VIII, it was "designed to ensure the state security and sovereignty of Ukraine, as well as to provide society with complete and accurate information" about the Orthodox denominations in Ukraine (*Parliament of Ukraine*, 2016). Also, the law was aimed to avert the "direct threat of the spread of destructive propaganda using the religious factor by the aggressor state" and the "potential risk" that arises because "the religious factor has a significant impact on the formation of public opinion" (*Parliament of Ukraine*, 2016).

The Ukrainian government has justified its intervention in church affairs as a means to protect Orthodox believers from misinformation and manipulation surrounding the names of Orthodox churches of different canonical jurisdictions in Ukraine (*Religious Information Service of Ukraine*, 2019). Indeed, it was in the state's interest as it sought to facilitate the formation of the autocephalous Orthodox Church of Ukraine (OCU), which is independent of Moscow, recognized by the Ecumenical Patriarch, and on equal footing with other Orthodox churches in the world.

In December 2018, on the eve of the adoption of the law, two Orthodox churches in Ukraine that were not previously recognized by world Orthodoxy came together at the unifying council in Kyiv to form a single OCU, with the participation of some UOC-MP bishops (*Radio Free Europe/Radio Liberty*, 2018a). On 5 January 2019, the newly established OCU received a *tomos* decree from His Holiness Bartholomew, the Ecumenical Patriarch, recognizing its independence and self-government (*Radio Free Europe/Radio Liberty*, 2019). A few months before, the Holy Synod of the Ecumenical Patriarchate abolished the patriarchal decree of 1686, which had granted the Moscow Patriarchate supremacy over the Kyiv Metropolis (*Ecumenical Patriarchate*, 2018). With this action, the newly created autocephalous OCU became the religious institution tasked with uniting Orthodox believers in support of Ukraine's state independence and sovereignty. Former Ukrainian President Petro Poroshenko emphasized the importance of the Church as the spiritual foundation of Ukraine's statehood, stating that "without our Church, there can be no state" (*Interfax-Ukraine*, 2019). Therefore, the autocephalous OCU is more favorable to the Ukrainian authorities due to its recognition by world Orthodoxy and the absence of canonical subordination to the Moscow Patriarchate.

The challenge is that since 1990 the UOC-MP has been officially known as the Ukrainian Orthodox Church and does not indicate affiliation with the Moscow Patriarchate. Also, it does not have the status of autocephaly and remains a structural unit of the Russian Orthodox Church with some autonomy rights. Conversely, the newly established autocephalous OCU has a double name as the "Orthodox Church of Ukraine (Ukrainian Orthodox Church)," emphasizing its canonical jurisdiction over the territory of Ukraine according to the decree of the Ecumenical Patriarchate. Thus, there is an obvious conflict of names, when two different Orthodox churches with different worldviews and different attitudes to the Russian aggression operate under almost the same name. This confusion may explain the state's desire to clarify the difference between both denominations so that Orthodox believers can make an informed choice about their denominational affiliation: whether to attend the autocephalous Orthodox Church of Ukraine or the Ukrainian Orthodox Church under the Moscow Patriarchate.

Comparing sociological and statistical data we can conclude that there is no correlation between the percentage of the actual number of believers in Ukraine who identify with a particular Orthodox church and the nominal number of parishes, as seen on the following data table:

Church's official name	*What denomination do you belong to?* Sociological survey of the Razumkov Centre (2020)	*Number of registered parishes and other legal entities* Statistical data of the State Service of Ukraine for Ethnopolitics and Freedom of Conscience (2021)
Ukrainian Orthodox Church (under the Moscow Patriarchate)	13.8%	33.5% (12,406)
Orthodox Church of Ukraine (autocephalous)	34.0%	19.4% (7,188)

The number of OCU believers is 2.5 times greater than the number of UOC-MP believers but the number of parishes and other structural units of the OCU is significantly less than in the UOC-MP. The prevailing opinion among Ukrainian researchers is that this discrepancy is because many members of UOC-MP parishes are unaware of the affiliation of their parish with the Moscow Patriarchate. After all, the official name states that it is the *Ukrainian* Orthodox Church. Instead, in sociological polls, respondents make a more informed choice when it comes to belonging to the "Ukrainian church" or the "Moscow church," because many Orthodox parishioners do not see the difference between patriarchates and do not even understand which church – Ukrainian autocephalous or affiliated with the Moscow patriarchate – they go to (Solodko, 2013).

Regardless of the increased sensitivity in Ukrainian society to the issue of affiliation with the Moscow Patriarchate following Russia's unleashing of a full-scale war, there was no significant wave of parishes transitioning from the UOC-MP to the canonical subordination of the OCU.[11] Considering this, the Ukrainian government argues that it is vital to publicly indicate the affiliation of the UOC-MP with the religious center in the aggressor state to avoid misinformation among the Orthodox faithful in Ukraine and give them options to make a conscious choice. The aim of Law #2662-VIII is to minimize the misinformation of Orthodox believers about their denomination's affiliation, eliminate manipulations due to the similarity of the names of two different Orthodox churches, and provide favorable conditions for the development of the newly established autocephalous Orthodox Church of Ukraine (OCU). However, such state intervention requires further examination to assess whether it has proven effective and to what extent it was proportionate to the pursued aim.

Law #2662-VIII gave nine months for local parishes and four months for other UOC-MP structural units to change their official name, forcing them to add affiliation with the ROC (*Про внесення зміни до статті 12 Закону України*. Ukraine. Parliament of Ukraine, 2018). In case of non-compliance with this requirement, the law stipulates that the statute of such religious organizations shall cease to be valid in the part which determines its full official name *(Про внесення зміни до статті 12 Закону України.* Ukraine. Parliament of Ukraine, 2018). However, the practical implementation of Law #2662-VIII on forced renaming proved to be excessively burdensome for both public authorities and the UOC-MP parishes.

It is obvious that the UOC-MP leadership did not agree with the requirement of forced renaming and took measures to block its implementation. On 19 January 2019, 49 parliamentarians initiated an appeal to the Constitutional Court of Ukraine demanding that Law #2662-VIII be declared unconstitutional. Next, the Kyiv Metropolis of the UOC-MP filed a suit in the District Administrative Court of Kyiv addressed to the Ministry of Culture of Ukraine, requesting recognition of the actions of the Ministry aimed at illegally implementing the law canceling the relevant decisions. While pending for more than three years, the court banned the Ministry of Culture from taking forced registration action against 266 UOC-MP religious organizations (*Kyiv Metropolis of the Ukrainian Orthodox Church v the Ministry of Culture of Ukraine* [2019]).

On 27 December 2022, the Constitutional Court of Ukraine recognized Law #2662-VIII on the forced renaming of the UOC-MP parishes and other structural units as complying with and not violating the Constitution of Ukraine.[12] Nevertheless, the law remains unfulfilled but creates difficulties for routine activities. Most UOC-MP parishes continue to operate with their current names and statutes. However, the legal restrictions remain for those who need to change their statutes or enter data in the state register regarding the new priest as the head of a legal entity, for example, in case of death (*Ukrainian Orthodox Church*, 2021). If any UOC-MP parish on its initiative applies to the religious affairs department for state registration of the new wording of its statute or for entering the updated information about the parish to the State Register of Legal Entities, it will be impossible without adding the provision of subordination to the ROC to its official name according to Law #2662-VIII. Despite the legal aim, registration procedures should not be used as a means of limiting the right to freedom of religion or belief of members of certain religious or belief communities to avoid discriminatory treatment in this regard (Bielefeldt, 2011).

Although the Constitutional Court of Ukraine and the District Administrative Court of Kyiv provided favorable decisions,[13] the religious affairs departments do not initiate lawsuits against the local UOC-MP parishes to force their renaming. Initiating lawsuits against more than 12,000 parishes and other UOC-MP legal entities is also a very costly and time-consuming affair for the state. As a result, the Ukrainian Parliament's interference in the UOC-MP's activities was carried out in a way that did not bring the expected result despite the legitimate aim.

3.3 An Introduction of the Easier Procedure of Changing the Affiliation of Local Parishes with a Religious Center (Denomination)

The next intervention to religious freedom by the Parliament of Ukraine was an introduction of the easier procedure of changing the affiliation of local parishes with a religious center (denomination). Law #2673-VIII of 17 January 2019 was adopted less than two weeks after the OCU received the *tomos* decree on autocephaly from the Ecumenical Patriarch and was allowed to become an alternative to the UOC-MP for millions of Ukrainian Orthodox believers who wanted to have an independent church without subordination to the Moscow Patriarchate (*Про внесення змін до деяких законів України.* Ukraine. Parliament of Ukraine, 2019). This significant historical fact and the desire of the state to promote the development of the autocephalous OCU led to the hasty adoption of this law, which did not consider the peculiarities of the activities of religious organizations of non-Orthodox denominations.

The Ukrainian authorities decided to facilitate the transition of local Orthodox parishes from the Moscow Patriarchate to the newly established OCU. In combination with the above-mentioned law on the forced renaming of all UOC-MP parishes, Law #2673-VIII aimed to simplify the procedure of changing the canonical subordination in the statutes of Orthodox parishes (*Про внесення змін до деяких законів України.* Ukraine. Parliament of Ukraine, 2019). The idea was that instead of fulfilling the obligation to reflect belonging to the Russian Orthodox Church in its name, the UOC-MP parishes would have to transit to the autocephalous OCU according to the new procedure.

The Ukrainian parliament wanted to respond to the legal issues arising because in many cases the parish statute's rules make the transition to another canonical subordination impossible. The statutory documents of most Orthodox parishes limit the right of its members to freely change their allegiance to another religious center other than the Moscow Patriarchate, despite the guarantee by Article 8 of the *Law of Ukraine on Freedom of Conscience and Religious Organizations* (*Про свободу совісті та релігійні організації.* Ukraine. Parliament of Ukraine, 1991). For example, without the signature of the parish priest or the written consent of a bishop of the eparchy, it was impossible. These legal obstacles are described in detail in the decision of the European Court of Human Rights in the case of *Svyato-Mykhaylivska Parafiya v Ukraine* [2007]. Given that the provisions of most statutes of the UOC-MP parishes prevent the transition from the Moscow Patriarchate to any other Orthodox Church, the Ukrainian Parliament decided to intervene in this area and legislate the procedure of changing canonical subordination for all religious organizations. Now the procedure for how the parish decides to change its canonical subordination (denomination) is determined not by its statute, but by the *Law of Ukraine on Freedom Conscience and Religious Organizations* (*Про свободу совісті та релігійні організації.* Ukraine. Parliament of Ukraine, 1991).

Law #2673-VIII implemented these new rules (*Про внесення змін до деяких законів України.* Ukraine. Parliament of Ukraine, 2019):

- The decision of changing the canonical subordination (affiliations with a denomination) is made by the general meeting of parish members.
- Parish members can initiate a general meeting to consider this issue.

- Two-thirds of the votes of the parish members from the quorum required for the legitimacy of the general meeting is sufficient to decide on the change of canonical subordination (affiliation with a denomination).
- This decision has to be signed by those members of the parish who voted for it.
- For the state registration of changes in the parish statute, a list of all participants of the general meeting, which approved these changes, is submitted to the religious affairs department.

On the one hand, the adoption of Law #2673-VIII simplified the process for Orthodox religious communities to change their affiliation to a religious center and ensured their rights to change canonical subordination freely. As a result, hundreds of UOC-MP parishes were able to legally formalize their transition to the OCU. However, the haste with which the Parliament adopted these legislative changes complicated the state registration procedure for all religious communities, which can be considered as exceeding the appropriate limits of state intervention. In order to comply with the principle of proportionality of state intervention, Ukrainian lawmakers are currently working on developing new legislative amendments to address these shortcomings.[14]

4 Draft Law 2023 on Severing Ties with Russian Religious Centers

On 1 December 2022, President Volodymyr Zelenskyy announced a draft law that would oblige religious organizations to sever ties with religious centers in Russia due to its aggression against Ukraine. Signing the decision of the National Security and Defense Council of Ukraine aimed at ensuring the "spiritual independence" of the state, President Zelenskyy (2022) said in his video address:

> Unfortunately, even Russian terror and a full-scale war have not convinced some figures that overcoming the temptation of evil is worth the effort. In this case, we must create conditions where any figures dependent on the aggressor state will not have any opportunity to manipulate Ukrainians and weaken Ukraine from within.

Numerous media outlets and experts hastily characterized this legislative initiative as a ban on the UOC-MP. Nevertheless, the changes suggested later by the Ukrainian government represent a moderately gradual yet not entirely perfect and clear approach to curbing Russia's influence on religious communities in Ukraine regardless of their denomination. Furthermore, the Ukrainian Parliament has not rushed to adopt draft law #8371 submitted by the government on 19 January 2023 (*Parliament of Ukraine*, 2023b). Instead, the Parliament is engaging in consultations with experts and the Ukrainian

Council of Churches and Religious Organizations (UCCRO), and preparing to refine the proposed amendments during the consideration process in several readings. After the meeting with the Parliament Chairman, UCCRO (2023) unanimously declared (a) the inadmissibility of the activities of any organizations in Ukraine, including religious ones, whose centers and leadership are located in the Russian Federation; (b) the inevitability of punishment for all persons involved in aiding the enemy and treason, regardless of which denomination and church they belong to and whether they have any rank; (c) equality before the law of representatives of all religions.

The general approach of governmental draft law #8371 can be summarized as follows:

- The State Service of Ukraine for Ethnic Policies and Freedom of Conscience is granted the right to conduct religious studies expertise on the activities of religious organizations to determine their affiliation with religious centers located in Russia, which is considered an aggressor state by the law.
- In case of affiliation with any Russian religious center, the State Service will issue an order for such religious organization to eliminate the violations identified during the religious studies expertise.
- If the religious organization fails to eliminate the violations within a one-month period from the date of the order, the State Service has the right to appeal to the court with an administrative claim to terminate the activities of the religious organization (*Parliament of Ukraine*, 2023b).

Several other legislative initiatives aimed at directly banning the UOC-MP are submitted to the Ukrainian parliament, but they have no prospects to pass because of the evident contradiction of international standards on religious freedom. In contrast, the advantage of the governmental draft law in the phased approach is to take measures against Ukraine's religious organizations affiliated with Russian religious centers. This approach is primarily aimed at encouraging the severing of ties to the aggressor state, rather than explicitly prohibiting a particular church or denomination. Of course, such state intervention in the internal affairs of religious organizations can also be considered as a separate violation of religious freedom. However, the Ukrainian government argues that this measure is appropriate and proportionate under martial law and given the Kremlin's complete control over all Russian religious centers in that Putin's authoritarian regime doesn't allow freedom of religion or belief at all.[15] The State Service expressed this position in response to a petition from UOC-MP faithful (Kominko, 2023):

> The Moscow Patriarchate is fully controlled by the Russian leadership and directed by it towards the destruction of Ukrainian statehood and the Ukrainian people, including the faithful of the UOC-MP. In this sense, the

> draft law pursues a legitimate goal and, at the same time, does not burden the conscience of the Orthodox faithful, since subordination to the Moscow Patriarchate is not part of Orthodox belief. In contrast, subordination to the inspirers of killers and rapists is difficult to justify with Christian conscience.

From law-making standards, draft law #8371 appears imperfect and requires further refinement to avoid broad discretion in the powers of officials who will conduct religious studies expertise, issue orders to religious organizations affiliated with the Russian religious centers, and prepare submissions to the court in cases of non-compliance with these orders. Specifically, the draft law needs to clearly define (a) the procedure and required conduct for conducting religious studies expertise, (b) the criteria for identifying connections with Russian religious centers that pose a threat to the state, its citizens' lives, and health, (c) the requirements for the form, content, and legal force of orders issued based on the results of religious studies expertise, (d) the possibility of extending the period for executing an order by more than one month, taking into account the probable need to undergo a lengthy state registration procedure to make changes to statutory documents, and (e) the consequences of a court decision to terminate the activities of a religious organization for non-compliance with the order, including its property, funds, and sacred objects.

Moreover, it is essential to consider how the legislative changes proposed in draft law #8371 will be implemented in practice if passed. It is in the interests of the Ukrainian government to ensure that these legislative amendments do not become a legal tool for the deliberate persecution of the UOC-MP and the redistribution of its property in favor of other Orthodox denominations. Remembering the experience of the legislative changes of 2018, which the UOC-MP ignored, the Ukrainian government should evaluate the prospect of missing the orders of the State Service by the leadership and local units of the UOC-MP. Furthermore, it is crucial to predict the potential implications for interfaith peace and social cohesion in Ukraine if an extreme measure like a court decision to terminate the activities of the UOC-MP metropolis or other leading structures or parishes as legal entities is implemented. And it is important to remember, akin to the matter of renaming the UOC-MP, the court cannot issue a verdict concerning the entire UOC-MP as a religious association, but must examine the issue of terminating the activity of each of the approximately 12,000 UOC-MP parishes and other individual structural units.

5 National Security <u>or</u> Religious Freedom?

The full-scale Russian invasion provided the Ukrainian government with strong arguments to take more decisive action to defend against Russian aggression, including in the religious sphere. Investigations actively initiated by the Security Service of Ukraine since November 2022 revealed dozens of priests and a few bishops of the UOC-MP who spread Russian propaganda and ideology of the Russian World from the church pulpit, collaborated with the Russian authorities and its occupation administrations, and among other crimes committed state treason.[16] As *Reuters* reported (Hunder et al., 2023), 61 UOC-MP clergy have had criminal cases opened against them since the start of 2022 with 7 found guilty by court verdicts. Created by the *Ministry of Culture and Information Policy of Ukraine* (2023), the commission documented misapplication facts in Kyiv-Pechersk Lavra, a sacred heritage site leased by the UOC-MP from the state. Moreover, the Security Service of Ukraine found millions of cash and identified suspicious citizens of the Russian Federation during searches of the Kyiv-Pechersk Lavra (Zubkova, 2022).

The criminal charges brought against the UOC-MP clergy should not be perceived as political persecution since Ukrainian society is dissatisfied for years with the impunity of the Church representatives for their crimes and abuses of religious freedom, due to the protection from pro-Russian parliamentarians and governmental officials. For example, the court decision on the house arrest of Metropolitan Pavlo (Lebed), the UOC-MP abbot of the Kyiv-Pechersk Lavra monastery, contains substantiated accusations and evidence of his state treason and other violations of the law (*Deutsche Welle*, 2023). Moreover, journalists have published investigations about the Russian citizenship of Metropolitan Onufriy (Berezovsky) and other UOC-MP leadership (Tkach, 2023). At the same time, the UOC-MP leadership doesn't take any measures to condemn the actions of some bishops and priests who openly collaborate with the Russian authorities and have been accused of state treason. There was neither public condemnation nor disciplinary action in the form of deprivation of the right to perform priestly duties. This position of the UOC-MP Primate and other bishops contradicts their own words about the formal separation from the ROC after the decisions of the UOC-MP Council in Kyiv on 27 May 2022 (*Radio Free Europe/Radio Liberty*, 2022b).

In times of martial law, the Ukrainian government faces the challenge of responding to new circumstances that reveal the compromised leadership of the UOC-MP and leave open the question of the Kremlin's use of this church structure to spread Russian World narratives, justify Russian aggression, weaken resistance from the Ukrainian people from within, and even adjust the fire of Russian troops and locate positions of Ukrainian defenders. In this case, certain bishops and priests of the UOC-MP pose not imaginary risks to national security but a genuine threat to the life and health of residents of Ukraine. Such concerns of the Ukrainian authorities and the whole society are heightened in connection with documented numerous war crimes committed by Russian military personnel that have signs of a genocidal intent, which is a separate crime under international humanitarian law (Vasin et al., 2022).

However, the question remains open whether the termination of activity of the UOC-MP as a religious association and its structural units will be able to solve the legitimate goals of the Ukrainian government to protect its people from Russian subversions through the use of religious communities that have remained a canonical connection with the Moscow Patriarchate. Will such state intervention be proportional in case draft law #8371 is adopted and implemented till the final stage? And will it not have the opposite effect by creating a halo of martyrdom for the UOC-MP and causing several thousand of its parishes to operate underground?

The restriction of religious freedom based on national security threats often has the opposite effect. For instance, the forced renaming of UOC-MP parishes led to Orthodox believers' anger, and to their joining active protests for the zealous protection of the interests of their denomination and a sense of being a victim of persecution for their faith (*Religiyna Pravda*, 2021). Nevertheless, the problems of Russian propaganda and misinformation remain unresolved, as such activities are mostly carried out by individual priests or bishops, rather than by a certain group of believers registered as a legal entity. As Vovk (2019, p. 48) noted, "It is still a challenge for the Ukrainian authorities to prove that the UOC-MP poses a threat to national security or territorial integrity in order to justify the restrictions imposed on that church." Although there have been more and more cases of state treason and collaborationism with Russia as an aggressor state investigated against the UOC-MP clergy in recent months, the Ukrainian parliament must carefully consider international obligations regarding religious freedom before resorting to extreme measures such as a termination of the activities of the entire Church, which has almost two million faithful (*Deutsche Welle*, 2022).

Legislative and administrative limitations in the name of national security, especially if they are very broad or applied arbitrarily, "can worsen rather than improve security" (*OSCE/ODIHR*, 2019, p. 6). The opposite effect of such measures taken by the state can be explained by the fact that contrasting national security and religious freedom is a disastrous approach. Instead of choosing between the two and pondering which aspect of freedom should be sacrificed for strengthening security, the concept of the interrelationship between security and religious freedom should be considered. In this context, the OSCE's comprehensive approach to security is relevant, because it "does not frame freedom of religion or belief and security as competing rights, but recognizes them as complementary, interdependent and mutually reinforcing objectives that can and must be advanced together" (*OSCE/ODIHR*, 2019, p. 6).

6 Conclusion: National Security and Religious Freedom

Given the interrelationship between security and religious freedom, several alternative proposals can be formulated for Ukrainian leaders to minimize the use of religion in Russian military aggression against Ukraine while respecting international obligations in the field of religious freedom. These proposals will be useful for other states facing similar challenges.

A Regarding the presence of UOC-MP chaplains in the Ukrainian Army, it would be expedient to provide alternative opportunities for the pastoral care of servicemen belonging to the UOC-MP. For example, to allow servicemen to have a short vacation for visiting a relevant Orthodox parish or to invite an Orthodox priest with an impeccable reputation to conduct services or sacraments on a volunteer basis (as a non-staff chaplain) and without his permanent presence at the military unit.

B In order to safeguard the Ukrainian people against Russian propaganda and the subversive activities of certain UOC-MP bishops and priests, it is advisable to maintain the current approach of individual criminal prosecutions of those who are suspected of offense, rather than impose a termination of the activities of all parishes and structural units of the UOC-MP. This approach would allow the Ukrainian government to address legitimate concerns about national security without excessively infringing on the religious freedoms of Ukrainian citizens. Individuals within the clergy, like any other citizens, must face personal criminal prosecution in the event of crimes against national security, as outlined in Articles 109–114 of the Criminal Code of Ukraine (*Кримінальний кодекс України*. Ukraine. Parliament of Ukraine, 2001). According to the OSCE/ODIHR's (2019, p. 34) recommendations,

> The fact that some individuals engage in such acts is not an indication that an entire religious or belief community shares these views or condones these activities. In such cases, personal and group actions and responsibilities should always be regarded as separate.

C If the illegal actions of the entire parish or certain religious administration like a metropolis or eparchy are proven, its activities may be terminated only by a court decision according to Article 16 of the *Law of Ukraine on Freedom of Conscience and Religious Organizations* (*Про свободу совісті та релігійні організації*. Ukraine. Parliament of Ukraine, 1991). Nevertheless, governmental draft law #8371 should ensure that the UOC-MP can continue to operate if the Church leadership takes all possible measures on its part to sever its subordination and canonical ties with the ROC and lose any affiliation with the Moscow Patriarchate.

It is essential to strike a balance between protecting national security and religious freedom. The Ukrainian government should avoid overly restrictive measures that could limit religious freedom on the local level and create a perception of martyrdom for the UOC-MP if it is forced to act underground. Therefore, draft law #8371 should provide clear and reasonable criteria for determining whether a particular church has ties with the

Russian religious center that threaten national security, and any legal action taken should be proportional and based on evidence of wrongdoing.

D Instead of demonizing the UOC-MP faithful as members of the church with a religious center in the aggressor state and inciting religious hatred against them, it would be more effective to encourage priests, bishops, and local parishes (as well as representatives of any other denomination) to strictly comply with the legislation of Ukraine. This can be achieved by punishing individual offenders, regardless of their position in the church. The response of law enforcement agencies to every crime against national security at the individual level would be a more effective preventive measure for other faithful and religious leaders of any denomination.

E Also, reducing intolerance toward the UOC-MP faithful could create a basis for a calmer and more natural process of formation of the autocephalous OCU, when believers could choose one or another denomination depending on the fruits of its pastoral and social activities, without being implacable enemies. After all, the enmity between the two Orthodox denominations in Ukraine does not promote the idea of uniting the Orthodox community into a single autocephalous church, but only destroys interreligious peace in the state and harms security interests. Ultimately, the goal should be to promote unity and peace within the Ukrainian society while protecting national security interests.

In conclusion, it can be summarized that abuses of religious freedom, which go unpunished, encourage the violators to commit even greater crimes. As an alternative, bringing guilty religious representatives to justice on an equal footing with other individuals is an indication of the state's ability to guarantee the security of the whole society based on equality before the law. In this case, the affiliation or non-affiliation of an individual to a particular parish or denomination, from one side, should not obstruct the application of statutory punishment for a guilty person and, from another side, should not lead to the persecution of innocent persons. In this way, the state can guarantee the security and freedom of religion or belief for all its citizens, regardless of their attitude to religion.

Notes

1 The Russian World is a concept based on the distorted representation of Russian history, culture, and religious roots, and used to relativize the borders between nation-states and to justify the Kremlin's interference in the internal affairs of foreign states, up to the full-scale military invasion like Moscow does against Ukraine (since 2014 until now). The conception favors the Russian Orthodox Church as a pillar and promoter of the Russian identity despite borders, which becomes the basis of the targeted persecution of religious minorities in Russia and the territories under its influence.

2 Quotations from Vladimir Putin's statement are provided by BBC News (2014).

3 Moscow Patriarch Kirill said this in Bulgaria on the air of Bulgarian National Television (*Radio Free Europe/Radio Liberty*, 2018b).

4 Moscow Patriarch Kirill repeated the narratives of the Kremlin propaganda in an interview with the author and host of the Vesti Nedeli program, Kremlin propagandist Dmitry Kiselev (*RBC-Ukraine*, 2016).
5 Radio Free Europe/Radio Liberty (2015) reported this incident on 9 May 2015.
6 In Russian-occupied Crimea, the C-400 missile system was consecrated by the priests of the Orthodox Church of the Moscow Patriarchate (*Crimea Realities*, 2018).
7 The Security Service of Ukraine has charged about a dozen UOC-MP priests with the crimes of treason and collaboration with Russia as an aggressor state. Charges against some of them have already resulted in court verdicts (see, for example, *Radio Free Europe/Radio Liberty*, 2023a).
8 The Russian Federation was recognized as an aggressor state by the Law of Ukraine #1207-VII of 15 April 2014 (*Про забезпечення прав і свобод*. Ukraine. Parliament of Ukraine, 2014).
9 These requirements are prescribed by Law of Ukraine #2662-VIII of 20 December 2018 (*Про внесення зміни до статті 12 Закону України*. Ukraine. Parliament of Ukraine, 2018).
10 This requirement is prescribed by Law of Ukraine #2673-VIII of 17 January 2019 (*Про внесення змін до деяких законів України*. Ukraine. Parliament of Ukraine, 2019).
11 As an example, on 28 April 2023 the Vechirniy Kyiv newspaper informed that since the beginning of the full-scale Russian invasion, not a single parish in Kyiv has left the UOC-MP (Novosvitnya, 2023).
12 Decision of the Constitutional Court of Ukraine (2022) #4-*p*/2022 of 27 December 2022.
13 On 15 May 2023, the Kyiv District Administrative Court confirmed the affiliation of UOC-MP with ROC. The court emphasized that the adoption of a new version of the UOC-MP's Statute of Governance at the Council on 27 May 2022 did not lead to the severance of the UOC-MP's ecclesiastical and canonical ties with ROC (Taranenko, 2023).
14 One of the legislative initiatives in this area is the draft Law on Amendments to Certain Legislative Acts of Ukraine on Improving the Legal Regulation of the Activity of Religious Organizations (Register No. 8262 dated 05.12.2022) (*Parliament of Ukraine*, 2023a).
15 Since 2017, USCIRF has recommended that the U.S. Department of State designate Russia as a "Country of Particular Concern," or CPC, for engaging in systematic, ongoing, and egregious violations of religious freedom, as defined by the International Religious Freedom Act (IRFA). In 2021, the State Department implemented this recommendation, recognizing the Russian government as one of the world's worst violators of religious freedom (*United States Commission on International Religious Freedom*, 2022).
16 On 2 December 2022, the Security Service of Ukraine (SSU) announced the completion of counterintelligence (security) measures at the facilities of the UOC-MP located in Zakarpattia, Rivne, and Zhytomyr regions (*Radio Free Europe/Radio Liberty*, 2022a). In January 2023, the SSU reported that similar counterintelligence inspections were conducted in the UOC-MP structures in the Kherson, Kirovohrad, Dnipropetrovsk, and Rivne regions (*Radio Free Europe/Radio Liberty*, 2023b).

References

BBC News (2014) 'Путин обещает "защищать русских" на Украине всегда' [Putin Promises to "defend Russians" in Ukraine Always], June 24 [Online]. Available at https://www.bbc.com/russian/russia/2014/06/140624_putin_deauthorisation_ukraine_reax (Accessed 3 March 2023).

Bielefeldt, H. (2011) *Report of the Special Rapporteur on Freedom of Religion or Belief*, New York, United Nations Human Rights Council. Available at https://digitallibrary.un.org/record/719392?ln=en#record-files-collapse-header (Accessed 27 April 2023).

Casanova, J. (2019) *Relihiya v Suchasnomu Sviti: Plyuralizm, Sekulyaryzatsiya, Hlobalizatsiya* [Religion in the Modern World: Pluralism, Secularization, Globalization], Lviv, Ukrainian Catholic University.

Censor.net (2014) 'Zhiteli Slavyanska obvinyayut svyashchennikov UPTS moskovskogo patriarkhata v sodeystvii rossiyskim terroristam' [Residents of Slavyansk Accuse Priests of the UOC of the Moscow Patriarchate of Assisting Russian Terrorists], 21 July [Online]. Available at https://censor.net/ru/video_news/294730/ (Accessed 27 April 2023).

Constitutional Court of Ukraine (2022) *у справі за конституційним поданням 49 народних депутатів України щодо відповідності Конституції України (конституційності) Закону України «Про внесення зміни до статті 12 Закону України "Про свободу совісті та релігійні організації" щодо назви релігійних організацій (об'єднань), які входять до структури (є частиною) релігійної організації (об'єднання), керівний центр (управління) якої знаходиться за межами України в державі, яка законом визнана такою, що здійснила військову агресію проти України та/або тимчасово окупувала частину території України» (справа щодо повної назви релігійних організацій)* [The Case Based on the Constitutional Submission of 49 People's Deputies of Ukraine Regarding the Compliance with the Constitution of Ukraine (Constitutionality) of the Law of Ukraine "On Amending Article 12 of the Law of Ukraine 'On Freedom of Conscience and Religious Organizations' Regarding the Name of Religious Organizations (associations) that Are Part of the Structure (Are Part of) of a Religious Organization (association), the Management Center (Management) of Which Is Located Outside of Ukraine in a State Recognized by Law as Having Carried Out Military Aggression against Ukraine and/or Temporarily Occupied Part of the Territory of Ukraine" (Case Regarding the Full Name of Religious Organizations)], 27 December [Online]. Available at https://ccu.gov.ua/docs/5777 (Accessed 27 April 2023).

Crimea Realities (2018) 'Rossiyskiye rakety v Krymu: pravoslavnyye svyashchenniki osvyatili ZRK S-400' [Russian Missiles in Crimea: Orthodox Priests Consecrated the S-400 Air Defense System], 30 November [Online]. Available at https://ru.krymr.com/a/video-rossiyskie-rakery-v-krymu/29629691.html (Accessed 27 April 2023).

Deutsche Welle (2023) 'Ukrainian Court Places Orthodox Cleric under House Arrest', 1 April [Online]. Available at https://www.dw.com/en/ukrainian-court-places-orthodox-cleric-under-house-arrest/a-65204773 (Accessed 27 April 2023).

Deutsche Welle (2022) 'КМІС: Кількість вірян УПЦ МП впала до чотирьох відсотків' [KIIS: Number of UOC-MP Believers Drops to Four Percent], 5 August [Online]. Available at https://www.dw.com/uk/opytuvannia-ponad-polovyna-ukraintsiv-viriany-ptsu-chotyry-vidsotky-upts-mp/a-62727186 (Accessed 31 May 2023).

Ecumenical Patriarchate (2018) 'Ἀνακοινωθὲν Ἁγίας καὶ Ἱερᾶς Συνόδου' [Announcement of the Holy and Sacred Synod], 11 October [Online]. Available at https://ec-patr.org/nakoinothen-gias-kai-er-s-synodoy-11-okt-2018/ (Accessed 31 May 2023).

Federation Council of the Federal Assembly of the Russian Federation (2014) 'Sovet Federatsii dal soglasiye na ispolzovaniye Vooruzhennykh Sil Rossii na territorii Ukrainy' [The Federation Council Agreed to the Use of the Russian Armed Forces on the Territory of Ukraine], 1 March [Online]. Available at http://council.gov.ru/events/news/39851/ (Accessed 27 April 2023).

Hunder, M., Ratynskyi, V., Starkov, N., and Ljunggren, D. (2023) 'Ukraine Cleric Accused of Glorifying Russia Invasion Given House Arrest', *Reuters*, 1 April [Online]. Available at https://www.reuters.com/world/europe/top-ukraine-cleric-accused-glorifying-russian-invasion-appears-court-2023-04-01/ (Accessed 27 April 2023).

Interfax-Ukraine (2019) 'Pravoslavnu tserkvu Ukrayiny v 2020 r vyznayut' shche kil'ka tserkov, a RPTS opynyt'sya v izolyatsiyi – Poroshenko' [The Orthodox Church of Ukraine in 2020 Will Be Recognized by Several More Churches, and the ROC Will Be in Isolation - Poroshenko], 15 December [Online]. Available at https://ua.interfax.com.ua/news/political/630557.html (Accessed 27 April 2023).

Kalaç v Turkey (1997) 'European Court of Human Rights, Application no. 20704/92' [Online]. Available at https://hudoc.echr.coe.int/eng?i=001-58042 (Accessed 27 April 2023).

Kominko, Y. (2023) 'Otzhe, petytsiya. Ta sama, yaka nabrala ponad 25000 holosiv na sayti Kabinetu Ministriv Ukrayiny i nazyvalasya "Ne zaboronyaty Ukrayins'ku Pravoslavnu Tserkvu"' [So, the Petition. The Same One that Received More than 25,000 Votes on the Website of the Cabinet of Ministers of Ukraine and Was Called "Do not ban the Ukrainian Orthodox Church"], 5 April [Online]. Available at https://www.facebook.com/iuliia.kominko/posts/pfbid02CiYBqdpvadXFz-BLv1ufpZqgTEsC3go73PWBTicBWr4QcR4udBDCLnK1s77NiHZQyl (Accessed 27 April 2023).

Kyiv Metropolis of the Ukrainian Orthodox Church v the Ministry of Culture of Ukraine (2019) 'Kyiv District Administrative Court, Case no. 640/4748/19' [Online]. Available at https://reyestr.court.gov.ua/Review/81332759 (Accessed 27 April 2023).

Ministry of Culture and Information Policy of Ukraine (2023) 'МКІП встановило ряд порушень з боку чоловічого монастиря УПЦ на території Києво-Печерської лаври' [The MCIP Documented a Number of Violations by the UOC Men's Monastery on the Territory of the Kyiv-Pechersk Lavra], 21 March [Online]. Available at https://mcip.gov.ua/news/mkip-vstanovylo-riad-porushen-z-boku-cholovichoho-monastyria-upts-na-terytorii-kyievo-pecherskoi-lavry/ (Accessed 4 October 2023).

National Institute for Strategic Studies (2017) *Analitychna dopovid' do shchorichnoho Poslannya Prezydenta Ukrayiny do Verkhovnoyi Rady Ukrayiny pro vnutrishni i zovnishni spravy v Ukrayini* [Analytical Report for the Annual Address of the President of Ukraine to the Verkhovna Rada of Ukraine on Internal and External Affairs in Ukraine], Kyiv, National Institute for Strategic Studies.

Novitchkova, A., Tomak, M., Valko, S., and Cooper, V. (2015) *When God Becomes the Weapon: Persecution Based on Religious Beliefs in the Armed Conflict in Eastern Ukraine*, Civic Solidarity Platform [Online]. Available at https://lockedfaith.org/files/2015.04_Report_Religious_persecution_in_occupied_Donbas_eng.pdf (Accessed 27 April 2023).

Novosvitnya, K. (2023) 'За останній рік жодна парафія УПЦ (МП) в Києві не перейшла на релігійний бік України, — Вікторія Муха' [Over the Past Year, Not a Single Parish of the UOC (MP) in Kyiv Has Switched to the Religious Side of

Ukraine — Viktoria Mukha], *Evening Kyiv*, 28 April [Online]. Available at https://vechirniy.kyiv.ua/news/82072/ (Accessed 28 April 2023).

OSCE/ODIHR (2019) *Freedom of Religion or Belief and Security: Policy Guidance*, Warsaw, OSCE/ODIHR [Online]. Available at https://www.osce.org/files/f/documents/e/2/429389.pdf (Accessed 27 April 2023).

OSCE/ODIHR (2004) *Guidelines for Review of Legislation Pertaining to Religion or Belief*, Warsaw, Advisory Panel of Experts on Freedom of Religion or Belief [Online]. Available at https://www.osce.org/files/f/documents/d/b/13993.pdf (Accessed 27 April 2023).

Parliament of Ukraine (2023a) 'Проект Закону про внесення змін до деяких законодавчих актів України щодо удосконалення правового регулювання діяльності релігійних організацій' [Draft Law on Amendments to Certain Legislative Acts of Ukraine on Improvement of Legal Regulation of Activities of Religious Organizations], Kyiv, Parliament of Ukraine [Online]. Available at https://itd.rada.gov.ua/billInfo/Bills/Card/40938 (Accessed 27 April 2023).

Parliament of Ukraine (2023b) 'Проект Закону про внесення змін до деяких законів України щодо діяльності в Україні релігійних організацій' [Amendments to the Law of Ukraine on Freedom of Conscience and Religious Organizations], Kyiv, Parliament of Ukraine [Online]. Available at https://itd.rada.gov.ua/billInfo/Bills/Card/41219 (Accessed 27 April 2023).

Parliament of Ukraine (2016) 'Проект Закону про внесення змін до Закону України "Про свободу совісті та релігійні організації" щодо назви релігійних організацій (об'єднань), які входять до структури (є частиною) релігійної організації (об'єднання), керівний центр (управління) якої знаходиться за межами України в державі, яка законом визнана такою, що здійснила військову агресію проти України та/або тимчасово окупувала частину території України' [Draft Law on Amendments to the Law of Ukraine "On Freedom of Conscience and Religious Organizations" Regarding the Name of Religious Organizations (Associations) that Are Part of (Are Part of) the Structure of a Religious Organization (Association), the Management Center (Management) of Which Is Located in Within the Borders of Ukraine in a State Recognized by Law as Having Carried Out Military Aggression against Ukraine and/or Temporarily Occupied Part of the Territory of Ukraine], Kyiv, Parliament of Ukraine [Online]. Available at https://w1.c1.rada.gov.ua/pls/zweb2/webproc4_1?pf3511=60346 (Accessed 27 April 2023).

Putin, V. (2021) 'On the Historical Unity of Russians and Ukrainians', President of Russia's Official Website, 12 July [Online]. Available at http://en.kremlin.ru/events/president/news/66181 (Accessed 27 April 2023).

Putin, V. (2018) 'Putin dal opredeleniye ponyatiyu Russkiy mir' [Putin Defined the Concept of Russian World], YouTube, October [Online]. Available at https://www.youtube.com/watch?v=EQyVzp07Uiw (Accessed 27 April 2023).

Radio Free Europe/Radio Liberty (2023a) 'СБУ повідомляє про затримання ще одного священника УПЦ (МП) на Сумщині' [The SBU Reports the Detention of Another UOC (MP) Priest in Sumy Oblast], March 3 [Online]. Available at https://www.radiosvoboda.org/a/news-sbu-zatrymannia-svyashchennyk-sumshchyna/32297903.html (Accessed 3 March 2023).

Radio Free Europe/Radio Liberty (2023b) 'Агітаційні листівки Медведчука і російські прапори: СБУ завершила обшуки в кількох єпархіях УПЦ (МП)' [Medvedchuk's Campaign Leaflets and Russian Flags: The SBU Completed Searches in Several Dioceses of the UOC (MP)], 6 January [Online]. Available at https://www.

radiosvoboda.org/a/news-sbu-obshuky-upts-mp-lystivky-medvedchuk/32211967.html (Accessed 3 March 2023).

Radio Free Europe/Radio Liberty (2022a) '«Методички» Кремля та нацистська символіка – СБУ про результати обшуків на об'єктах УПЦ (МП) у трьох областях' [Kremlin "methodics" and Nazi Symbols - SBU on the Results of Searches at UOC (MP) Facilities in Three Regions], 2 December [Online]. Available at https://www.radiosvoboda.org/a/news-sbu-upts-mp-obsuky/32159431.html (Accessed 27 April 2023).

Radio Free Europe/Radio Liberty (2022b) 'Ukrainian Orthodox Church, Loyal to Russia Since 2019 Schism, Now Cuts Ties over War', 27 May [Online]. Available at https://www.rferl.org/a/orthodox-church-kirill-war-russia/31872141.html (Accessed 27 April 2023).

Radio Free Europe/Radio Liberty (2019) 'Decree on Independence Handed Over to New Orthodox Church in Ukraine', 6 January [Online]. Available at https://www.rferl.org/a/ukraine-bartholomew-presents-tomos-chirch-independence/29693771.html (Accessed 27 May 2023).

Radio Free Europe/Radio Liberty (2018a) 'Ukraine Announces Creation of Independent Church, Selects Leader', 15 December [Online]. Available at https://www.rferl.org/a/ukraine-orthodox-priests-to-hold-historic-meeting-in-kyiv/29657742.html (Accessed 27 May 2023).

Radio Free Europe/Radio Liberty (2018b) 'Патріарх РПЦ Кирило і сайт угруповання «ДНР» просувають тезу Кремля щодо війни на Донбасі' [Patriarch of the Russian Orthodox Church Kyrylo and the Website of the "DNR" Group Promote the Kremlin's Thesis Regarding the War in Donbas], 3 March [Online]. Available at https://www.radiosvoboda.org/a/29075729.html (Accessed 3 March 2023).

Radio Free Europe/Radio Liberty (2015) 'УПЦ (МП): митрополит не встав під час вшанування Героїв України, бо «проти війни»' [UOC (MP): The Metropolitan Did Not Stand Up During the Commemoration of the Heroes of Ukraine, Because He Is "against the war"], 9 May [Online]. Available at https://www.radiosvoboda.org/a/news/27005934.html (Accessed 3 March 2023).

Razumkov Centre (2020) 'Konfesiyna ta tserkovna nalezhnist hromadyan Ukrayiny' [Confessional and Ecclesiastical Affiliation of Citizens of Ukraine], 3 February [Online]. Available at https://razumkov.org.ua/napriamky/sotsiologichni-doslidzhennia/konfesiina-ta-tserkovna-nalezhnist-gromadian-ukrainy-sichen-2020r (Accessed 27 April 2023).

RBC-Ukraine (2016) 'Kirill: Dlya menya Ukraina – eto to zhe samoye, chto i Rossiya' [Kirill: For Me, Ukraine Is the Same as Russia], 7 January [Online]. Available at https://styler.rbc.ua/rus/zhizn/kirill-dlya-menya-ukraina-eto-samoe-rossiya-1452177422.html (Accessed 27 April 2023).

Religious Information Service of Ukraine (2019) 'Ministr kultury Volodymyr Borodyans'kyy: U relihiyniy sferi vazhlyvo maty chesni vidnosyny' [Minister of Culture Volodymyr Borodyanskyi: In the Religious Sphere, It Is Important to Have Honest Relations], 6 November [Online]. Available at https://risu.ua/ministr-kulturi-volodimir-borodyanskiy-u-religiyniy-sferi-vazhlivo-mati-chesni-vidnosini_n100930 (Accessed 27 April 2023).

Religious Information Service of Ukraine (2018) 'Girkin pryznavsya, shcho chentsi Svyatohirs'koyi lavry blahoslovlyaly yoho na viynu, a yerarkhiya UPTS (MP) ne pidtrymala vidkryto' [Girkin Admitted that the Monks of the Svyatogorsk Lavra Blessed Him for the War, and the Hierarchy of the UOC-MP Did Not Openly

Support], 12 October [Online]. Available at https://risu.ua/girkin-priznavsya-shcho-chenci-svyatogirskoji-lavri-blagoslovlyali-yogo-na-viynu-a-yerarhiya-upc-mp-ne-pidtrimala-vidkrito_n93687 (Accessed 27 April 2023).

Religiyna Pravda (2021) 'Viryany UPTS MP vyyshly na molytovne stoyannya proty pereymenuvannya na RPTsvU' [Believers of the UOC-MP Went on a Prayer Stand against the Renaming to the ROCU], 15 June [Online]. Available at https://religionpravda.com.ua/?p=70188 (Accessed 27 April 2023).

Roshchyna, V. (2023) 'Kolaboranty v ryasi? Shcho chekaye na Ukrayins'ku pravoslavnu tserkvu (ne) Moskovskoho patriarkhatu' [Collaborators in Cassocks? What Awaits the Ukrainian Orthodox Church (Not) of the Moscow Patriarchate], Ukrainska Pravda, 11 January [Online]. Available at https://www.pravda.com.ua/articles/2023/01/11/7384308/ (Accessed 27 April 2023).

Schwirtz, M., and Reinhard, S. (2022) 'How Russia's Military Is Positioned to Threaten Ukraine', *The New York Times*, 7 January [Online]. Available at https://www.nytimes.com/interactive/2022/01/07/world/europe/ukraine-maps.html (Accessed 7 January 2022).

Shumylo, S. (2022) 'Pravoslavnyy shakhidyzm ta neoyazychnyts'ka teolohiya viyny moskovskoho patriarkha Kyryla' [Orthodox Martyrdom and the Neo-pagan Theology of War of the Moscow Patriarch Kirill], *Radio Free Europe/Radio Liberty*, 28 September [Online]. Available at https://www.radiosvoboda.org/a/kyrylo-hundyayev-russkyy-myr-ideolohiya-viyny/32054793.html (Accessed 27 April 2023).

Smith, P. (2022) 'Moscow Patriarch Stokes Orthodox Tensions with War Remarks', *The Associated Press*, 8 March [Online]. Available at https://apnews.com/article/russia-ukraine-putin-religion-europe-moscow-0670305be2e010e02a4e195ced2b7523 (Accessed 27 April 2023).

Solodko, P. (2013) 'Istoriya i suchasnist' ukrayins'koho pravoslav'ya. Statystyka' [History and Modernity of Ukrainian Orthodoxy. Statistics], Ukrayins'ka Pravda, 25 July [Online]. Available at https://www.istpravda.com.ua/articles/2013/07/25/131816/ (Accessed 27 April 2023).

State Service of Ukraine for Ethnopolitics and Freedom of Conscience (2021) *Zvit pro merezhu relihiynykh orhanizatsiy v Ukrayini stanom na 1 sichnya 2021 roku* [Report on the Network of Religious Organizations in Ukraine as of January 1, 2021], Kyiv [Online]. Available at https://dess.gov.ua/wp-content/uploads/2021/05/Form1-2021-public3.xls (Accessed 27 April 2023).

Svyato-Mykhaylivska Parafiya v Ukraine (2007) 'European Court of Human Rights, Application no. 77703/01' [Online]. Available at https://hudoc.echr.coe.int/eng?i=001-81067 (Accessed 27 April 2023).

Taranenko, V. (2023) 'УПЦ МП – підрозділ російської церкви. Рішення суду публікується вперше' [UOC-MP Is a Subdivision of the Russian Church. The Court Decision Is Published for the First Time], *Glavkom*, 19 May [Online]. Available at https://glavcom.ua/publications/upts-mp-je-pidrozdilom-rosijskoji-tserkvi-rishennja-sudu-928354.html (Accessed 27 May 2023).

TASS (2015) 'Putin: Kyiv ispol'zoval mirnuyu peredyshku dlya peregruppirovki sil' [Putin: Kyiv Used Peaceful Respite to Regroup Forces], 26 January [Online]. Available at https://tass.ru/politika/1722618 (Accessed 27 April 2023).

Tkach, M. (2023) 'Hrazhdanin Onufriy. Ukrayinska Pravda publikuye rosiyski pasporty svyashchennosluzhyteliv UPTS' [Citizen Onufriy. Ukrainska Pravda Publishes the Russian Passports of UOC Clerics], *Ukrainska Pravda*, 7 April [Online].

Available at https://www.pravda.com.ua/articles/2023/04/7/7396895/ (Accessed 27 April 2023).

UCCRO (2023) 'The Council of Churches Condemns Russia's Abuse of Religious Sentiments in Its Aggressive and Unjust War against Ukraine', Ukrainian Council of Churches and Religious Organizations, 12 January [Online]. Available at https://vrciro.ua/en/events/rada-tserkov-zasudzhue-zlovzhivannya-rosiyskoyu-federatsieyu-religiynimi-pochuttyami-v-agresivniy-i-nespravedliviy-viyni-proti-ukraini (Accessed 27 May 2023).

Ukraine. Parliament of Ukraine (2019) *Про внесення змін до деяких законів України щодо підлеглості релігійних організацій та процедури державної реєстрації релігійних організацій зі статусом юридичної особи* [On Amendments to Some Laws of Ukraine Regarding the Subordination of Religious Organizations and the Procedure for State Registration of Religious Organizations with the Status of a Legal Entity], Kyiv, Parliament of Ukraine (BBP, 2019, No. 6, Article 40, or Law #2673-VIII) [Online]. Available at https://zakon.rada.gov.ua/laws/show/2673-19#Text (Accessed 27 April 2023).

Ukraine. Parliament of Ukraine (2018) *Про внесення зміни до статті 12 Закону України "Про свободу совісті та релігійні організації" щодо назви релігійних організацій (об'єднань), які входять до структури (є частиною) релігійної організації (об'єднання), керівний центр (управління) якої знаходиться за межами України в державі, яка законом визнана такою, що здійснила військову агресію проти України та/або тимчасово окупувала частину території України* [On Amending Article 12 of the Law of Ukraine "On Freedom of Conscience and Religious Organizations" Regarding the Name of Religious Organizations (Associations) that Are Part of (Are Part of) the Structure of a Religious Organization (Association), the Management Center (Management) of Which Is Located in Within the Borders of Ukraine in a State Recognized by Law as Having Carried Out Military Aggression against Ukraine and/or Temporarily Occupied Part of the Territory of Ukraine], Kyiv, Parliament of Ukraine (BBP, 2019, No. 3, Article 23, or Law 2662-VIII) [Online]. Available at https://zakon.rada.gov.ua/laws/show/2662-19 (Accessed 27 April 2023).

Ukraine. Parliament of Ukraine (2014) *Про забезпечення прав і свобод громадян та правовий режим на тимчасово окупованій території України* [On Ensuring the Rights and Freedoms of Citizens and the Legal Regime in the Temporarily Occupied Territory of Ukraine], Kyiv, Parliament of Ukraine (BBP, 2014, No. 26, Article 892) [Online]. Available at https://zakon.rada.gov.ua/laws/show/1207-18 (Accessed 27 April 2023).

Ukraine. Parliament of Ukraine (2001) *Кримінальний кодекс України* [Criminal Code of Ukraine], Kyiv, Parliament of Ukraine (BBP, 2001, No. 25-26, Article 131) [Online]. Available at https://zakon.rada.gov.ua/laws/show/2341-14 (Accessed 27 April 2023).

Ukraine. Parliament of Ukraine (1991) *Про свободу совісті та релігійні організації* [Law of Ukraine on Freedom of Conscience and Religious Organizations], Kyiv, Parliament of Ukraine (BBP, 1991, No. 25, Article 283) [Online]. Available at https://zakon.rada.gov.ua/laws/show/987-12 (Accessed 27 April 2023).

Ukrainian News (2018) 'Skandalnoho protoiyereya UPTS zasudyly do 6 rokiv vyaznytsi za posobnytstvo boyovykam na Donbasi' [The Scandalous Archpriest of the UOC-MP Was Sentenced to 6 Years in Prison for Assisting the

Militants in Donbas], 13 December [Online]. Available at https://ukranews.com/ua/news/601967-skandalnogo-protoiyereya-upc-zasudyly-do-6-rokiv-v-yaznyci-za-posobnyctvo-boyovykam-na-donbasi (Accessed 27 May 2023).

Ukrainian Orthodox Church (2021) 'U Kyyevo-Pechers'kiy Lavri vidbuvsya kruhlyy stil Try roky sprob prymusovoho pereymenuvannya Ukrayins'koyi Pravoslavnoyi Tserkvy: naslidky, otsinky, komentari' [Round Table "Three Years of Attempts to Forcibly Rename the Ukrainian Orthodox Church: Consequences, Assessments, Comments" Took Place in Kyiv-Pechersk Lavra], 20 December [Online]. Available at https://news.church.ua/2021/12/20/u-kijevo-pecherskij-lavri-vidbuvsya-kruglij-stil-tri-roki-sprob-primusovogo-perejmenuvannya-ukrajinskoji-pravoslavnoji-cerkvi-naslidki-ocinki-komentari/ (Accessed 27 April 2023).

Ukrinform (2018) 'Zvernennya uchasnykiv ATO shchodo diyalnosti tserkov Moskovskoho Patriarkhatu' [Appeal of the ATO Participants Regarding the Activities of the Churches of the Moscow Patriarchate], 22 January [Online]. Available at https://www.ukrinform.ua/rubric-presshall/2383398-zvernenna-ucasnikiv-ato-sodo-dialnosti-cerkov-moskovskogo-patriarhatu.html (Accessed 27 April 2023).

United Nations (1966) *International Covenant on Civil and Political Rights* [Online]. Available at https://www.ohchr.org/en/instruments-mechanisms/instruments/international-covenant-civil-and-political-rights (Accessed 27 May 2023).

United States Commission on International Religious Freedom (2022) *Backgrounder: Russia*, Washington, DC, March [Online]. Available at https://www.uscirf.gov/sites/default/files/2022-03/2022%20Russia%20Backgrounder.pdf (Accessed 27 April 2023).

van den Berg, S., and Sterling, T. (2022) 'Dutch Court Sentences Three to Life in Prison for 2014 Downing of MH17 over Ukraine', *Reuters*, 18 November [Online]. Available at https://www.reuters.com/world/europe/judges-rule-murder-trial-2014-downing-flight-mh17-over-ukraine-2022-11-17/ (Accessed 27 April 2023).

Vasin, M., Koval, D., Kozlovskyy, I., and Zaiets, A. (2022) *Russian Attacks on Religious Freedom in Ukraine: Research, Analytics, Recommendations*, Kyiv, Institute for Religious Freedom [Online]. Available at https://irf.in.ua/files/publications/2022.09-IRF-Ukraine-report-ENG.pdf (Accessed 27 April 2023).

Vasin, M., Zaiets, A., and Zaiets, O. (2018) *Religious Freedom at Gunpoint: Russian Terror in the Occupied Territories of Eastern Ukraine*, Kyiv, Institute for Religious Freedom [Online]. Available at https://irf.in.ua/files/publications/2018.10.24-IRF-Report-ENG.pdf (Accessed 27 May 2023).

Vovk, D. (2019) 'Dynamics of Church-state Relations in Ukraine and the Military Conflict with Russia', in Clark, E., and Vovk, D. (eds) *Religion During the Russian-Ukrainian Conflict*, London, Routledge, pp. 32–53.

Zelenskyy, V. (2022) 'We Will Guarantee Spiritual Independence to Ukraine', *The Presidential Office of Ukraine*, 1 December [Online]. Available at https://www.president.gov.ua/en/news/mi-garantuyemo-ukrayini-duhovnu-nezalezhnist-zvernennya-prez-79577 (Accessed 27 April 2023).

Zubkova, D. (2022) 'SSU Finds Millions of Cash and Identified Russian Citizens During Searches of Kyiv-Pechersk Lavra and Other Churches', *Ukrainian News*, 23 November [Online]. Available at https://ukranews.com/en/news/896990-ssu-finds-millions-of-cash-and-identified-russian-citizens-during-searches-of-kyiv-pechersk-lavra (Accessed 27 April 2023).

PART III

Religion, Security, and Identities

6

TOWARDS RESOLVING THE CONFLICT BETWEEN NATIONAL AND MUSLIM IDENTITIES IN NIGERIA

Azizat Omotoyosi Amoloye-Adebayo

1 Introduction

This chapter argues that Nigerian religious and national identities conflict in this religiously pluralistic and culturally divergent country. Islam will be the frame of analysis of religious identity for two main reasons. First, the current techniques for managing the conflict between religious and national identities are unsatisfactory and have contributed significantly to the development of such groups as *Boko Haram* as a third identity for some Nigerians. Even though most Nigerian Muslims would vehemently assert that Boko Haram's ideology is alien to Islam, the group continually seeks to validate its violent activities through Islam. Thus, this third identity seeks to take its legitimacy not only from a religious perspective but it has grave implications for political stability and national security as most Nigerians are aware. Also, this third identity as shall later be examined is neither fully religious nor national.

Second, Islam is one of three major religions in Nigeria and the author is a Nigerian Muslim. Islam teaches that Muslims may only depart from their religious identity as a temporary measure out of necessity but not as a way of life. This further complicates the split identity problem for Nigerian Muslims. According to Islamic textual sources, if the national and religious identities cannot be reconciled, a permanent solution such as migration to a place where Islamic identity may be enjoyed unfettered should be sought. For national identity, this chapter contends that a sense of nationality could emerge from an individual's connectedness to public ideals as expressed in the Nigerian Constitution. However, current constitutional provisions are not sufficiently instructive for Nigerian Muslims to forge a religious identity that is compatible with national ideals. This has serious implications for

DOI: 10.4324/9781003453086-10

peaceful coexistence and social cohesion. What follows in this chapter is an analysis of the stated perspective and suggestions for future development. The methodology adopted is doctrinal, consisting of a constitutional analysis of relevant provisions of the Nigerian constitution as well as a library-based review of existing literature.

2 Nigeria, Nationality, and Religion

Nigeria, with a population of around 200 million divided across over 500 lingual and ethnic groups, is the most populous African country ranking number seven in world population (*World Bank*, 2021). Within this great diversity, there are a few unifying factors, and the most notable are a national constitution, the English language as the lingua franca, and adherence to religion. On the religious demography in Nigeria, the following statement by Nwauche (2008, pp. 569–570) aptly captures the situation:

> What is generally accepted is that Muslims dominate the northern states of Nigeria and Christians dominate the rest of the country, with the margin being closer in the Middle Belt and southwestern part of the country where there is a significant Muslim population. There seems to be broad agreement that Muslims constitute a slightly larger, if not equal, section of the population than that constituted by Christians, and that there are a substantial number of persons who practice traditional indigenous religions as well as a good number of non-religious believers. It is fair to conclude that Islam and Christianity are the dominant religions in Nigeria.

Of the three unifying factors, religion appears to be the least appreciated and often overlooked factor of socialization and aggregation. In terms of African traditional belief, religion is also the only factor amongst the three that is indigenous to Nigeria as to origin and historical source (Grillo et al., 2019, p. 17). Despite this fact, religion constitutes a divisive factor, and several violent Nigerian conflicts have had to do with religion (Shah et al., 2012, p. 2). This perhaps accounts for why there are always attempts to push religion as far away as possible from political discussions so that the focus will be on national identity. Even though Nigeria has endeavoured through its constitution (Nigeria. *Constitution of 1999 as amended*), particularly in Section 10 (that no religion shall be adopted as state religion at all levels of government) and in Section 38 (on components of religious freedom from belief, practice, observance, and propagation to instruction of children by their parents, etc.), to maintain a distinction between religion and politics while also encouraging freedom of religion, it has not been successful. This is perhaps not surprising given the fact that even in European and North American societies that have gone through various processes of secularization, religion and politics are not always as neatly separated as is sometimes suggested (Grillo et al., 2019, pp. 150–152).

There are 11 references to religion in the Nigerian constitution. The first point of reference is in Section 10 which states that neither the federal government nor any of its federation units as states "shall adopt any religion as State Religion" (*Constitution of Nigeria*, as amended, Section 10. National Assembly, 1999). Section 15 (1) states the motto of the Nigerian Federation as "Unity and Faith, Peace, and Progress" (*Constitution of Nigeria*, as amended, Section 15(1). National Assembly, 1999). Arguably, the word "faith" is another word for religion and perhaps is the 12th reference to religion in the constitution. More particularly in 15 (2) it is stated that national integration should be actively encouraged (*Constitution of Nigeria*, as amended, Section 15(2). National Assembly, 1999). This is to be achieved by prohibiting discrimination on the "grounds of place of origin, sex, religion, status, ethnic or linguistic association or ties" (*Constitution of Nigeria*, as amended, Section 15(2)). National Assembly, 1999). Further, under Chapter IV of the Constitution on "Fundamental Rights," Section 38 (1–4) states the fundamental right of all Nigerians to "freedom of thought, conscience, and religion" (Section 38(1–4). National Assembly, 1999). This right includes the freedom to change one's religion or belief as well as the freedom (either alone or in community with others, and in public or in private) to manifest and propagate one's religion or belief in matters of "worship, teaching, practice and observance" (*Constitution of Nigeria*, as amended, Section 38(1). National Assembly, 1999). On the one hand, Subsection 2 of Section 38 protects all Nigerians in all avenues of education against religious instructions and observance contrary to those of the beliefs of the individual concerned (*Constitution of Nigeria*, as amended, Section 38(2). National Assembly, 1999). On the other hand, Subsection 3 gives the right to religious communities or denominations to give religious instruction to pupils "in any place of education maintained wholly by that community or denomination" (*Constitution of Nigeria*, as amended, Section 38(3). National Assembly, 1999).

Additionally, religion is recognized in Section 42 as one of the grounds upon which a person may neither be subjected to "disabilities or restrictions" nor become the recipient of "any privilege or advantage" (*Constitution of Nigeria*, as amended, Section 42(1)(a). National Assembly, 1999) simply because they belong to such a religion. This is regardless of whether the disability/restriction or the privilege/advantage is a result of the express or practical operation of any law in force in Nigeria as well as any executive or administrative action. The other grounds stated in this section alongside religion concern particular community, ethnic group, place of origin, sex, and political opinion (*Constitution of Nigeria*, as amended, Section 42. National Assembly, 1999). The final reference to religion in the Nigerian constitution is contained in Part III, which is the segment on Supplemental provisions. The provision concerned is Section 222 under segment (D) on political parties. The section provides in its subsection (a) and (b) that:

> No association by whatever name called shall function as a party, unless –
>
> a the names and addresses of its national officers are registered with the Independent National Electoral Commission;
> b the membership of the association is open to every citizen of Nigeria irrespective of his (sic) place of origin, circumstance of birth, sex, religion or ethnic grouping (*Constitution of Nigeria*, as amended, Section 222. National Assembly, 1999).

Contrary to the many constitutional references to religion as discussed above, it appears that academic literature on Nigerian politics pays very little attention to it despite its great political influence (Grillo et al., 2019, pp. 150–152; Shah et al., 2012, pp. 2–3). This stance ignores the fact that religion is an important component of the Nigerian identity. For example, in the 2006 national census, religion was deleted as one of the specific parameters (Nwauche, 2008, p. 569). One reason for the exclusion appears to be that public discourse between religion, politics, and nationality could not be mediated because of the many differences in religious beliefs.

3 Conflicts in Identity Formation Process and Resources in the Public Space

One of the foremost religious figures of Catholicism in Nigeria (Retired Archbishop of the Diocese of Abuja, Mr. John Olorunfemi Onaiyekan) once wrote in the foreword to a book (1993, p. vii) that "It is the same concrete human person who assumes both political and religious identity, and one necessarily affects the other." Available materials and resources on the position of religion in the public domain such as the constitutional provisions examined above and those in other legal instruments as is exemplified below continue to lend themselves to different interpretations by private individuals on the matter of religion in the public space. The implication of this is that such public resources may fuel notions of disconnectedness in some parts of the citizenry. For example, in a country that supposedly proscribes the establishment of any religion as a state religion, Islamic law is a constitutionally recognized legal source supported by a court system established by public funds. These constitutional references are mainly contained in Chapter VII, Parts I and II, entitled "The Judicature," which provides for the establishment of federal and state courts under the 1999 Constitution. Specifically, Sections 260–264 and 275–279 provide for the establishment, composition, and jurisdiction of a Sharia Court of Appeal for the federal capital territory and any of the federating units (*Constitution of Nigeria*, as amended, Sections 260–264, 275–279. National Assembly, 1999). Aside from this, there is also an observable bias for Christianity in the Nigerian marriage laws (Nwauche, 2008; Boparai, 1982) and under the criminal code. For instance, a wife in a Christian marriage is exculpated from liability in certain circumstances, such as being an accessory after the fact, and couples in a Christian marriage cannot be charged for conspiracy within themselves (*Criminal Code Act 1990*, Sections 10, 34. Government of the Third Republic, 1990). In the same vein, part of the legal holidays for the Nigerian courts called *dies non juris* follow the Christian religious holidays such as any week beginning with Easter Monday or Christmas and Boxing Day as is illustrated in Order 52, Rule 4, of the High Court of Federal Capital Territory Abuja Rules of Court (Order 52, Rule 4. Justice Bello, 2018).

Consequently, private constructions of the relationship between religion, an individual, and the state on the one hand and between Nigerian citizens of diverse religious affiliations on the other, in the absence of common value direction, often work against each other and obstruct the path to a common national identity. Nigerian scholars such as Terwase (2014), Obadere (2018), and Basil (2022) have provided useful analyses of the nuances within this engagement. As regards the constitutional status of the Islamic legal system, for example, the agelong (Kukah, 1993, pp. 115–144), non-Muslim citizen's perception is evident in the following argument that it is "functionless in a pluralistic and complex society. It is an act of provoking a war in place of harmony, brotherhood and peace" (*The Daily Sketch*, 1997, p. 7). This comment was contained in one of the foremost Nigerian newspapers in 1997 and was made in response to a call in the same publication by some Nigerian Muslims for the establishment of Islamic law courts in southern Nigeria (*The Daily Sketch*, 1997, p. 7). What was interesting was that even though the call for establishment of Islamic law courts was and (continues to be) perceived by non-Muslim Nigerians as problematic, the initial call by Muslims was also in reaction to the perceived Christian origins of English law that is a significant part of the Nigerian legal system.

A scholar of Nigerian history, Adesina (2017, p. 6), wondered whether it is possible for Nigerians to "engage in historical reconstruction in a national context, devoid of geopolitical partisanship and primordial ethnic bias." In view of discussions so far, religious affiliation could also be added to the list of parameters for bias. The implication, therefore, is that Nigerians adopt identities for national or religious purposes depending on the perspective of the individual concerned and the interests perceived to be earliest rather than a sense of collective interest. At any rate, the public resources such as the constitution and other legal provisions do not inspire the individual towards common values and goals. As Constantin (1993) contends, this phenomenon appears to be common to the specific character of modern nation-states in

Africa that emerged out of colonized territories. Not only do these states, Nigeria included, have existential challenges, but they must also grapple with contrasting values (Constantin, 1993). These contrasting values arose from multiple religious, non-religious, and imported ideologies and it is no wonder that most of the provisions in the national constitutions (for instance, the 1999 Constitution in Nigeria) and other laws appear disjointed.

This argument is persuasive because as the 1999 Constitution exemplifies, the provisions must aspire to unify diverse aspirations that often appear to be mutually exclusive. Where this is not realized, there are grave consequences for identity crises that could and often do result in security challenges (Terwase, 2014). Put another way, a perceived challenge to religious or national identity when viewed as mutually exclusive often leads to the breakdown of law and order by a resort to self-help measures. For example, academic analysis of the emergence and consolidation of the *Boko Haram* group in Nigeria suggests a disconnectedness with existing strategies for civic engagement and political administration (*Center for Contemporary Islam*, 2019, pp. 4, 24). They are regarded as "Western" relics of colonial and missionary activities in Nigerian political history and thus un-Islamic (Kukah, 1993, p. 3).

To further aggravate the situation are the conflicting indications from political and religious leaders as to the best model of religion-state relationships that can aid individual constructions. For instance, the Late Chief Obafemi Awolowo, one of the foremost nationalist and political leaders in the struggle for Nigerian independence, after the coup of 1966 (vividly reported by Robertson, 2017) commented from a Christian perspective from the Calabar prison where he was incarcerated:

> Nigeria should be a secular state. The existing association between the State and the Church should be completely severed. It is an old British custom which is apish, unreflecting and discriminatory for us to preserve .... The whole thing is ludicrous. God is everywhere and His ever-ready responsiveness to our supplications is not confined to any Church or place. To be sure, it is a very good thing indeed for the churches, the mosques, and other religious gatherings, to pray, from time to time, for the success of the Government of the day, if they are convinced that its plans and programmes are good and promote the welfare and happiness of the people. But it would be wrong, and of course futile, (sic) for them to pray, as they did in recent years for the success of a manifestly satanic administration. For the reformation of such a government, they certainly must pray. By participating in state ceremonies, and getting too much involved in official functions, some religious leaders find it difficult to speak out with freedom, forthrightness, and courage, in condemnation of what they know to be evil in the doings of the state ... as far as possible, there should be separation of activities of the state on the one hand, and religious bodies on the other.
> *(Awolowo, 1966, pp. 150–151)*

Also, Alhaji Shehu Shagari as the first executive president of Nigeria in its planned second republic 1979–1983 was quoted from a Muslim perspective:

> Though ours is a secular state with diverse religious creeds we do, in fact, live in harmony among ourselves, respect each other's religious beliefs and rise as one people [to strengthening] the moral fibre of our people which is about love and brotherhood, honesty, integrity, and respect for those traditions that make a nation.
>
> *(Ojigbo, 1981, pp. 387–388)*

After the tumultuous aftermath of the annulment of the June 12, 1993, elections for a proposed third republic, General Sani Abacha as the Nigerian military president inaugurated in 1994 a National Constitutional Conference Commission and remarked:

> Nigeria is a secular state. We have acknowledged this in all our previous constitutions, and it is not advisable that we deviate from this course. Religion is an instrument for building moral bricks in our society and it should remain within the realms of personal faith and group choice. It must never be allowed to interfere with our collective desire to build a unified and indivisible nation. The quest to combat indiscipline and corruption in our society is an ongoing struggle which draws its inspiration from several provisions in existing Constitutions. Our quest for accountability in public life should move away from emphasis on pious appeals to conscience to institutionalised legislation enforced within the context of respect for individual rights and lawful aspirations.
>
> *(Umar, 1995, p. xlviii)*

It is surmisable from the above quotations that even though these national leaders employed the word "secular" about Nigeria very differently, they did not intend that the issue of religion was irrelevant. Awolowo was concerned about the integrity of religion and clerics who he believed should be holding politicians accountable rather than currying favour with them. Shagari and Abacha's considerations were for the respect and protection of various forms of religious beliefs under one nation. Striking and instructive, however, is the concluding part of the comment noted earlier by the former Archbishop of the Diocese of Abuja, Mr. John Olorunfemi Onaiyekan:

> The strident call for a separation of politics from religion often becomes a slogan used according to the convenience of the moment. The reality is that both are tied together, by the very nature of things – and this for at least two reasons: First, there is something inherently sacred about political power. History has shown that it can only be properly exercised when handled with sacred attention. In religious jargon, we say, "all powers

> belong to God." Secondly, it is the same concrete human person who assumes both political and religious identity, and one necessarily affects the other. No wonder, even nations which make much of separation of religion and politics find many ways in practice to act against this principle. It seems to me that this is why our prolonged debate over the "secular" nature of the Nigerian state has remained inconclusive. "Secular state" means different things to different people. It is surely more useful to tackle concrete issues of interaction of politics and religion and from there evolve just and fair solutions to our problems of peaceful co-operation.
>
> *(Kukah, 1993, p. vii)*

Onaiyekan is correct that there are different conceptions of secularism and even though it incorporates the notion of separating the spiritual (religion) from the temporal (politics), the reality often is opposite. The argument that even the so-called secular societies inevitably mix religion with politics is certainly true of the practice of the UK Parliament as is evident in Awolowo's remarks, while the U.S. practice will be discussed in Section 4. In the Nigerian situation, if the nation is truly secular then the question of the Islamic law as a constitutionally recognized source of law with a supporting court system is an anathema. The issue appears to be that, as Onaiyekan noted, secularism is only a convenient slogan in Nigerian politics that has become instrumentalized just like religion itself.

4 Third Identity: Friend of State or Foe?

In striving to achieve a balance between national and religious identities given the nature of the available public resources, it is observed that religious individuals construct a third identity which is a fusion of the religious and national identities. The only challenge is that one component is reinforced more than the other depending on the perspective of the individual concerned. Research in Nigerian national newspapers from the late 1980s to early 1990s indicates religious conflicts in Nigeria are political conflicts that have instrumentalized religion. Nigerians of whatever religious identity often resort to an affirmation of that identity over their national identities, for the following reasons: (1) as a convenient strategy for rallying political support to oust political authority that is perceived to have failed; (2) to resist political domination and articulate minority concerns; and (3) when there is a sense of religious domination as noted from the citizens exemplified in the newspaper publication because of competition amongst adherents of different religious faiths.

The Constitution and other legal documents play an all-important role in any religiously pluralistic and culturally divergent society such as Nigeria (which appears to be a common feature of all modern nation-states and democratic regimes). These laws become a common ideology for all citizens despite the sentiments that threaten national cohesion and peace. Taking account of the discussion in the introductory section of this chapter as well as the analysis of the constitutional provisions above, the question may be asked: what brand of religion-state relationship has the Nigerian state adopted thus far? That there are two competing theories by religious and political leaders is clear from discussions in the preceding section. Thus, the first theory affirms the multi-religious nature of Nigerian polity which does not accommodate favouring any religion over others. The other theory carries the notion of secularism which denotes essentially that religion is a private affair. Unfortunately, the jurisprudence of the Nigerian Supreme Court as the apex court is unclear on which theory underpins Nigeria's notion of religious freedom as contained in the Constitution. This means every Nigerian has individual notions regarding the intersection of religion and nationality. This reality continues to polarize opinions and perspectives and contributes to the emergence of groups comprising individuals fostering dangerous ideologies such as the infamous *Boko Haram* group and many more.

What becomes problematic is that both the secular and multi-religious arguments in terms of the religion-state relationship in Nigeria are sustainable based on Section 10 of the Constitution. It is better to hold to the multi-religious theory rather than the secular theory for Nigeria. The notion of secularism is merely a political instrument to foist alien religious ideologies on non-adherents through craftily constructed *supposedly religiously neutral* strategies. To give a contemporary example, the Constitution of the United States of America is perhaps the most illustrious instance of secularism as a model of the religion-state relationship. The First Amendment's Establishment Clause to the U.S. Constitution prohibits any government action "respecting an establishment of religion" (U.S. Constitution, amend. I). Yet in the 2019 case of *American Legion v American Humanist Association* [2019], the U.S. Supreme Court held that the display of a 32-foot-tall cross of the Christian faith on public land with its ownership and maintenance through public funds by the Maryland National Capital Park and Planning Commission did not violate the Establishment Clause. The perspective of the Court is that the religion clauses of the Constitution "aim to foster a society in which people of all beliefs can live together harmoniously" and that the cross "had acquired additional layers of historical meaning" where "its removal or radical alteration would be seen by many not as a neutral act but as the manifestation of a hostility toward religion" (2019).

Interestingly, this American case is reminiscent of the Nigerian situation. For the proponents of secularism, the question may be asked as to the presence of a religious law (Islamic law) supported by a constitutionally recognized legal system and court structure in Nigeria. This question has been taken up elsewhere in that the recognition of Islamic law as a legal source in

Nigeria is not favouritism to Islam and its adherents but a historical component of the emergence of Nigeria itself as a body politic (Amoloye-Adebayo, 2019). As shown in the American case, the historical argument of state connection with a particular religion in a multi-religious context is unassailable. The contention of this chapter is therefore that in both the American and Nigerian contexts, the secularism theory is fallacious. For Nigeria, Section 10 should be read as aiming to "foster a society in which people of all beliefs can live together harmoniously" as held in the *American Legion* case (2019). Thus, the presence of the Islamic legal system in the Nigerian Constitution is understood in its correct historical sense and will not be the basis of controversial remarks by non-adherent Nigerians (see, for instance, Ordu, 2015) in ways that can trigger violence and instability. It can then be said that the import of Section 10 of the Nigerian Constitution encapsulates the notion of "freedom of religion" and not "freedom from religion."

There is also a strong basis for the impact of Section 10 for religious peace and stability in Nigeria if other constitutional provisions on religion are combined, namely, Sections 15, 38, 42, and 222. A combined reading of Sections 38, 42, and 222 shows the issue of religion can constitute a basis of discrimination threatening national cohesion (*Constitution of Nigeria*, as amended, Sections 38, 42, 222. National Assembly, 1999). Thus, expressions of religious beliefs and observance in private and public spheres are protected. Not only that but there is also protection against proselytizing in educational institutions even though public proselytizing is permissible, recognizing religion is one of the pillars of existence for Nigerian society which can bring about private and public consequences to non-adherent minorities or individuals. In particular, the subsections of Sections 38, 42, and 222 attempt to regulate these consequences while not limiting religious freedom. Undoubtedly, this careful balance is necessary for peace, stability, and national cohesion.

However, Section 15 has serious negative implications for religious peace and stability especially as it is contained in the Fundamental Objectives and Directive Principles of State Policy. As earlier said, this argument has been presented more fully elsewhere (Amoloye-Adebayo, 2023). Out of all the cited constitutional provisions, only Section 15 is about interpersonal relationships amongst citizens concerning religion along with ethnic and tribal affiliations. The other sections are more concerned with the role of religion and its regulation in the public sphere. For ease of consideration, the relevant portion of the provision of the section is reproduced as follows:

> 15. (1) The motto of the Federal Republic of Nigeria shall be Unity and Faith, Peace and Progress...
>
> (3) For the purpose of promoting national integration, it shall be the duty of the State to....

(c) encourage inter-marriage among persons from different places of origin, or of *different religion*, ethnic or linguistic association or ties.

(Constitution of Nigeria, *as amended, Section 15. National Assembly, 1999, emphasis added)*

Rather than *national integration* here, "national cohesion" appears to the current author to be a better construction. Integration carries the sense of mixing with and joining a society or a group of people, often changing to suit their way of life, habits, and customs.

Conversely, *cohesion* is indicative of being in close agreement and working well together. In the current author's opinion, it is more realistic to work towards cohesion in matters involving deeply held convictions such as religious beliefs rather than working towards integration through norms that may be at variance with the religious identities of some people. An instance of such possible conflict is part of the provision cited above which seeks to promote national integration through marriage. This is clearly at variance with the Islamic position on marriage. The Islamic textual sources are detailed on who can marry whom, and most Muslims would consider themselves bound by the relevant textual provisions on the matter. According to the dictates of Qur'ān 5:5, interfaith marriages are strictly regulated such that a Muslim man may marry from the Jewish and Christian faiths but not a follower of traditional religion. However, a Muslim woman can marry only a Muslim man (Qur'ān 5: 5). The example of interfaith marriage encouraged by the constitution and the Islamic position is not cited with the notion that strategies for promoting national cohesion and not integration should be "Muslim-centric." Far from this, the purpose of the example is to underscore one fact. The fact is that dissonance between a central/core value of any religion and what is supposed to be common aspirational values underpinning constitutional provisions for all citizens is likely to create sustained tensions and conflicts between adherents of that religious faith and others.

Put differently, where it is manifestly impossible to respect a constitutional value and a religious dictate on the same point, the incompatibility can create multiple identities that serve different purposes for the adherent. This shift between identities will no doubt detract from the level of commitment to patriotic values for national cohesion and lead to a lack of inner spiritual peace. There are also broader ripple effects from the perspective of other citizens who are non-adherents to the religious faith concerned. Where the identity presented is one of adherence to religious value at the expense of the constitutional dictates, such individuals are viewed by the non-adherents as unreasonable in the process of nation-building and nationhood, thus shrinking the spirit of accommodation. The resolution of the internal conflict by the adherents is then tagged as "fundamentalism," "extremism," or a downright commitment to destroy what is perceived as a common objective or value. The person is viewed as being non-tolerant and non-patriotic. To illustrate this point is the following observation of Bishop Matthew Hassan Kukah of Sokoto Catholic Diocese:

> [W]e still continue to see ourselves only as Christians and Muslims. Rather than focusing on our common citizenship, we behave as if our Islam and Christian identities dropped from heaven ... These identities have now become markers that seem to determine where we shall be and how far we can grow in our society.... Some parts of the country as in other parts of the world, families comprising Christian and Muslims live together, marry and intermarry and so on. In the North, this is anathema. Every time such issues come up; people say that this is what Islam teaches, that the religion allows Muslim men to marry Christian girls (and hopefully make them Muslims) while Christian men cannot marry Muslim women. How do we progress with this given that marriage is such a key institution for national integration? We must sift the chaff from the grain.
>
> *(Kukah, 2015, pp. 2–3)*

This non-Muslim perspective on the position of Muslims on interfaith marriages demonstrates the understandable confusion of a non-adherent in the face of what is perceived as a laudable constitutional value. Under Islamic family law, however, there are basic assumptions regarding roles and responsibilities that are matters of religious observance such as that the burden of all material and economic provisions for the family rests squarely on the husband (Qur'ān 4: 34). Thus, non-maintenance and ill-treatment is a ground for the dissolution of marriage in Islam (Qur'ān 4: 128), which is enforceable in Islamic law courts and constitutes a religious sin. In the event of marriage between a Muslim man and a Jewish or Christian woman, the woman is entitled to the same rights of dower (Qur'ān 5: 5) and maintenance as well as the protection of the Islamic court. But how will Islamic law compel a non-Muslim man married to a Muslim woman in the same circumstance? As a religious law, Islamic law is understandably only enforceable on adherents and non-adherents who willingly submit to its jurisdiction. The Muslim woman in that circumstance is thus outside the ambit of protection of Islamic law, and this appears to be the wisdom behind the prohibition. In view of this, Section 15 may justifiably be viewed by Muslims as a clear opposition to their religious tenets, a stance not amenable to religious peace and stability.

5 Conclusion

There is an urgent need for collective deep reflection on the role of religion in the constitution and the construction of the Nigerian identity. Put another way, the government must continually engage with the citizenry to foster a common understanding of what constitutes religious freedom in Nigeria, as the general conclusion to this edited volume indicates, given its historical and political context as well as the demography of its citizenry. For example, the National Orientation Agency in Nigeria has the main purpose, in accordance with Decree 100 of 1993, of ensuring that the citizenry is well acquainted with governmental programmes and policies. The implication of provisions on religion in the constitution and as well as the various notions of religious identities within the Nigerian demography are appropriate matters, to the current author, that should be taken up by the agency. This chapter's expectation is that such engagement will ensure a significant reduction of friction between people of diverse religious faiths and affiliations. It is also hoped it should encourage cross-fertilization of ideas amongst people of diverse faiths, thereby fostering public and collective appreciation of the core values of the various religions. It is expected that the process of such dialogue and public engagements will drive constitutional revisions of provisions such as Section 15 in both semantic and substantive content as discussed. As the Constitution is the norm that binds all Nigerians together regardless of all forms of division, no Nigerian should feel alienated by any of its provisions so that even where a third identity is created, it is an identity that is not at variance with the continued existence of Nigeria as a body politic.

References

Adesina, O. C. (2017) 'Nigerian History and the Problems of Selective Memory', in Adesina, O. C. (ed) *Nigeria in the Twentieth Century: History, Governance and Society*, Ibadan, Connel Publications. pp. 2–13.

American Legion v American Humanist Association (2019) 204 L. Ed. 2d 452.

Amoloye-Adebayo, A. O. (2018) 'Islamic Law, the 1999 Constitution and the Challenges of Interfaith Relations in Nigeria' *Journal of Islam in Nigeria*, vol. 3, no. 1, pp. 33–46.

Amoloye-Adebayo, A. O. (2019) 'The Nigerian Constitution and the Sharīʿah Question in Southwestern Nigeria', in Opeloye, M. O., Bidmos, M. A., and Afis, O. (eds) *Islam in Yorubaland: History, Education and Culture*, Lagos, University of Lagos Press. pp. 259–276.

Awolowo, O. (1966) *Thoughts on Nigerian Constitution*, Ibadan, Oxford University Press.

Basil, E. (2022) 'Conflict, Religion and Ethnicity in the Post-colonial Nigerian State', *Australian Review of African Studies*, vol. 30, no. 2, pp. 47–67.

Boparai, H. (1982) 'The Customary and Statutory Law of Marriage in Nigeria', *The Rabel Journal of Comparative and International Private Law*, vol. 46, no. 3, pp. 530–557.

Center for Contemporary Islam (2019) *Debating Boko Haram* [Online]. Available at https://core.ac.uk/download/pdf/267981729.pdf (Accessed 30 April 2023).

Constantin, F. (1993) 'Leadership, Muslim Identities and East African Politics', in Brenner, L. (ed) *Muslim Identity and Social Change in Sub-Saharan Africa*, Bloomington, Indiana University Press. pp. 36–58.

Grillo, L. S., van Klinken, A., and Ndzovu, H. J. (2019) *Religions in Contemporary Africa: An Introduction*, London and New York, Routledge.

Kukah, M. H. (2015) 'Religion and National Integration', Keynote Address Presented at the 2015 Annual Conference of Islam in Nigeria, Islamic Welfare Foundation, Nigeria. On file with the author.

Kukah, M. H. (1993) *Religion, Politics and Power in Northern Nigeria*, Ibadan, Spectrum Books Limited.

Nigeria (2018) *High Court of the Federal Capital Territory, Abuja: Civil Procedure Rules, 2018* [Online]. Abuja, Justice Ishaq Usman Bello. Available at https://olumidebabalolalp.com/wp-content/uploads/2021/01/FCT-High-Court-Civil-Procedure-Rules-2018.pdf.pdf (Accessed 30 April 2023).

Nigeria (1999) *Constitution of the Federal Republic of Nigeria 1999* as amended [Online]. Abuja, National Assembly. Available at https://www.constituteproject.org/constitution/Nigeria_2011.pdf (accessed 30 April 2023).

Nigeria. *Criminal Code Act 1990* as amended [Online]. Abuja, Government of the Third Republic of Nigeria. Available at https://jurist.ng/act/criminal_code_act (Accessed 30 April 2023).

Nwauche, E. S. (2008) 'Law, Religion and Human Rights in Nigeria', *African Human Rights Law Journal*, vol. 8, no. 2, pp. 568–595.

Obadere, E. (2018) *Pentecostal Republic, Religion, and the Struggle for State Power in Nigeria*, London, Zeb Books.

Ojigbo, O. (1981) *Shehu Shagari: The Biography of Nigeria's First Executive President*, Yugoslavia, Mladinska knijiga.

Onaiyekan, J. O. (1993) 'Foreword', in Kukah, M. H. (ed) *Religion, Politics and Power in Northern Nigeria*, Ibadan, Spectrum Books Limited. pp. ix–x.

Ordu, G. E. (2015) 'Sharia Law in Nigeria: Can a Selective Imposition of Islamic Law Work in the Nation?', *Journal of Islamic Studies and Culture*, vol. 3, no. 2, pp. 66–81.

Qur'ān 4: 34, 128; 5: 5.

Robertson, J. (2017) 'Nigeria in 1965', in Adesina, O. C. (ed) *Nigeria in the Twentieth Century: History, Governance and Society*, Ibadan, Connel Publications. pp. 21–25.

Shah, T. S., Stefan, A., and Toft, M. D. (eds) (2012) *Rethinking Religion and World Affairs*, Oxford, Oxford University Press.

Terwase, I. (2014) 'Religion and the Nigerian State: Situating the De Facto and De Jure Frontiers of State-Religion Relations and Its Implications for National Security', *Oxford Journal of Law and Religion*, vol. 3, no. 2, pp. 311–339.

The Daily Sketch, No. 21, 312, 30 September 1997.

Umar, A. M. (ed) (1995) *Constitutional Conference 1994/95 Official Handbook and WHO IS WHO*, Abuja, Heritage Press.

World Bank (2021) *Population 2021* [Online]. Available at https://databankfiles.worldbank.org/public/ddpext_download/POP.pdf (Accessed 26 April 2023).

7

REJECTING SECURITY

A Comparative Analysis of the Rejection of Security, Public Safety, and Public Order Concerns as a Ground for Restricting Freedom of Religion in Religious Dress Cases

Renae Barker

1 Introduction

In May 2010, a person wearing a *burqa*[1] robbed a man in a Sydney carpark (Barker, 2016, p. 209). The event prompted controversial Senator Cory Bernardi[2] to call for a ban on the wearing of face veils in Australia. Bernardi's call for a so-called "*burqa* ban," as well as the original event itself, led to a national debate about the Islamic face veil and its place in contemporary multicultural and multi-faith Australia (Barker, 2012, pp. 144–148). While numerous justifications were put forward for a ban on the Islamic face veil (Barker, 2016), chief among them concerned security, public safety, and public order.

Security remains a powerful argument in support of restrictions on the wearing of religious symbols and dress. Religious attire such as the *niqab* or *burqa* obscures the face, frustrating the use of CCTV, facial recognition software, and eyewitness evidence as to identity. Religious headwear such as the *hijab*, *habit*, turban, *pagri*, or *chunni* may change a person's appearance in identity photographs, or be used to conceal contraband (See Barker, 2020, p. 167).[3] Similarly, loose-fitting religious clothing such as the *chador*, *khimar*, robes, or cassocks may be used to conceal a weapon, bomb, or other contraband. Some religious symbols, such as the *kirpan*, have the potential to be used as weapons themselves. It is therefore unsurprising that some states seek to ban or restrict the wearing of certain religious symbols or dress in the interests of promoting security, public safety, or public order.

Claims by states that the wearing of a particular religious symbol or dress poses a threat to security, public safety, or public order are not always accepted by the court. This chapter considers cases where the court has rejected

DOI: 10.4324/9781003453086-11

security, public safety, or public order as a legitimate reason for restricting the wearing of religious symbols or dress. It is not the intention of this chapter to cover every such case. Instead, it aims to provide a sampling of cases from the 2000s through to the 2010s from a range of Western jurisdictions. As is the nature of these types of cases, some jurisdictions and religious groups are overrepresented in the case law, and some repetition is therefore inevitable.

While this chapter focuses on cases where security, safety, or public order have been rejected as a ground for restricting freedom of religion, it is important to note that these grounds are often accepted by courts, in some cases with little in-depth discussion of the actual threat posed. For example, in *Mann Singh v France* [2008] the European Court of Human Rights (ECtHR) accepted that requiring a Sikh man to remove his turban and appear "bareheaded" in a photograph on his driver's licence was necessary for public safety (Howard, 2020, p. 138). The Court accepted the government's argument that the measure was necessary for public security in light of increased fraud and falsification of driver's permits. The Court did not elaborate on how removing a turban for the identity photograph, presumably worn while driving, would reduce fraud. Similar conclusions have been reached in other cases such as *El Morsli v France* [2008] and *Phull v France* [2005].

This chapter is divided into four parts. Part One provides an outline of the chapter and some introductory and background comments. Part Two summarises the nature of Freedom of Religion and Belief (FoRB), the limitations that may be placed upon it, and the role of security, public safety, and public order as a legitimate aim justifying the abrogation of FoRB. Part Three considers a number of cases where the relevant court has rejected security as a justification for abrogating the manifestation of FoRB via the wearing of religious symbols or dress. Finally, Part Four provides concluding observations.

A number of different jurisdictions are considered in this chapter. As a result, the outcome may vary from jurisdiction to jurisdiction – even where the facts appear, on their face, to be identical (Howard, 2020, p. 212). This may be the result of several factors including differently worded provisions regarding FoRB or the result of different, or arguably more or less rigorous, reasoning processes by the judiciary. As will be discussed below, the ECtHR and the United National Human Rights Committee (UNHRC) regularly come to differing conclusions when presented with nearly identical facts.

Cases concerning the right to manifest a person's religion or belief via the wearing of religious symbols or dress often invoke multiple rights. Rights such as the right to education, freedom of association, the right to a livelihood, freedom of expression, the right to privacy, and freedom of religion may all be relevant (Cox, 2019, p. 76). This chapter will focus on just one of these rights, FoRB. Similarly, states often offer a range of justifications for limitations on the wearing of religious symbols or dress (Cox, 2019, p. 78). This chapter, however, will focus on those cases where security, public safety, or public order was argued to be a legitimate aim.

2 Public Safety as a Limitation on FoRB

FoRB is a fundamental human right, protected by international,[4] transnational,[5] and domestic law.[6] As one Australian High Court judge has put it, "[f]reedom of religion, the paradigm freedom of conscience, is of the essence of a free society" (*Church of the New Faith v Commissioner of Pay-Roll Tax* [1983], paragraph 6). Religion touches upon almost all aspects of a person's life. It may influence what they eat and drink, what they wear, whom they associate with, how they raise their children, when they wake up and when they go to sleep, which day they work and which they rest (*Adelaide Co. of Jehovah's Witnesses Inc. v Commonwealth* [1943], p. 124). It can even influence how they interact within civil society and, in a democracy, whom they vote for.

While international, transnational, and domestic law recognises the importance of FoRB, it also recognises the need to limit that freedom. For example, Article 18(3) of the *International Covenant on Civil and Political Rights* (ICCPR) states:

> Freedom to manifest one's religion or beliefs may be subject only to such limitations as are prescribed by law and are necessary to protect public safety, order, health or morals or the fundamental rights and freedoms of others.
>
> *(United Nations General Assembly, 1966)*

Determining when it may be appropriate to limit FoRB and the necessary pre-conditions is not always easy. Different jurisdictions have come up with different tests to determine the issue. For example, in Australia, Latham CJ determined that there would be a breach of the freedom of religion provision in Section 116 of the *Australian Constitution* where there was an "undue infringement of religious freedom" (*Adelaide* [1943], p. 131). In Canada, the test, first outlined in *R v Oakes* ([1986], p. 105), is whether the limitation on freedom of religion is "reasonable and demonstrably justified in a free and democratic society." Article 9(2) of the European Convention on Human Rights (ECHR) adopts a similar formulation to the ICCPR. The manifestation of religion or belief may only be subject to:

> such limits as are prescribed by law and are necessary in a democratic society in the interests of public safety, for the protection of public order, health or morals, or for the protection of the rights and freedoms of others.
>
> *(European Union. European Court of Human Rights, 1950)*

As the ECtHR explained in *Kokkinakis v Greece* ([1994], paragraph 31), limitations are justified as:

> it recognises that in democratic societies, in which several religions coexist within one and the same population, it may be necessary to place

> restrictions on this freedom in order to reconcile the interests of various groups and ensure that everyone's beliefs are respected.

In the USA, various tests are applied at the state and federal level. While the "strict scrutiny" or "compelling state interest test" has been eroded by successive judgments, including *Employment Division, Department of Human Resources of Oregon v Smith* [1990], this relatively strict test for limiting FoRB has been re-enacted in many states, as well as in specific federal contexts such as federal prisons (Durham and Scharffs, 2019, pp. 252–256). As a result, different standards apply across the USA, highlighting the difficulty in determining the appropriate formulation for limitations on FoRB.

A common ground upon which limitations on FoRB are justified is public safety, security, and order. While Article 18(3) ICCPR and Article 9(2) of the ECHR do not include national security as a ground for limiting FoRB, other jurisdictions consider this a legitimate ground. For example, during wartime, Australian High Court judge Latham CJ considered national security may be a legitimate ground for limiting FoRB (*Adelaide* [1943], p. 147). In 1941, the Australian federal government declared Jehovah's Witnesses to be unlawful under the *National Security (Subversive Associations) Regulation* (1940). This led to their property being seized, including the Kingdom Hall in Adelaide. The Adelaide Company of Jehovah's Witnesses challenged the seizure of their property under Section 116 of the *Australian Constitution* in *Adelaide Co. of Jehovah's Witnesses Inc. v Commonwealth*.

Section 116 of the Australian Constitution states:

> The Commonwealth shall not make any law for establishing any religion, or for imposing any religious observance, or for prohibiting the free exercise of any religion, and no religious test shall be required as a qualification for any office or public trust under the Commonwealth.
>
> *(Australia. Queen Victoria, 1900)*

Despite its textual similarities with the First Amendment of the US Constitution, it has been interpreted more narrowly by the Australian High Court. In the case of the Jehovah's Witnesses and the seizure of the Adelaide Kingdom Hall, Latham CJ noted that Section 116 of the Australian Constitution:

> is not required for the protection of the religion of the majority. The religion of the majority of the people can look after itself. Section 116 is required to protect the religion (or absence of religion) of minorities, and, in particular unpopular minorities.
>
> (Adelaide *[1943], p. 124)*

Despite this, Latham CJ ultimately concluded that the *National Security (Subversive Associations) Regulation* (1940) did not infringe Section 116. He based his conclusion on his interpretation of "free" in "free exercise of religion." In his view free did not mean licence. Rather, it meant free within the confines of a free society noting that "[i]t is consistent with the maintenance of religious liberty for the state to restrain actions and courses of conduct which are inconsistent with the maintenance of civil government or prejudicial to the continued existence of the community" (*Adelaide* [1943], p. 131).[7]

In regard to the wearing of religious symbols and dress, threats to security, public safety, and public order manifest in both direct and indirect "threats" (Cox, 2019, p. 72). Direct threats include:

- religious dress or symbols which may be used as a weapon (*Multani v Commission Scolaire Marguerite-Bourgeoys* [2006]);
- religious dress hindering identification, acting as a disguise or enabling those intent on committing a crime or terrorist act from evading detection or capture (Barker, 2016, pp. 209–210; Cox, 2019, p. 72; Howard, 2020, p. 38); and
- religious dress being used to hide a weapon, bomb, or other contraband (Barker, 2016, pp. 209–210; Cox, 2019, p. 72).

Indirect threats include:

- religious dress or symbols being used or seen as "fundamentalist" or "extreme" symbols and symptomatic of the existence of a fundamentalist network, which may threaten the security of the state (Barker, 2016, p. 211; Cox, 2019, p. 72; Howard, 2020, pp. 37–38); and
- religious dress or symbols used to proselytise or put pressure on others to convert to a more extreme form of religion, which may threaten the security of the state (*Dahlab v Switzerland* [2001]; Howard, 2020, p. 38).

As this list demonstrates, the nature of the threat posed to security, public safety, and public order is likely to vary significantly between different forms of religious dress. The level of threat posed by religious dress will also vary between different settings. Concerns over the hiding of weapons, bombs, or other contraband and the need to immediately identify someone are likely to be heightened in high-security settings such as airports, banks, government buildings, and crowded public gatherings. Similarly, the nature of indirect threats posed by a particular form of religious dress will vary between jurisdictions depending on the socio-political climate of that country. The following section examines a number of cases from a range of Western, predominantly European, jurisdictions. While the court's assessment of the threat posed by various forms of religious dress to security, public safety, and public order will be discussed at a high level of generality, it is important to keep in mind the specific jurisdictional setting of each case.

3 Case Law

A number of cases have specifically considered whether security, public safety, and public order justify limiting manifestations of religion in the form of the wearing of religious symbols or dress. This section considers several such cases, primarily from the ECtHR and UNHRC – although cases from other jurisdictions will also be considered. The cases are presented in roughly chronological order to show the progression of judicial thought on this question over time. However, the time taken to hear and decide cases in some jurisdictions is lengthy. As a result, the date of the actual incident and the final court determination may be years apart. The date given for each case is the date the judgment was handed down, decided, or adopted.

3.1 Multani v Commission Scolaire Marguerite-Bourgeoys *[2006]*

As discussed above, the wearing of religious dress or symbols can pose a threat to security, public safety, or public order due to the symbolic nature of the dress or symbol. As I have argued elsewhere, symbols can be very powerful (Barker, 2016, p. 211). However, the message that a particular symbol may convey is likely to be different for different groups. While *Multani v Commission Scolaire Marguerite-Bourgeoys* is ostensibly about physical safety in schools, the need to regulate the wearing of religious symbols in this case also arguably revolved around the interpretation of the *kirpan*. The *kirpan* is a religious symbol worn by baptised Orthodox Sikh men. It resembles a dagger or knife and is made of metal. In this case, a school saw the *kirpan* as little more than a weapon, describing it as "essentially a dagger, a weapon designed to kill, intimidate or threaten others" (Barker, 2016, pp. 281–282). By contrast, as Chaplain Manjit Singh explained in the case, "The word *kirpan* comes from *kirpa*, meaning 'mercy' and 'kindness,' and *aan*, meaning 'honour'" ([2006], p. 281). In its judgment, the Canadian Supreme Court acknowledged that viewing the *kirpan* as little more than a weapon was "indicative of a simplistic view of freedom of religion" ([2006], p. 295).

3.1.1 Facts

This Canadian Supreme Court case involved an Orthodox Sikh schoolboy, Gurbaj Singh Multani, who wanted to wear his *kirpan*[8] at school (*Multani* [2006]). The wearing of the *kirpan* to school first came to the attention of the school when he "accidentally dropped the *kirpan* he was wearing under his clothes in the yard of the school" (*Multani* [2006], p. 266). Following the incident, the family was initially able to reach an accommodation with the school for Gurbaj to continue wearing the *kirpan* so long as it remained sealed inside his clothing. The school board, however, was not prepared to endorse the accommodation as, in their view, the carrying of the *kirpan* was in breach of the school *code de vire* (code of conduct) which, *inter alia*, prohibited the carrying of weapons (*Multani* [2006], p. 266). The school board offered to allow Gurbaj to wear a symbolic *kirpan*, made from a material other than metal (i.e. wood) or in the form of a pendant. Other Sikh children attending the school already opted for this option. However, Gurbaj and his family sincerely believed he was required to wear a real *kirpan* made of metal (*Multani* [2006], p. 266). He was, however, prepared to accept restrictions on how he wore it, such as that "[t]he *kirpan* must be enclosed in a wooden sheath and the sheath must be sewn inside a cloth envelope, which must itself be attached to a shoulder strap worn under the student's clothing" (*Multani* [2006], p. 305).

3.1.2 Arguments Regarding Security

The school's primary argument centred on its view that the *kirpan* "is essentially a dagger, a weapon designed to kill, intimidate or threaten others" (*Multani* [2006], pp. 281–282). They argued it was a threat to the safety of other students and teachers. In relation to the threat posed by the *kirpan*, the school made three specific arguments. First, the *kirpan* was a threat in and of itself as a weapon that may be used by either the person wearing it or another to injure or harm students or staff members. Second, allowing *kirpans* in schools would lead to a proliferation of weapons, and, third, that it would have a negative impact on the school environment. The Canadian Supreme Court ultimately rejected all three augments.

In its initial analysis, the Court accepted that the *kirpan* could "be used wrongly to wound or even kill someone," while at the same time rejecting an analysis of the question based "only on the physical makeup of the *kirpan*" (*Multani* [2006], p. 281). The Court also accepted that ensuring safety in schools was sufficiently important to justify limiting FoRB. However, the Court was not prepared to accept at face value the school's assertion that the *kirpan* was a sufficient threat to safety in schools. The Court noted that according to the Canadian Human Rights Commission, the level of safety required is "reasonable safety, not absolute safety" (*Multani* [2006], p. 283). In particular, the Court noted that:

> The application of a standard of absolute safety could result in the installation of metal detectors in schools, the prohibition of all potentially dangerous objects (such as scissors, compasses, baseball bats and table knives in the cafeteria) and permanent expulsion from the public school system of any student exhibiting violent behaviour.
>
> (Multani *[2006], pp. 283–284)*

Such a standard would not only be impossible to obtain but it would compromise the provision of universal access to education (Multani [2006], p. 283).

The Court carefully considered the question of whether the *kirpan* posed an actual risk to safety in schools. The Court considered four possible justifications for limiting the wearing of *kirpans* in schools on this basis: use by Gurbaj Singh, use by Gurbaj Singh's classmates, actual uses of the *kirpan* as a weapon, and the potential use as a weapon. The first two bases were dismissed relatively quickly on the basis that Gurbaj Singh did not have behaviour problems and had never used violence at school and the near impossibility of a classmate taking the *kirpan* from him (*Multani* [2006], p. 288).

The Court gave extensive consideration to the history of *kirpans* in schools and Canadian society generally. The Court noted government and media reports on the use of *kirpans* as weapons, as well as the permissibility of wearing *kirpan* in other settings where security, public safety, or public order are a matter of concern. In particular, the Court noted that in over 100 years of Sikhs attending schools in Canada, there had never been an incident where a *kirpan* had been used as a weapon (*Multani* [2006], p. 288). Finally, the Court considered the school's argument that it should "not be necessary to wait for harm to occur before correcting the situation" (*Multani* [2006], p. 291). While the Court agreed with the basic proposition, the Court was of the view that "the existence of concerns relating to safety must be unequivocally established for the infringement of a constitutional right to be justified" (*Multani* [2006], p. 293).

The remaining two arguments that permitting the *kirpan* would lead to a proliferation of weapons and negatively impact the school environment were similarly rejected by the Supreme Court. As the Court noted:

> The argument that the wearing of kirpans should be prohibited because the kirpan is a symbol of violence and because it sends the message that using force is necessary to assert rights and resolve conflict must fail. Not only is this assertion contradicted by the evidence regarding the symbolic nature of the kirpan, it is also disrespectful to believers in the Sikh religion and does not take into account Canadian values based on multiculturalism.
>
> (Multani *[2006], p. 294)*

In relation to an argument that other students may see it as "unfair" that Sikh students were permitted to carry a *kirpan* while they were not permitted to carry a knife, the Court was of the view that:

> If some students consider it unfair that Gurbaj Singh may wear his kirpan to school while they are not allowed to have knives in their possession, it is incumbent on the schools to discharge their obligation to instil in their students this value that is ... at the very foundation of our democracy.
>
> (Multani *[2006], p. 296)*

In other words, the presence of a *kirpan* in school would arguably have the potential for a positive impact on the school environment as a teaching opportunity about Canadian values, rather than the negative one asserted by the school.

3.2 Ahmet Arslan and Others v Turkey *[2010]*

Ahmet Arslan and Others v Turkey [2010] is the first case in which the ECtHR considered restrictions on the wearing of religious symbols or clothing in the public sphere. Previous cases considering the wearing of religious symbols had primarily concerned public institutions, where the need to maintain state neutrality outweighed individual freedom of religion (Powell, 2013, p. 138). The Court noted that as the applicants were ordinary citizens, they could not be said to represent the state in the same way as public officials or teachers (*Arslan* [2010], paragraph 48). Similarly, the Court noted that previous decisions regarding students at educational institutions did not apply in this case (*Arslan* [2010], paragraph 49).

In previous cases involving Turkey, such as *Leyla Şahin v Turkey* [2005] and *Kurtulmuş v Turkey* [2006], the ECtHR had been prepared to accept that in the context of a public institution, restrictions on the wearing of religious symbols and dress were permissible in the interests of protecting "public safety, public order and the rights and freedom of others." Such restrictions were particularly relevant in Turkey where the character of Turkey's secularism demanded absolute neutrality from the state (*Arslan* [2010], paragraph 26; Cox, 2019, pp. 218–219). For example, in *Leyla Şahin*, the ECtHR commented that:

> [T]he Court considers this notion of secularism to be consistent with the values underpinning the Convention. It finds that upholding that principle, which is undoubtedly one of the fundamental principles of the Turkish State which are in harmony with the rule of law and respect for human rights, may be considered necessary to protect the democratic system in Turkey. An attitude which fails to respect that principle will not necessarily be accepted as being covered by the freedom to manifest one's religion and will not enjoy the protection of Article 9 of the Convention.
>
> *([2005], paragraph 114; see also* Refah Partisi (the Welfare Party) and Others v Turkey *[2003])*

The laws which the applicants were convicted under in *Arslan* had been originally passed some 70 years earlier, to safeguard the secularity of the Turkish Republic (*Arslan* [2010], paragraph 26).

3.2.1 Facts

The applicants were members of the Aczmendi Tarikati religion. In October 1996, 127 members of the group gathered in Ankara outside the Kocatepe

Mosque for a religious celebration. They wore a distinctive form of dress, which included a headdress or turban which they believed was required by their religion (*Arslan* [2010], paragraph 7; Howard, 2020, p. 79; Powell, 2013, p. 136). The group was arrested and later brought before the State Security Court. At the first hearing, the applicants appeared dressed in their religious dress and were advised to remove their head coverings as a sign of respect for the Court.[9] While some members of the group complied, others refused to do so. All were found guilty of breaches of Turkish law with respect to both their gathering in October 1996 and their appearance in Court wearing religious dress (*Arslan* [2010], paragraphs 8–18).

3.2.2 Arguments Regarding Security

The Turkish government argued that the law prohibiting the wearing of certain forms of religious dress in public areas was necessary in the interests of "public safety, for the protection of public order," and "for the protection of the rights of others." In particular, it was necessary to safeguard the secular character of the Turkish Republic (*Arslan* [2010], paragraph 26). Further, the government argued that the applicant's actions amounted to proselytism and propaganda, which was, therefore, a threat to security (*Arslan* [2010], paragraph 29). As discussed above, the nature of Turkey's path to secularism means that issues such as religious dress take on a significance not seen in other parts of Europe (Howard, 2020, p. 79). The Turkish government also argued that in refusing to remove their headdresses, the applicants had shown disrespect to the Court (*Arslan* [2010], paragraph 28).

While the ECtHR accepted that the protection of public safety, public order, and the rights of others were legitimate aims, the Court ultimately rejected Turkey's arguments. The Court distinguished the applicant's case from previous ECtHR case law on the basis that the applicants were ordinary citizens and not state officials, teachers, or students attending a state institution (*Arslan* [2010], paragraphs 48–49). The Court noted that no evidence of any threat posed by the group had been presented and, as a result, found that there had been a violation of Article 9 of the ECHR (*Arslan* [2010], paragraph 50). As Malcom Evans (2010, p. 367) puts it, "[i]n short, the European Court's judgment suggests that the group posed no particular threat to anyone or anything."

Ahmet Arslan and Others v Turkey is an important high-water mark in the ECtHR application of Article 9, and, in particular, the limitations that may be imposed on religious expression. While in previous cases, the Court had accepted state arguments that restrictions were necessary in the interests of public order with limited evidence of the actual threats posed, in *Ahmet Arsland and Others v Turkey* the Court required actual evidence of the threat (Howard, 2020, pp. 139–140). It is important to note, however, that the

ECtHR was careful to distinguish the case from instances where restrictions had been applied to state officials, teachers, and students attending state educational institutions.

3.3 Ranjit Singh v France *[2011] and* Shingara Mann Singh v France *[2013]*

In 2008, a number of cases were brought to the UNHRC regarding restrictions faced by Sikhs in France. The cases included *Ranjit Singh v France* [2011], *Shingara Mann Singh v France* [2013], and *Bikramjit Singh v France* [2012]. In each case, the French government relied on pre-existing judgments from the ECtHR's finding in their favour. The UNHRC, however, took a different approach, resulting in the emergence of a discrepancy between the jurisprudence of the ECtHR and UNHRC.

3.3.1 Facts

The authors in both *Ranjit Singh v France* [2011] and *Shingara Mann Singh v France* [2013] applied to have their identity documents renewed by the French government.[10] Both men submitted photographs of themselves as part of the renewal process wearing turbans as required by their Sikh faith. Despite previously obtaining identity documents with photographs of them wearing their turbans, the French government refused to use the provided photographs as the men did not appear "bareheaded" as required by the relevant regulations (*Ranjit Singh* [2011], paragraph 2.1; *Shingara Mann Singh* [2013], paragraphs 2.1–2.2). As a consequence, Ranjit Singh was unable to obtain his residency permit. This had the effect of rendering his residency in France illegal and removed his access to France's free public health system, unemployment benefits, housing benefits, and reduced transit fees – all of which would otherwise have been available to him (*Ranjit Singh* [2011], paragraphs 3.2–3.3). Similarly, Shingara Mann Singh was unable to renew his passport limiting his ability to travel internationally (*Shingara Mann Singh* [2013], paragraph 3.6).

3.3.2 Arguments Regarding Security

In both cases the French government argued that the requirement for people to appear bareheaded in photographs for identity documents was necessary to minimise the risk of fraud or falsification (*Ranjit Singh* [2011], paragraph 5.3; *Shingara Mann Singh* [2013], paragraph 6.6). The UNHRC accepted that this pursued the legitimate aim of protecting public safety and public order (*Ranjit Singh* [2011], paragraph 8.4; *Shingara Mann Singh* [2013], paragraph 9.4). However, the UNHRC was not prepared to accept that a prohibition on the wearing of a head covering in photographs for identity documents was necessary. In reaching this conclusion, the Committee noted that France had not explained how requiring a person to appear bareheaded "avert[ed] the risk of fraud or falsification" (*Ranjit Singh* [2011], paragraph 8.4; *Shingara Mann Singh* [2013], paragraph 9.4). Similarly, the Committee noted that France had not explained why

> the wearing of a Sikh turban covering the top of the head and a portion of the forehead but leaving the rest of the face clearly visible would make it more difficult to identify the author than if he were to appear bareheaded since he wears his turban at all times.
>
> (Ranjit Singh *[2011], paragraph 8.4; see also* Shingara Mann Singh *[2013], paragraph 9.4)*

As a result, unlike in early ECtHR cases, the UNHRC found that France's bans on religious headgear in identity photographs had violated FoRB. The reasoning in the decisions in these two cases is perhaps best encapsulated by the argument made by the author in *Shingara Mann Singh v France* ([2011], paragraph 3.2):

> Identical treatment of persons in very different situations can constitute a form of discrimination. What is important is for people to have the opportunity to equally enjoy the same rights.

3.4 **Bikramjit Singh v France** *[2012]*

Like *Multani v Commission Scolaire Marguerite-Bourgeoys*, the case of *Bikramjit Singh v France* [2012] concerned a Sikh schoolboy who was excluded from classes, and eventually expelled, for wearing a religious symbol. While in *Bikramjit Singh v France* the religious symbol took the form of a head covering, rather than a *kirpan*, similar issues were at stake. While the supposed threat posed by Bikramjit Singh's *keski* was arguably less direct than Gurbaj Multani's *kirpan*, in both cases the court ultimately determined that no evidence had been adduced of the threat posed by the religious symbol or dress.

3.4.1 Facts

In 2004 the French government passed a law prohibiting the wearing of religious symbols and dress by students and staff in state schools (*Bikramjit Singh* [2012], paragraph 2.1; see also Barker, 2020, pp. 163–165). Prior to the ban, Bikramjit Singh wore a *patka*, and subsequently a *keski* from the age of 17 (*Bikramjit Singh* [2012], paragraph 2.3). As the UNCHR explained:

> The *keski* (like the turban for adult men) is not meant as an external display of faith but is rather intended to protect the long uncut hair, which

> is considered as a sacred, inherent, and intrinsic part of the religion. The turban is not worn with a view to proselytise – a concept which is foreign to the Sikh religion (*Bikramjit Singh* [2012], paragraph 2.3).

Following the introduction of the ban, Bikramjit Singh refused to remove his *keski* and was subsequently removed from class and then expelled after he requested that a disciplinary board be convened (*Bikramjit Singh* [2012], paragraphs 2.4–2.9).

3.4.2 Arguments Regarding Security

The French government argued, *inter alia*, that the 2004 ban on the wearing of religious symbols in public schools was introduced following "a worrying increase in tension connected to the claims of communities, after the Stasi Commission had indicated that identity-related conflicts could become a factor of violence in schools" (*Bikramjit Singh* [2012], paragraph 3.3). In support of its assertion the French government noted that the number of incidents reported had decreased since the ban had come into force (*Bikramjit Singh* [2012], paragraph 5.8).

The UNHRC, however, rejected France's argument that the ban was necessary. In particular, the Committee noted that France had "not furnished compelling evidence that, by wearing his *keski*, the author would have posed a threat ... to order at the school" (*Bikramjit Singh* [2012], paragraph 8.7). The UNHRC went further noting "the State party imposed this harmful sanction on the author, not because his personal conduct created any concrete risk, but solely because of his inclusion in a broad category of persons defined by their religious conduct" (*Bikramjit Singh* [2012], paragraph 8.7). As a result, the UNHRC found that France had not shown that the ban was either necessary or proportionate.

3.5 **S.A.S. v France** *[2014]*

In October 2011, France became the first European country to ban the wearing of face coverings in all public places. Unlike previous laws, the French ban was not restricted to specific high-security places, such as airports, banks, and public buildings, nor was it restricted to people fulfilling public roles such as schoolteachers, attending public institutions such as schools, or enforced for public officials. Instead, the ban applied to all public spaces. Subsequently, several other European jurisdictions have passed similar laws. While the French law did not refer to Islamic face veils specifically, the law, and those like it, have become colloquially known as "*burqa* bans."[11] While neutral in its wording, the history of the French law, along with its application in practice, strongly suggests that its primary purpose was to prohibit the wearing of the Islamic *burqa* and *niqab*.

3.5.1 Facts

The applicant was a devout French Muslim woman who regularly wore the *niqab*. She was, however, inconsistent in when and where she wore the *niqab*. "She was thus content not to wear the *niqab* in public places at all times but wished to be able to wear it when she chose to do so, depending in particular on her spiritual feelings" (*S.A.S. v France* [2014], paragraph 12). The ECtHR noted that this was not a bar to her bringing a claim under Article 9 of the ECtHR as there was no obligation to demonstrate that a specific religious practice was required, merely that it was motivated by religious belief in order to bring it within the ambit of Article 9 (*S.A.S. v France* [2014], paragraphs 55–56).

3.5.2 Arguments Regarding Security

S.A.S. v France has become (in)famous for the ECtHR's acceptance of the French government's argument that the ban on the wearing of face coverings in public was to protect the "rights and freedoms of others," namely, a condition of "living together" (*le vivre ensemble*) (*S.A.S. v France* [2014]). However, the French government also advanced a number of other arguments in support of the ban. This included that the ban "satisfied the need to identify individuals so as to prevent danger for the safety of persons and property and to combat identity fraud" (*S.A.S. v France* [2014], para. 82).

In considering the public safety and public order arguments advanced by France, the ECtHR noted that it had not found there to be a violation of Article 9 of the ECHR in cases where a person had been asked to remove religious clothing for the purposes of security checks (*Phull* [2005]; *El Morsli* [2008]) or to appear bareheaded in identity photographs (*Mann Singh v France* [2008]) (*S.A.S. v France* [2014], paragraphs 133, 138). However, the ECtHR distinguished these cases from the present cases noting:

> [I]n view of its impact on the rights of women who wish to wear the full-face veil for religious reasons, a blanket ban on the wearing in public places of clothing designed to conceal the face can be regarded as proportionate only in a context where there is a general threat to public safety.
>
> *(*S.A.S. v France* [2014], paragraph 139)*

In the Court's view, the French government had not demonstrated that such a context existed. Instead, the Court noted that the government's stated objective could be achieved "by a mere obligation to show their face and to identify themselves where a risk for the safety of persons and property has been established, or where particular circumstances entail a suspicion of identity fraud" (*S.A.S. v France* [2014], paragraph 139).

The lack of proportionality of the ban on face coverings weighed heavily on the Court's assessment. The Court commented that the effect of the ban was to ask women to "give up completely an element of their identity" where a more targeted approach would have sufficed to satisfy the government's objectives regarding public safety (*S.A.S. v France* [2014], paragraph 139).

As alluded to above, while the ECtHR rejected France's arguments based on security, public safety, and public order, the Court found that the limitations were justified in order to protect the rights and freedoms of others, namely, a condition of "living together" (*le vivre ensemble*). Two subsequent face-veil cases, *Belcacemi and Oussar v Belgium* [2017] and *Dakir v Belgium* [2017], have followed the Court's approach in *S.A.S.*, finding that similar bans in Belgium are permissible on the basis of the minimum condition of "living together" (Howard, 2020, pp. 90–91).

While the ECtHR ultimately found that the ban did not violate Article 9, it confirmed that restrictions based on concerns for public safety can only be a legitimate aim where there is evidence of a genuine threat (Howard, 2020, p. 82).

3.6 Yaker v France *[2018] and* Hebbadj v France *[2018]*

Article 9(2) of the ECHR and Article 18(3) of the ICCPR are nearly identical in their terms. They both restrict limitations on the manifestation of religious belief or practices to circumstances where it is prescribed by law, and where it is necessary to protect certain specific public goods. These public goods are also nearly identical, covering public safety, order, health or morals, and the rights and freedoms of others. The ECHR adds that not only must any limitation be necessary in general terms, but it must also specifically be necessary "in a democratic society."

> Article 9(2)
>
> Freedom to manifest one's religion or beliefs shall be subject only to such limitations as are prescribed by law and are necessary in a democratic society in the interests of public safety, for the protection of public order, health or morals, or for the protection of the rights and freedoms of others.
>
> *(European Union. European Court of Human Rights, 1950)*

> Article 18(3)
>
> Freedom to manifest one's religion or beliefs may be subject only to such limitations as are prescribed by law and are necessary to protect public safety, order, health, or morals or the fundamental rights and freedoms of others.
>
> (United Nations General Assembly, *1966)*

While it might be expected that two nearly identical provisions would result in identical outcomes, as has been alluded to above, this is not always the case. *Yaker v France*, *Hebbadj v France*, and *S.A.S. v France* have similar facts and concern the same law restricting the wearing of facial coverings in France, yet they reached different conclusions. Critically, however, both rejected security as justification for the ban on full face coverings.

3.6.1 Facts

Sonia Yaker and Miriana Hebbadj were both stopped for an identity check in Nantes, France, in October and November 2011, respectively (*Yaker* [2018], paragraph 2.1; *Hebbadj* [2018], paragraph 2.1). They were subsequently charged and convicted of a breach of the offence of wearing a garment to conceal their face in public and ordered to pay the maximum penalty of 150 euros (*Yaker* [2018], paragraphs 2.1–2.2; *Hebbadj* [2018], paragraphs 2.1–2.2). Both women contended that they wore a face veil for religious reasons in compliance with their Muslim faith (*Yaker* [2018], paragraph 3.2; *Hebbadj* [2018], paragraph 3.2).

3.6.2 Arguments Regarding Security

Like *S.A.S. v France*, the French government in *Yaker v France* and *Hebbadj v France* presented numerous justifications for limiting freedom of religion by banning the wearing of full face coverings in public (*Yaker* [2018], paragraphs 7.1–7.11; *Hebbadj* [2018], paragraphs 5.1–5.11). In relation to public order and public safety, France argued that:

[I]t must be able to identify all individuals when necessary in order to avert threats to the security of persons or property and to combat identity fraud. That implies that people reveal their faces, a requirement that is all the more crucial in the context of the global threat of terrorism (*Yaker* [2018], paragraph 7.8; see also *Hebbadj* [2018], paragraph 5.8).

The UNHRC rejected this argument. While the UNHRC recognised "the need for States in certain contexts, to be able to require individuals to show their faces" (*Yaker v France* [2018], paragraph 7.8), this should be limited to one-off instances in specified circumstances. By contrast, the French law comprehensively prohibits the wearing of certain face coverings in public at all times (*Yaker v France* [2018], paragraph 7.8). The UNHRC was particularly critical of the French government's failure to demonstrate that the ban was proportionate to its objectives commenting:

> Even if the state party could demonstrate the existence of a specific and significant threat to public safety and order in principle, it has failed to demonstrate that the prohibition contained in Act No. 2010-1192 is proportionate to that objective, in view of its considerable impact on the

author as a woman wearing the full-face veil. Nor has it attempted to demonstrate that the ban was the least restrictive measure necessary to ensure the protection of the freedom of religion or belief.

(Yaker v France *[2018], paragraph 8.8)*

Unlike *S.A.S. v France,* however, the UNHRC rejected France's argument that the ban could be justified on the basis of protecting the rights and freedoms of others. In particular, the UNHRC noted that in order to rely on this justification, the specific human rights affected and the persons affected needed to be identified (*Yaker v France* [2018], paragraph 8.10). The vaguer concept of the requirements of "living together" did not meet this threshold.

3.7 Lachiri v Belgium *(2018)*

The ability for religious parties and witnesses to be able to take part in court proceedings is vital for the effective administration of justice. However, the wearing of religious symbols and dress can pose particular challenges in the courtroom. For example, the wearing of the Islamic face veil by witnesses in common law courtrooms has presented a particular challenge. Courts have needed to balance the interests of justice of all parties and witnesses (including those who wish to wear the face veil) alongside the need to respect FoRB (See Barker, 2017, 2018). While *Lachiri v Belgium* concerned the wearing of a *hijab*, rather than a *burqa* or *niqab*, it raises similar issues with respect to access to justice – in this case for a civil party to criminal proceedings – for religious adherents who wear particular forms of religious symbols or dress.

3.7.1 Facts

The applicant was a civil party to criminal proceedings relating to the death of her brother. She, along with other family members, was appealing against a decision to commit her brother's attackers on a charge of assault and wounding rather than murder. On the day of the hearing, the applicant arrived at the courtroom door wearing a hijab. She was requested to remove her head covering in accordance with Article 759 of the Judicial Code. She refused to remove her hijab and was therefore unable to enter the courtroom (Kaushik, 2018).

3.7.2 Arguments Regarding Security

Article 759 of the Judicial Code, *inter alia*, prohibited the wearing of headgear in court. The Belgium government argued that this restriction was necessary to prevent disrespectful behaviour towards the judiciary and prevent disruption to the smooth running of court proceedings (Kaushik, 2018, paragraph 38). The ECtHR accepted that this was a legitimate aim in order to protect "public order" (Kaushik, 2018, paragraph 38). However, the Court found that Belgium had not established that such a measure was necessary for a democratic society. The Court considered a number of factors in coming to this conclusion. The Court noted that the applicant was an ordinary citizen rather than a representative of the state (such as a judge or other court official) and therefore was not exercising a public function. Unlike those exercising a public function, a private citizen has no obligation to exercise discretion in the manifestation of their religious beliefs (Kaushik, 2018, paragraph 44). The Court further noted that while a courtroom was a public space (unlike a workplace), it was more akin to a school or other public establishment. As a result, an argument may have been open to the Belgium government that the ban on the wearing of headgear was necessary to promote and protect the neutrality of the state (Kaushik, 2018, paragraph 45). Belgium made no such argument. Instead, it relied solely on an argument based on the need to protect "public order" (Kaushik, 2018, paragraph 38). The Court, therefore, concluded that as the applicant had not engaged in any explicitly disrespectful or disruptive behaviour the Belgium government had not demonstrated that such a ban was, in fact, necessary (Kaushik, 2018, paragraph 46).

4 Analysis and Concluding Comments

As demonstrated by the cases considered above, security, public order, and public safety is a common argument advanced to justify the banning of certain forms of religious symbols and dress such as the *niqab*, *burqa*, *hijab*, *kirpan*, turban, and *keski*. While security, public safety, and public order are a powerful argument for limiting FoRB, it is not always accepted by the courts. Despite significant jurisdictional differences in how the threats posed by religious symbols and dress are assessed by the Courts, two broad commonalities can be deduced from the proceeding cases.

First, in ECtHR decisions, where the ban is imposed on members of the general public, as opposed to those engaged in public roles such as teachers or government officials, the Court is more likely to be sceptical of the necessity and proportionality of the restriction. This scepticism is heightened further when the ban is comprehensive, covering all public spaces, rather than targeted at particular institutions. In both *Ahmet Arslan and Others v Turkey* and *S.A.S. v France*, the ECtHR rejected arguments based on public safety and public order largely based on the broad application of the bans to the general public. Similarly, in *Lachiri v Belgium*, the ECtHR emphasised that the ban applied to ordinary citizens and not public officials, although a courtroom was a public institution. Given the wide margin of appreciation usually afforded to state parties by the ECtHR, the rejection of public safety and public order in these cases is a powerful statement of the limits of restriction on FoRB on that basis.

Second, where the state party does not provide sufficient evidence of the actual threat posed by the wearing of the particular religious symbol or dress, the argument is more likely to be rejected. This is most evident in the UNHRC cases such as *Ranjit Singh v France*, *Shingara Mann Singh v France*, *Bikramjit Sing v France*, *Yaker v France*, and *Hebbadj v France*. However, it can also be seen in the Canadian Supreme Court decision in *Multani v Commission Scolaire Marguerite-Bourgeoys* and the ECtHR decision in *Ahmet Arslan and Others v Turkey*. While the level of evidence required varies between jurisdictions, the party imposing the ban needs to provide at least some evidence to support their assertion that the religious symbol or dress possesses an actual threat to security, public safety, or public order.

While a threat to security, public safety, and public order will remain powerful arguments for the restriction of FoRB, as the cases discussed demonstrate, they are not a panacea justifying any and all restrictions on the wearing of religious dress and symbols a state may believe to be necessary. States considering the restriction of the wearing of religious dress and symbols would be wise to limit such restrictions to those fulfilling public functions or where a real threat can be established.

Notes

1 The *niqab* and *burqa* are a form of dress worn by some Muslim women which envelops the body and covers the face of the wearer.

2 In 2017 Mr. Bernardi left the Liberal Party to form his own political party, Australian Conservatives. The Australian Conservatives was disbanded in 2019 and voluntarily deregistered by the Australian Electoral Commission. Mr. Bernardi resigned from parliament in November 2019.

3 This is the reason often cited by schools in the USA for a blanket ban on "headwear."

4 See, e.g., the 1948 Universal Declaration of Human Rights (*United Nations General Assembly*, 1948); the 1966 International Covenant on Civil and Political Rights, Art. 18 (*United Nations General Assembly*, 1966); and the 1989 Convention on the Rights of the Child, Art. 14 (*United Nations General Assembly*, 1989).

5 See, e.g., the 1950 Convention for the Protection of Human Rights and Fundamental Freedoms, Art. 9 (European Union. European Court of Human Rights, 1950).

6 See, e.g., US Const. (Amend. I); Austl. Const. ch. V, §116 (Australia. Queen Victoria, 1900); Constitution Act (Canada. Queen Elizabeth II, 1982), Pt. 1 cl. 11; Const. of South Africa (Constitutional Assembly, 1996), ch. 2, §15.

7 For a more detailed discussion of the case and its background, see Barker (2019, pp. 92–93, 195, 201).

8 The orthodox Sikh dress code requires men to wear religious symbols known as the five Ks: the *kesh* (uncut hair), the *kangha* (wooden comb), the *kara* (a steel bracelet), the *kaccha* (undergarment), and the *kirpan* (metal; dagger or sword). See *Multani* ([2006], p. 280).

9 The Court explained the men were expected to appear bareheaded in court while women could appear either bareheaded or with a head cover.
10 *Ranjit Singh v France* [2011] concerned the renewal of a residency permit, while *Shingara Mann Singh v France* [2013] concerned the renewal of a French passport.
11 Despite the inaccuracy of this term, the alliteration in this assignation has proven too irresistible for journalists, commentators, politicians, and academics alike.

References

Adelaide Co. of Jehovah's Witnesses Inc. v Commonwealth [1943] 67 CLR 116.
Ahmet Arslan and Others v Turkey [2010] No. 41135/98, ECtHR.
Australia. Australian Parliament (1940) *National Security (Subversive Associations) Regulation 1940*, Canberra.
Australia. Queen Victoria (1900) *Commonwealth of Australia Constitution Act 1900*, Canberra.
Barker, R. (2020) 'Children in Schools: The Battle Ground of Religious Belief', *The University of Western Australia Law Review*, vol. 47, no. 1, pp. 152–174.
Barker, R. (2019) *State and Religion: The Australian Story*, Abingdon, Routledge.
Barker, R. (2018) 'Of Burqas (and Niqabs) in courtrooms: the neglected women's voice', in Rex Ahar (ed) *Research Handbook on Law and Religion*, Cheltenham, Edward Elgar Publishing.
Barker, R. (2017) 'Burqas and Niqabs in the Courtroom: Finding Practical Solutions', *The University of Western Australia Law Review*, vol. 91, no. 3, pp. 225–243.
Barker, R. (2016) 'Rebutting the Ban the Burqa Rhetoric: A Critical Analysis of the Arguments for a Ban on the Islamic Face Veil in Australia', *Adelaide Law Review*, vol. 37, pp. 191–218.
Barker, R. (2012) 'The Full Face Covering Debate: An Australian Perspective', *The University of Western Australia Law Review*, vol. 36, no. 1, pp. 143–157.
Belcacemi and Oussar v Belgium [2017] No. 37798/13, ECtHR.
Bikramjit Singh v France [2012] CCPR/C/106/D/1852/2008, United Nations Human Rights Committee.
Canada. Queen Elizabeth II (1982) *Constitution Act 1982*, Toronto.
Church of the New Faith v Commissioner of Pay-Roll Tax [1983] 154 CLR 120.
Cox, N. (2019) *Behind the Veil: A Critical Analysis of European Veiling Laws*, Cheltenham, Edward Elgar Publishing.
Dahlab v Switzerland [2001] No. 42393/98, ECtHR.
Dakir v Belgium [2017] No. 4619/12, ECtHR.
Durham, C. and Scharffs, B. (2019) *Law and Religion, National, International and Comparative Perspectives*, 2nd edn, Boston, Aspen Publishing.
El Morsli v France [2008] ECtHR, No. 15585/06.
Employment Division, Department of Human Resources of Oregon v Smith [1990] 109 S.Ct. 1526.
European Union. European Court of Human Rights (1950) *European Convention on Human Rights*, as amended. Rome, Strasbourg [Online]. Available at https://www.echr.coe.int/documents/convention_eng.pdf (Accessed 15 March 2021).
Evans, M. (2010) 'From Cartoons to Crucifix: Current Controversies Concerning the Freedom of Religion and the Freedom of Expression before the European Court of Human Rights', *Journal of Law and Religion*, vol. 26, no. 1, pp. 345–370.
Hebbadj v France [2018] CCPR/C/123/D/2807/2016, United Nations Human Rights Committee.

Howard, E. (2020) *Law and the Wearing of Religious Symbols in Europe*, 2nd edn, Abingdon, Routledge.

Kaushik, P. (2018) 'Lachiri v Belgium', *Oxford Journal of Law and Religion*, vol. 7, no. 3, pp. 569–570.

Kokkinakis v Greece [1994] No. 14307/88, ECtHR 3/1992/348/421.

Kurtulmuş v Turkey [2006] No. 65500/01, ECtHR.

Leyla Şahin v Turkey [2005] No. 44774/98, ECtHR.

Mann Singh v France [2008] No. 24479/07, ECtHR.

Multani v Commission Scolaire Marguerite-Bourgeoys [2006] 1 SCR 256.

Phull v France [2005] No. 35753/03, ECtHR 2005-I.

Powell, L. (2013) 'The Constitutionality of France's Ban on the Burqa in Light of the European Convention's Arslan v Turkey Decision on Religious Freedom', *Wisconsin International Law Journal*, vol. 31, no. 1, pp. 118–146.

R v Oakes [1986] 1 SCR 103.

Ranjit Singh v France [2011] CCPR/C/102/D/1876/2009, United Nations Human Rights Committee.

Refah Partisi (the Welfare Party) and Others v Turkey [2003] Nos. 41340/98, 41342/98, 41343/98, and 41344/98, ECtHR.

S.A.S. v France [2014] No. 43835/11, ECtHR.

Shingara Mann Singh v France [2013] CCPR/C/108/D/1928/2010, United Nations Human Rights Committee.

South Africa. Constitutional Assembly (1996) *Constitution of the Republic of South Africa*, Cape Town.

United Nations General Assembly (1989) *Convention on the Rights of the Child*, New York, United Nations, Document A/RES/44/25 [Online]. Available at https://www.un.org/en/development/desa/population/migration/generalassembly/docs/globalcompact/A_RES_44_25.pdf.

United Nations General Assembly (1966) *International Covenant on Economic, Social and Cultural Rights, International Covenant on Civil and Political Rights and Optional Protocol to the International Covenant on Civil and Political Rights*, New York, United Nations, Document A/RES/2200(XXI) [Online]. Available at https://undocs.org/Home/Mobile?FinalSymbol=A%2FRES%2F2200(XXI)&Language=E&DeviceType=Desktop&LangRequested=False (Accessed 15 January 2023).

United Nations General Assembly (1948) *Universal Declaration of Human Rights*, Paris, United Nations [Online]. Available at https://www.un.org/en/universal-declaration-human-rights/ (Accessed 30 January 2022).

United States Constitution. Amendment I.

Yaker v France [2018] CCPR/C/123/D/2747/2016, United Nations Human Rights Committee.

8

RELIGION-BASED BOUNDARIES

Restricting Pluralism through Symbolic Barriers

Tania Pagotto

1 Religion as a Thin Boundary between Insiders and Outsiders

The problems of migration and asylum-seeking are crucial issues in political programs, policies, action plans, and governments' agendas around the world.[1] During the last decades, international migration flows have increased, both on a geographical scale and in quantitative terms (Dauvergne, 2021; Menjívar and Ness, 2019; Weinar et al., 2018).[2] For example, in 2016 should all international migrants have gathered in one single country, it would have been the world's fifth most populated (Connor and López, 2016).

Political responses by States' governments, however, have not been unified. Destination countries capable of external border controls to prevent entry by foreign nationals have made these newcomers' exercise of fundamental rights more difficult. At the same time, other States have straightened their "inner boundaries", whether real, symbolic, or legal, by widening the gap between the legal treatment of citizens and non-citizens.

These trends have led political theorists and legal academics to raise several key questions, such as the political representation of newcomers in the receiving countries' communities (Pedroza, 2019; Forest, 2006), the current *status quo* on borders security (Shaw-Taylor and McCall, 2020), and even the legitimacy of boundaries themselves (Espejo, 2020). Broader questions have been raised as well, on equality, human rights compliance, justice, and socio-economical inclusion (Sager, 2016; Bauböck, 2009; Benhabib, 2004).

Part I of this chapter focuses on a narrow, although significant, concern: the practice of "testing" that some European countries carry out on prospective migrants and citizens. It does so by focusing on the role of religion, directly or indirectly, and by reading responses under the lens of public

DOI: 10.4324/9781003453086-12

security that emerged globally after the terrorist attacks of September 11, 2001 (9/11) in the US and the other deadly bombings in Europe. Countries have addressed their concerns about identity clashes posed by newcomers within the framework of public security in migration and citizenship testing.

Part II traces the theoretical and legal framework of the chapter, deepening the interconnections between migration, pre-entrance tests, and religion. Tightening immigration law has been justified by the compelling need to safeguard internal security. In practice, however, it affects both pluralism and religious diversity.

Part III introduces citizenship tests and describes how restricting religious pluralism arose through attempts to prevent clashes between religious norms, on the one hand, and State values, on the other hand. European case studies demonstrate these tests were first applied to third-country nationals before their entrance and administered through immigration law. However, this practice has also been extended to would-be citizens, at the moment of acquiring citizenship.

Finally, Part IV concludes that perceived threats coming from the outside and related to third-country nationals have now been internalized, touching upon the very notion of citizenship.

There are not only physical borders, which circumscribe countries' territory, but also undefined, psychological borders, which identify the *demos* (Shachar, 2020). As the case of pre-departure and naturalization tests shows, this second type of border can be built on the wave of national security-insecurity and based on generalized and religiously oriented presumptions. This symbolic border can be located outside national borders, or it can be located within them, based also on "a representation of Islam as a problem" (Denaro, 2014, p. 271).

2 The Link between Religion and the Regulation of Mobility: The "External" Test Dimension

The ties between mobility and the governance of religion have a long and well-established track record that intersects in many different aspects: diversity of the host country and its religious pluralism. Indeed, regardless of the reasons to migrate, either humanitarian or economic, such a contested distinction in the literature (van Hear et al., 2009), the movement of personal identities itself has been always understood as impacting the social makeup of the nation-states, including the religious component.

Two testing examples from the US illustrate the bond between restricting access and governing religious diversity. In 1917, the US government introduced the literacy test. Upon arrival at Ellis Island, would-be immigrants had to prove their literacy in any language by reading a short passage to the officer. This measure was "intended to curtail immigration of Catholics from southern and eastern Europe, Jews from eastern Europe, and immigrants from the Middle East" (Finkelman, 2003, p. 335).[3] One century later, in 2017, Trump's administration restricted admission to the US by citizens of several different countries, i.e. Muslim-majority nations, to protect "the nation from foreign terrorist entry" (Trump, 2017a, 2017b). Ultimately upheld by the Supreme Court (*Trump v Hawaii* [2018]), the "travel bans" have been contested on religious discrimination grounds as well as under the Establishment Clause, beyond being portrayed as being motivated by anti-Muslim sentiment and at odds with the inclusive principles of American identity (Barrow, 2018; Maltz, 2018; Blackman, 2017).

Today, as in 1917, alarming uncertainties posed by increased religious, ethnic, and cultural diversity are still shaping national laws on migration. However, contrary to the beginning of the 20th century, the features of migration flows have changed, as well as the scenarios where they take place. First, after the terrorist attacks of 9/11 and the rise of global terrorism, fears toward newcomers are more evident. In addition, the broad discourse on danger not only relates to entrances but has been extended to the whole process of integration (Bosworth and Guild, 2008).

Second, while in the first half of the 20th century, migration flows sketched routes from Europe to the US, now Europe has become a destination for foreign nationals. With a remarkable number of migrants coming mostly from Africa and Asia, Europe perceives itself as an immigration space (Kaya, 2002).

Third, the fact that migrants can bear cultures and identities that challenge Western liberal values is widely accepted (Laqueur, 2007; Fukuyama, 2006). On the one hand, the perceived clashes between Western and non-Western religious values adhered to by some immigrants, especially Muslim ones, have gained public and political visibility, destabilizing vulnerable societies (King and Lulle, 2016; Koenig et al., 2016; Triandafyllidou and Maroukis, 2012). On the other hand, State *vis-à-vis* non-State affiliations, such as religious communities, have fueled demands for accommodations and have led to hundreds of applications lodged before European courts (Orgad, 2010; Soysal, 1997).[4]

Against this theoretical background, European laws and administrative procedures related to both entrance and integration policies are worthy of attention, since not only do they reinstate the us-versus-them narratives, but they also externalize integration issues outside the borders of national communities.

Since Western European Union (EU) nations frame migration policy as a response to the need for security, limiting who comes across the borders tends to be achieved through the criminal law (Gatta, 2021; Wonders and Jones, 2019). This criminalization process has developed indicators for "suitable" migrants, and rather than affecting border flow as an overall phenomenon, it targets border crossers as persons (Horsti and Pellander, 2015, p. 753). ID papers, reporting-in requests, biometric profiling, and electronic tagging are evidence of these policies (Feldman, 2011; Broeders, 2007). They are aimed at targeting only certain segments of migration and controlling certain others under the prism of crime, "especially those viewed as 'undesirables' typically based on class, race, ethnicity, gender, and/or post-colonial histories" (Wonders and Jones, 2019, p. 138), including religious aspects of diversity.

Regarding integration, religion has been employed as an exclusionary element even outside borders. Indeed, since 2006, several EU countries have started to subject migrants, their spouses, and family migrants to pre-departure integration requirements (FitzGerald et al., 2018, p. 34). The Netherlands was the first nation to introduce the "civic integration abroad" test (*Wet inburgering in het buitenland.* Queen Beatrix, 2006; see also *Ministry of Social Affairs and Employment*, n.d.) and paved the way for its adoption in France (*Loi n° 2007-1631.* French Parliament, 2007), Germany (*Gesetz zur Umsetzung Aufenthalts.* German Parliament, 2007), Denmark (*Lov om ændring af udlændingeloven.* Danish Parliament, 2007), Austria (*Fremdenrechtsänderungsgesetz.* Austrian Parliament, 2011), and the UK (Bonjour, 2014; de Vries, 2013).

The wave of pre-departure integration tests has been justified on the grounds of facilitating and increasing employability in the labor market and integration in the receiving society. Although some differences can be identified from country to country, newcomers usually must prove proficiency in the new language, legislation, and culture, before their journey to Europe starts (FitzGerald et al., 2018, p. 10). For example, Denmark asks for "awareness of the receiving society", while France for knowledge of Republican values (Bonjour, 2014).

In the years following the implementation of pre-integration tests in the countries mentioned above, while immigration has generally increased, flows from predominantly Muslim countries have declined (FitzGerald et al., 2018, p. 15). Research has shown that pre-entry tests target *de facto* third-country nationals, unskilled adults who wish to settle permanently, and people "generally associated with … immigrants from rural areas and/or Muslim countries" (Bonjour, 2014, p. 209; Scholten et al., 2012, p. 55).

What are some of the theoretical rationales justifying such an important impact of pre-entry tests on some religious groups in the name of integration? Looking at the supranational level is useful to articulate the reply.

The European Union (EU), indeed, has promoted coordination and coherence over national policies not only by adopting harmonization measures but also by establishing national contact points for integration.[5] However, when it comes to integration and religion, such a crucial value in the EU context (Ninatti and Gennusa, 2016), the EU integration policy is aligned with the idea that everyone is expected to share European core values. In November

2004, the Justice and Home Affairs Council adopted the *Common Basic Principles for Immigrant Integration Policy in the EU*, a set of 11 principles guiding the integration of newcomers residing in one of the EU Member States (*Council of the European Union*, 2004).

These principles required, for example, "basic knowledge of the host society's language, history, and institutions" and "respect for the basic values of the European Union" but also underlined that "[s]hared forums, intercultural dialogue, education about immigrants and immigrant cultures ... enhance the interactions between immigrants and Member State citizens" (*Council of the European Union*, 2004). According to the document, moreover, adherence to core EU values is the duty of every "resident" (*Council of the European Union*, 2004). Moreover, "[v]iews and opinions that are not compatible with such basic values might hinder the successful integration of immigrants into their new host society and might adversely influence the society as a whole" (*Council of the European Union*, 2004).

The condition to have the theoretical capacity to integrate before entering the EU space probably accounts for the initial position suggested by the EU Court of Justice, which considered legitimate two types of measures either conditioning or restricting the entrance of people or investments.

On the one hand, the Court found it legitimate to subject minors' potential capacity to integrate to pre-entry tests (*European Parliament v Council of the European Union* [2006]), when minor-aged people arrive at the EU independently from the rest of the family, under the right to family reunification (*Council of the European Union*, 2003a). The Court of Luxembourg, for example, had to decide whether Member States were allowed to verify if a 12-year-old child met integration criteria, before authorizing his or her entry and residence; moreover, it had to adjudicate on whether such tests violated the obligation to respect the right to family life of migrants and migrant families (*Parliament v Council* [2006]).[6] The Court ultimately held that preemptively testing the capacity of minors to integrate in the so-called "host society" does not appear *as such* in violation of the right to respect for family life as protected by binding human rights treaties (*Parliament v Council* [2006]).[7] By contrast, it considered that "the necessity for integration may fall within a number of the legitimate objectives" and may serve as a legitimate scope for limiting the right to respect for family life (*Parliament v Council* [2006]).[8]

On the other hand, in different cases still relevant today, the Court of Luxembourg has accepted as legitimate in principle the reasons for public policy and public security in support of the restrictions imposed on the freedom of movement of people, capitals, or goods. This was the case, for example, in judgments which made certain direct investments linked to the Church of Scientology subject to prior authorization by the national State concerned

(*Association Eglise v Prime Minister* [2000]) or when the competent authorities refused to allow a woman entering the UK to accept employment as a secretary with the Church of Scientology, whose activities were considered socially detrimental (*Yvonne van Duyn v Home Office* [1974]). Moreover, in other rulings, the Court drew attention to "moral, religious or cultural considerations" when assessing the legitimacy of national measures restricting activities often considered immoral, such as betting, lotteries, and gambling (*Criminal Proceedings Against Gambelli* [2003]; *Markku Juhani Läärä v Kihlakunnansyyttäjä* [1999]; *Questore di Verona v Zenatti* [1999]; *Her Majesty's Customs v Schindler* [1994]).

These cases and others stand for the European idea of fostering integration hand in hand with the enhancement of the principles of freedom and democracy, assuming that not all religious convictions are compatible with the European set of values. However, this purpose may be distorted if read in light of a broader political context and contrasted with national experiences. Straightening boundaries and limiting mobility have been justified by governments under the compelling need to safeguard internal domestic security. In practice, however, control over borders and entrances of newcomers spilled over into policies of integration and values (Pin, 2019; Angelucci, 2017; Ferrari, 2009).

This section has shown that the religious identity of migrants has become relevant even outside the country's borders (Houtum and Pijpers, 2007)[9] and while national (in)security conflated with the limitation of diversity and religious pluralism, this form of integration has migrated abroad and become expected before entrance (Dobrowolsky, 2007).

3 The Link between Religion and Citizenship Acquisition: "Internal" Test Dimension

Tests can be performed not only before newcomers cross borders, but also once they have integrated into the national community and applied for citizenship (Bauböck and Tripkovic, 2017; Shachar et al., 2017).

Integration and citizenship are entwined in an ambivalent relationship, having "a strong rhetorical dimension in forging understandings of what it is to belong to a community, and in shaping a country's sense of its own identity" (Pillai and Williams, 2017, p. 554). Painting with a broad brush, on the one hand, the multicultural theory considers citizenship as a tool for integration since the rights attached to settlement and nationality are keys toward a further sense of belonging (Stewart and Mulvey, 2014, p. 1026). On the other hand, citizenship is conceived as the result of successful integration. The latter concept assumes that integration is possible only when migrants become citizens and fully part of society. According to the assimilationist approach (Joppke and Morawska, 2003), foreign nationals undergo "a slow process of demonstrating value to the nation and assimilation to its culture" (Abrams, 2009, p. 39).

Regardless of different conceptualizations (Ajani, 2015; Miller, 2000), while integration has always been something dealing with "the Other", in the aftermath of 9/11 and the world's subsequent attention to the rise of the Islamic State, something new emerged. Not only have Western States faced international terrorism, but terrorism has also become a threat within European countries (Vedaschi, 2018, p. 179). European citizens participated in attacks or left their own countries as foreign terrorist fighters (Murphy, 2019). Due to radicalization, granting citizenship along with global anxiety about religious fanatism became salient political issues, alongside a general distrust toward religious and cultural diversity (Motilla, 2018).

In this context, since the early 2000s, several European countries have introduced language and citizenship tests as new requirements for migrants to access both long-term residence and, most importantly, naturalization. Citizenship tests were first applied in the US (*United States Congress*, 1917, 1907),[10] Canada (*Canadian Museum of Immigration at Pier 21*, n.d.),[11] and Australia (*Australian Citizenship Act 2007*. Australia. Australian Parliament, 2014).[12] Justification for testing varies in several schools of thought but, as far as this chapter is concerned, the tests assessed if would-be citizens shared values or practices deemed protected, sustained, agreed upon, and promoted in the country on a linguistic, social, and cultural level (Etzioni, 2007).

Beyond language proficiency (von Busekist and Boudou, 2018), tests generally survey knowledge of democracy, rights, freedoms, and duties as well as history, traditions, and geography of a country. They can also include questions on religious differences and cultural pluralism, and, consequently, make diversity relevant to citizenship acquisition (Ajani, 2015, p. 26).

The Netherlands, for example, requires people to apply for Dutch nationality through naturalization by having sufficient knowledge of the language and Dutch society and asking applicants to take a civic integration exam. According to some data, about 28% of the questions related to politics, history, and geography; another 46% to the public economy; and, finally, about 16% to morality and "etiquette", i.e. "how-to" questions on the acceptance of social norms, asking would-be citizens to share their opinions in a way to avoid bothering others who behave differently concerning religion. As a matter of illustration, the candidate should know that in the Netherlands certain ways of dressing in public should not be interpreted as unchaste (Michalowski, 2011, 2010a, p. 759).

Denmark has one of the most strenuous citizenship application processes. Critics of this test point to its overreliance on history, to the lack of clarity of some questions on Danish culture, and to the intrusive nature of the test (Groenendijk and van Oers, 2010). In particular, some questions challenge the applicants' religious beliefs by asking, for example, whether the laws of the society should prevail over religious beliefs (*Global Citizenship Observatory*, 2016). In February 2021, the press reported that the national center-right party wanted to add five new questions on "Danish values", e.g. whether women should be allowed to choose romantic partners (*The Local*, 2021).

Finally, German citizenship regulation has received a lot of scholarly attention due to a reform that took place at the turn of the 21st century. Some amendments occurred in the wake of international terrorism, and they represent a good case study, since they can track and contrast two different trends, before and post 9/11.

German nationality today relies on a mixture between *ius sanguinis* (when citizenship is acquired on the basis of the nationality or ethnic origin of one or both parents) and *ius soli* attribution (when a child's nationality is determined by its birthplace),[13] but that has not always been the case. In 2000 a reform to the law on nationality took place (*Staatsangehörigkeitsgesetz*. Germany. German Parliament, 2022): a form of *ius soli* attribution was introduced for second-generation qualified immigrants and residence for naturalization was reduced from 15 to 8 years (*Staatsangehörigkeitsgesetz*. Germany. German Parliament, 2022, Article 10(1)). At that time, integration was perceived also, although not exclusively, in terms of governance of religious diversity. In the early 2000s, for example, the German Federal Commissioner for Migration, Refugees, and Integration used to refer to "integration with R" to indicate that integration has a religious dimension that public policies should address (Koenig, 2005, p. 220).

The softening trend of naturalization was brought to a halt after 2001 when the necessity to exclude potential terrorists from German naturalization became an urgent and pressing need, increasingly persistent in the discourse of some political parties. In the following years, not only were naturalization requirements progressively sharpened but language and culture tests (*Einbürgerungstest*) were also introduced (van Oers, 2014, p. 152).[14] Due to the federal structure of the German State, citizenship tests have been subject to different amendments and practices throughout the German States (*Länder*). The latter enjoyed a margin of maneuvering with selected questions acknowledging the command of the German democratic order and the so-called "declaration of loyalty" to the free and democratic constitutional set of values (Michalowski, 2010b, p. 195).

In 2006 the State of Baden-Württemberg introduced the "interview manual", known in the press as the "Muslim test" (Hawley, 2006), a list of questions to be used to determine whether the applicant understood the content of the declaration of loyalty (Farahat and Hailbronner, 2020, p. 22). Questions covered the applicant's attitude toward criticizing religion, opinions on the obedience of women to their husbands,[15] nudism, and the lawfulness of religious conversions under State law (Welfens and Pisarevskaya, 2020).

Hesse, located in the central-western part of Germany, introduced a 100-question form as part of the declaration of loyalty section. Officials were allowed to question people's convictions and ask concerning the possibility of women appearing in public or traveling alone without a male member of the family.[16]

Reforms are still taking place; and some citizenship laws have been amended at the German federal level toward a more liberal imprint (van Oers, 2014, p. 78); indeed, these cases remain significant examples of how citizenship itself, and naturalization practices, in particular, can be leveraged as exclusionary tools (Meer, 2014, p. 3).

Citizenship tests, indeed, represent a thorny issue. First, scrutinizing the inner religious beliefs of applicants is highly problematic as a possible violation of fundamental rights. Human rights law and international treaties generally recognize the right to deeply held beliefs, religious or not.[17] This right is not only absolute but also unconditional and unqualified and covers the right to have, not to have, or to change any belief whatsoever. Limitations can be introduced only on the manifestation side of beliefs and convictions, and under given conditions; they must usually be prescribed by law, necessary in a democratic society, and protect one of the aims provided for by international human rights treaties, i.e. public safety and order, morality and health, and the protection of other people's rights and freedoms (Temperman et al., 2019; Bond, 2018; Murdoch, 2012; Doe, 2011; McCrea, 2010; Knights, 2007; Uitz, 2007; Evans, 2001). The absolute right to hold a belief protects individuals from any form of the State's interference. By contrast, these tests, formerly blind regarding religion and immigrant culture, "include questions directed at specific immigrant groups, seeking to make these immigrants transparent" (Löwenheim and Gazit, 2009, p. 156).

Second, one may ask if these questions are genuinely relevant for granting citizenship or maybe fostered by an ideological bias. Some of the same topics chosen to acknowledge the loyalty to the democratic order of would-be citizens (obedience to religious values v. obedience to secular laws) are still contested and yet these issues remain unsolved among citizens themselves. For example, in 2014, the Grand Chamber of the European Court of Human Rights delivered a judgment that garnered much media coverage and international attention, in the case of a French citizen prevented from wearing a burqa in public by national legislation. The Court held that the ban did not breach the European Convention on Human Rights (*S.A.S. v France* [2014]). Four years later, an Algerian Muslim woman refused to shake hands with male officials at a French naturalization ceremony. The circumstance was considered a sign of defective assimilation, and citizenship was denied, although the application for naturalization had been successful (*Conseil d'État* [2018]). The French Council of State adjudicated the claim and stated that the government's decision was legitimate given that the episode occurred "in a place and at a moment that is symbolic (*Conseil d'État* [2018])".[18]

In the previous section, we have seen that clashes between religious norms and Western values have been addressed through immigration law and labeled as security policies to protect citizens. It can be added that the same observation can be raised as to citizenship tests, introduced to prevent potential terrorists from acquiring nationality.[19]

4 Final Remarks: "Religion-Based Boundaries"

The role of the law and administrative procedures in regulating migration has increased dramatically (Torpey, 1999, p. 151). So is regulating citizenship, where the modern State now determines for whom citizenship is secured, conferred, and also revoked (Shachar, 2001, p. 21).

With the rise of testing practices, the cry for security has penetrated not only the domain of migration but also the domain of citizenship.

On the one hand, the need to ensure security from objective threats (terrorism) has conflated with the need to ensure security from subjective threats (identitarian clashes). In doing so, the attempt to promote the integration of migrants and to safeguard citizens' security has become an opportunity to address the complex and delicate management of cultural and religious pluralism (Zanfrini, 2020; Njaim, 2018; Karyotis, 2007).

On the other hand, in the aftermath of global terrorism, these measures and policies started to have a broader scope, addressed only to third-country nationals. Through the introduction of naturalization tests and, above all, by posing applicants with intrusive variants of questions, the State can regulate the emergence of possible dissent or minority beliefs (Löwenheim and Gazit, 2009; Wright, 2008).

This brings consequences not only for third-country nationals or would-be citizens, to whom these measures are primarily addressed, but for everyone subject to State laws, including citizens themselves. Seeing pre-entry tests and citizenship tests as two faces of the same coin and considering that the route to citizenship, other than by birth, usually starts by migrating to another country could be a sufficient reason to make the case for a closer juxtaposition in migration and citizenship laws (Aleinikoff and Klusmeyer, 2011; Bauböck, 2006; Klusmeyer and Aleinikoff, 2000).

In addition, pre-entry tests and citizenship tests show that citizenship, conventionally attached to the principle of inclusion and stability, can in practice become "mixed up with immigration policy and ambitions of control" (Carrera and Guild, 2010, p. 37). Since the French Revolution, European citizenship has been affirmed as a unitary notion bringing an equal status.

From diversity, citizenship creates political unity, toward which every legal order is oriented. But it is also a sign of equality because the bundle of rights, freedoms, and duties it confers on every individual moves to the idea of equal dignity among all people (Leydet, 2017).

The cases presented in this chapter contrast these two traditional attributes. They illustrate policies driven by pursuing security from supposed illiberal outsiders. At the same time, however, these policies erode the liberal threat of citizenship for all insiders,[20] and they do so along "religion-based boundaries (real or imagined)" (Hirschl and Shachar, 2018, p. 440).

Notes

1 This chapter is a re-work and an updated version of a paper in Italian language published as T. Pagotto, "L'uso di indici presuntivi, e religiosamente orientati, nell'ambito dei test di pre-partenza condotti all'estero e di naturalizzazione", DPCE ONLINE, 2021(3), 2857–2874.

As to legal definitions, migrant and refugee are terms that correspond to two distinctive concepts (Motomura, 2020). Being aware of the differences, however, for the purposes of this chapter, I consider all newcomers and third-country nationals as an all-encompassing category.

2 A bundle of different reasons leads people to migrate, including wars, human rights violations, economic hardship, climate changes, urbanization, socio-economic inequalities, environmental degradation, and others.

3 The only exception was for those fleeing their country of origin for religious persecution (Finkelman, 2003, p. 335).

4 Liav Orgad (2010, p. 57) talks about "inside-out" communities, physically residing inside the country but culturally remaining outside, while Yasemin Nuhoğlu Soysal (1997, p. 515) identifies transnational communities connected by local groups that mobilize legal claims and voting rights.

5 For example, in 2007, the European Fund for the Integration of Third-Country Nationals was established, and in 2009 the European Migration Forum. See also, among many directives on migrants, "Council Directive 2003/86/EC of 22 September 2003 on the Right to Family Reunification" (*Council of the European Union*, 2003a) and "Council Directive 2003/109/EC of 25 November 2003 Concerning the Status of Third-Country Nationals Who Are Long-Term Residents" (*Council of the European Union*, 2003b).

6 See Art. 7 of the Charter of Fundamental Rights of the European Union (2016) and Art. 8 of the European Convention on Human Rights (European Union. European Court of Human Rights, 1950).

7 See the previous note.

8 Paragraph 66 of Parliament v Council of the European Union.

9 According to Van Houtum and Pijpers (2007, p. 297), newcomers have started to be "valued on the basis of their other country of birth, colour, creed, religion or culture".

10 Section 8 of the 1906 Naturalization Act introduces for the first time the knowledge of English language as a requirement to obtain citizenship (*United States Congress*, 1907, pp. 35, 44); the literacy test has been introduced by the 1917 Immigration Act, Section 3 (*United States Congress*, 1917, p. 877).

11 See Section 10(1)(e)(f).

12 See in particular Sections 21(2)(d)–(f), 21(2)(A), 23(A), 46(1)(A), and 53(2).
13 "German Nationality Act of 22 July 1913 as Last Amended by Article 1 of the Act of 20 November 2019", Pub. L. No. 1913, Federal Law Gazette I p. 1626, accessed March 15, 2021, https://www.gesetze-im-internet.de/englisch_stag/index.html. Of course, naturalization is also possible, indeed, generally after a period of six to eight years of legal residence in Germany.
14 See also Art. 10(5) of the *Staatsangehörigkeitsgesetz* (Germany. German Parliament, 2022, Article 10(5)). This provision introduces the naturalization test, while Art. 10(4) specifies language requirements (*Staatsangehörigkeitsgesetz*. Germany. German Parliament, 2022, Article 10(4)).
15 For other questions, see van Oers (2014, p. 77): "What is your attitude towards criticising a religion? Do you think that is allowed? What do you think about the statement that a woman should obey her husband and that her husband is allowed to beat her, if she is disobedient? What is your opinion about forced marriages? Do you think such marriages are compatible with human dignity?"
16 For other questions, see van Oers (2014, p. 78).
17 See, e.g., European Convention on Human Rights, Art. 9 (European Union. European Court of Human Rights, 1950) and Charter of Fundamental Rights of the European Union, Art. 10 (2016).
18 "[U]n tel comportement, dans un lieu et à un moment symboliques, révélait un défaut d'assimilation (*Conseil d'État* [2018])."
19 According to Zedner (2010, p. 181), "it is no coincidence that in the bid to reassert one territorially bounded good – national security – governments have had recourse to another territorially bounded concept – citizenship".
20 A similar argument has elaborated by Italian scholarship as to citizenship revocation (see Mitrotti, 2019; Raimondo, 2019; Viola, 2019).

References

Abrams, K. (2009) 'Becoming a Citizen: Marriage, Immigration, and Assimilation', in McClain, L. C. and Grossman, J. L. (eds) *Gender Equality: Dimensions of Women's Equal Citizenship*, Cambridge, Cambridge University Press, pp. 39–59.

Ajani, M. (2015) *Citizenship, the Self and the Other: Critical Discussions on Citizenship and How to Approach Religious and Cultural Difference*, Newcastle upon Tyne, Cambridge Scholars Publishing.

Aleinikoff, T. A. and Klusmeyer, D. (2011) *Citizenship Policies for an Age of Migration*, Washington, DC, Carnegie Endowment for International Peace.

Angelucci, A. (2017) 'Libertà religiosa e cittadinanza integrativa. Alcune note sul "vivere assieme" in una società plurale', *Stato, Chiese e Pluralismo Confessionale*, no. 39, pp. 1–13 [Online]. Available at https://doi.org/10.13130/1971-8543/9289 (Accessed 15 March 2021).

Association Eglise de Scientologie de Paris and Scientology International Reserves Trust v The Prime Minister [2000] Case C-54/99, European Court Reports 2000 I-01335.

Australia. Australian Parliament (2014) *Australian Citizenship Act 2007*. Canberra, Australian Parliament (Act No. 20 of 2007) [Online]. Available at https://www.refworld.org/docid/4cf3ac052.html (Accessed 14 March 2021).

Austria. Austrian Parliament (2011) *Bundesgesetz, mit dem das Niederlassungs - und Aufenthaltsgesetz, das Fremdenpolizeigesetz 2005, das Asylgesetz 2005, das*

Grundversorgungsgesetz - Bund 2005 und das Staatsbürgerschaftsgesetz 1985 geändert werden (Fremdenrechtsänderungsgesetz 2011). Vienna, Bundesgesetzblatt (BGBl. I Nr. 38/2011) [Online]. Available at https://www.ris.bka.gv.at/eli/bgbl/I/2011/38/20110523 (Accessed 14 March 2021).

Barrow, J. L. (2018) 'Trump's Travel Ban: Lawful but Ill-advised', *Harvard Journal of Law & Public Policy*, vol. 41, no. 2, pp. 691–718.

Bauböck, R. (2009) 'Global Justice, Freedom of Movement and Democratic Citizenship', *European Journal of Sociology/Archives Européennes de Sociologie*, vol. 50, no. 1, pp. 1–31 [Online]. Available at https://doi.org/10.1017/S000397560900040X (Accessed 14 March 2021).

Bauböck, R. (2006) *Migration and Citizenship: Legal Status, Rights and Political Participation*, Amsterdam, Amsterdam University Press.

Bauböck, R. and Tripkovic, M. (2017) (eds) *The Integration of Migrants and Refugees: An EUI Forum on Migration, Citizenship and Demography*, Fiesole, European University Institute.

Benhabib, S. (2004) *The Rights of Others: Aliens, Residents, and Citizens*, Cambridge, Cambridge University Press.

Blackman, J. (2018) 'The Travel Bans', in Shapiro, I. et al. (eds) *2017–2018 Cato Supreme Court Review*, Washington, DC, Cato Institute, pp. 29–58.

Bond, M. (2018) *An Introduction to the European Convention on Human Rights*, Strasbourg, Council of Europe.

Bonjour, S. (2014) 'The Transfer of Pre-departure Integration Requirements for Family Migrants among Member States of the European Union', *Comparative Migration Studies*, vol. 2, pp. 203–226 [Online]. Available at https://doi.org/10.5117/CMS2014.2.BONJ (Accessed 15 March 2021).

Bosworth, M. and Guild, M. (2008) 'Governing through Migration Control: Security and Citizenship in Britain', *British Journal of Criminology*, vol. 48, no. 6, pp. 703–719 [Online]. Available at https://doi.org/10.1093/bjc/azn059 (Accessed 14 March 2021).

Broeders, D. (2007) 'The New Digital Borders of Europe: EU Databases and the Surveillance of Irregular Migrants', *International Sociology*, vol. 22, no. 1, pp. 71–92 [Online]. Available at https://doi.org/10.1177/0268580907070126 (Accessed 14 March 2021).

Canadian Museum of Immigration at Pier 21 (n.d.) 'Canadian Citizenship Act, 1947' [Online]. Available at https://pier21.ca/research/immigration-history/canadian-citizenship-act-1947 (Accessed 15 March 2021).

Carrera, S. and Guild, E. (2010) 'Are Integration Tests Liberal? The "Universalistic Liberal Democratic Principles" as Illiberal Exceptionalism,' in Joppke, C. and Bauböck, R. (eds) *How Liberal Are Citizenship Tests?*, Fiesole, European University Institute, pp. 29–34.

Charter of Fundamental Rights of the European Union (2016) *Official Journal of the European Union*, C202, vol. 59, pp. 389–405.

Connor, P. and López, G. (2016) '5 Facts about the U.S. Rank in Worldwide Migration', *Pew Research Center*, 18 May [Online]. Available at https://www.pewresearch.org/fact-tank/2016/05/18/5-facts-about-the-u-s-rank-in-worldwide-migration/ (Accessed 14 March 2021).

Conseil d'État, 2ème - 7ème Chambres Réunies [2018] Case 412462, Conseil d'État.

Council of the European Union (2003a) *Council Directive 2003/86/EC of 22 September 2003 on the Right to Family Reunification*, Brussels, 22 September [Online]. Available at https://eur-lex.europa.eu/legal-content/EN/ALL/?uri=CELEX%3A32003L0086 (Accessed 14 March 2021).

Council of the European Union (2003b) *Council Directive 2003/109/EC of 25 November 2003 Concerning the Status of Third-Country Nationals Who Are Long-Term Residents*, Brussels, 25 November [Online]. Available at https://eur-lex.europa.eu/legal-content/en/ALL/?uri=CELEX%3A32003L0109 (Accessed 14 March 2021).

Council of the European Union (2004) *Common Basic Principles for Immigrant Integration Policy in the EU*, Brussels, 19 November [Online]. Available at https://ec.europa.eu/migrant-integration/library-document/common-basic-principles-immigrant-integration-policy-eu_en (Accessed 15 March 2021).

Criminal Proceedings Against Piergiorgio Gambelli and Others [2003] Case C-243/01, European Court Reports 2003 I-13031.

Dauvergne, C. (ed) (2021) *Research Handbook on the Law and Politics of Migration*, Cheltenham, Edward Elgar Publishing.

Denaro, R. (2014) 'La Costituzione spiegata ai migranti: Un Muslim test tra le righe della Carta dei valori', in Spena, M. R. and Carbone, V. (eds) *Il Dovere di Integrarsi: Cittadinanze Oltre il Logos Multiculturalista*, Rome, Armando Editore, pp. 271–284.

Denmark. Danish Parliament (2007) *Lov om ændring af udlændingeloven og lov om aktiv socialpolitik*. Copenhagen, Danish Parliament (Lov nr 379 af 25/04/2007) [Online]. Available at https://www.retsinformation.dk/eli/lta/2007/379 (Accessed 14 March 2021).

de Vries, K. M. (2013) *Integration at the Border: The Dutch Act on Integration Abroad and International Immigration Law*, London, Hart Publishing.

Dobrowolsky, A. (2007) '(In)Security and Citizenship: Security, Im/migration and Shrinking Citizenship Regimes', *Theoretical Inquiries in Law*, vol. 8, no. 2, pp. 629–662.

Doe, N. (2011) *Law and Religion in Europe: A Comparative Introduction*, Oxford, Oxford University Press.

Espejo, P. O. (2020) *On Borders: Territories, Legitimacy, and the Rights of Place*, Oxford, Oxford University Press.

Etzioni, A. (2007) 'Citizenship Tests: A Comparative, Communitarian Perspective', *The Political Quarterly*, vol. 78, no. 3, pp. 353–363 [Online]. Available at https://doi.org/10.1111/j.1467-923X.2007.00864.x (Accessed 14 March 2021).

European Parliament v Council of the European Union [2006] Case C-540/03, European Court Reports, I-05769.

European Union. European Court of Human Rights (1950) *European Convention on Human Rights*, as amended. Rome, Strasbourg [Online]. Available at https://www.echr.coe.int/documents/convention_eng.pdf (Accessed 15 March 2021).

Evans, C. M. (2001) *Freedom of Religion Under the European Convention on Human Rights*, Oxford, Oxford University Press.

Farahat, A. and Hailbronner, K. (2020) *Report on Citizenship Law: Germany*, Fiesole, Global Citizenship Observatory [Online]. Available at https://cadmus.eui.eu/handle/1814/66430 (Accessed 15 March 2021).

Feldman, G. (2011) *The Migration Apparatus: Security, Labor, and Policymaking in the European Union*, Redwood City, CA, Stanford University Press.

Ferrari, S. (2009) 'Tra manifesto e contratto: La Carta dei valori, della cittadinanza e dell'integrazione degli immigrati in Italia', *Anuario de Derecho Eclesiástico del Estado*, vol. XXV, no. 25, pp. 469–483.

Finkelman, P. (2003) 'Immigration and Naturalization Law and Religion', in Finkelman, P. (ed) *Religion and American Law: An Encyclopedia*, Abingdon, Routledge, pp. 231–236.

FitzGerald, D. S., Cook-Martín, D., García, A. S. and Arar, R. (2018) 'Can You Become One of us? A Historical Comparison of Legal Selection of "Assimilable" Immigrants in Europe and the Americas', *Journal of Ethnic and Migration Studies*, vol. 44, no. 1, pp. 27–47 [Online]. Available at https://doi.org/10.1080/1369183X.2017.1313106 (Accessed 15 March 2021).

Forest, J. J. F. (ed) (2006) *Homeland Security: Borders and Points of Entry*, Westport, CT, Praeger Security International.

France. French Parliament (2007) *Loi n° 2007-1631 du 20 novembre 2007 relative à la maîtrise de l'immigration, à l'intégration et à l'asile (1)*. Paris, Journal Officiel de la République Française (Law 2007-1631) [Online]. Available at https://www.legifrance.gouv.fr/loda/id/JORFTEXT000000524004/ (Accessed 14 March 2021).

Fukuyama, F. (2006) 'Identity, Immigration, and Liberal Democracy', *Journal of Democracy*, vol. 17, no. 2, pp. 5–20.

Gatta, G. L. (2021) 'Global Trends in "Crimmigration" Policies: From the EU to the USA', in Gatta, G. L., Mitsilegas, V. and Zirulia, S. (eds) *Controlling Immigration through Criminal Law: European and Comparative Perspectives on 'Crimmigration'*, London, Hart Publishing, pp. 47–80.

Germany. German Parliament (2022) *Staatsangehörigkeitsgesetz*. Berlin, Bundesgesetzblatt [Online]. Available at https://www.gesetze-im-internet.de/stag/BJNR005830913.html (Accessed 14 March 2021).

Germany. German Parliament (2007) *Gesetz zur Umsetzung Aufenthalts – und asylrechtlicher Richtlinien der Europäischen Union*. Berlin, Bundesgesetzblatt [Online]. Available at https://www.bmi.bund.de/SharedDocs/downloads/DE/gesetzestexte/Richtlinienumsetzungsgesetz.html (Accessed 15 March 2023).

Global Citizenship Observatory (2016) 'Two Thirds Failed the New Danish Citizenship Test,' 7 July [Online]. Available at https://globalcit.eu/two-thirds-failed-the-new-danish-citizenship-test/ (Accessed 15 March 2021).

Groenendijk, K. and van Oers, R. (2010) 'How Liberal Tests Are Does Not Merely Depend on Their Content, but Also Their Effects', in Joppke, C. and Bauböck, R. (eds) *How Liberal Are Citizenship Tests?*, Fiesole, European University Institute, pp. 9–10.

Hawley, C. (2006) 'Muslim Profiling: A German State Quizes Muslim Immigrants on Jews, Gays and Swim Lessons', *Der Spiegel*, 31 January [Online]. Available at https://www.spiegel.de/international/muslim-profiling-a-german-state-quizes-muslim-immigrants-on-jews-gays-and-swim-lessons-a-397482.html (Accessed 15 March 2021).

Her Majesty's Customs and Excise v Gerhart Schindler and Jörg Schindler [1994] Case C-275/92, European Court Reports 1994 I-01039. Hirschl, R. and Shachar, A. (2018) 'Competing Orders? The Challenge of Religion to Modern Constitutionalism', *The University of Chicago Law Review*, vol. 85, no. 2, pp. 425–455.

Horsti, K. and Pellander, S. (2015) 'Conditions of Cultural Citizenship: Intersections of Gender, Race and Age in Public Debates on Family Migration', *Citizenship*

Studies, vol. 19, no. 6–7, pp. 751–767 [Online]. Available at https://doi.org/10.1080/13621025.2015.1008998 (Accessed 15 March 2021).

Houtum, H. V. and Pijpers, R. (2007) 'The European Union as a Gated Community: The Two-Faced Border and Immigration Regime of the EU', *Antipode*, vol. 39, no. 2, pp. 291–309 [Online]. Available at https://doi.org/10.1111/j.1467-8330.2007.00522.x (Accessed 14 March 2021).

Joppke, C. and Morawska, E. T. (eds) (2003) *Toward Assimilation and Citizenship: Immigrants in Liberal Nation-States*, London, Palgrave Macmillan [Online]. Available at https://doi.org/10.1057/9780230554795 (Accessed 15 March 2021).

Karyotis, G. (2007) 'European Migration Policy in the Aftermath of September 11: The Security-migration Nexus', *Innovation: The European Journal of Social Science Research*, vol. 20, no. 1, pp. 1–17.

Kaya, B. (ed) (2002) *The Changing Face of Europe – Population Flows in the 20th Century* (trans. M. Campbell and C. Reynolds), Strasbourg, Council of Europe Publishing.

King, R. and Lulle, A. (2016) *Research on Migration: Facing Realities and Maximising Opportunities. A Policy Review*, Brussels, European Commission.

Klusmeyer, D. B. and Aleinikoff, T. A. (eds) (2000) *From Migrants to Citizens: Membership in a Changing World*, Washington, DC, Carnegie Endowment for International Peace.

Knights, S. (2007) *Freedom of Religion, Minorities, and the Law*, Oxford, Oxford University Press.

Koenig, M. (2005) 'Incorporating Muslim Migrants in Western Nation States – A Comparison of the United Kingdom, France, and Germany', *Journal of International Migration and Integration*, vol. 6, no. 2, pp. 219–234.

Koenig, M., Maliepaard, M. and Güveli, A. (2016) 'Religion and New Immigrants' Labor Market Entry in Western Europe', *Ethnicities*, vol. 16, no. 2, pp. 213–235 [Online]. Available at https://doi.org/10.1177/1468796815616159 (Accessed 15 March 2021).

Laqueur, W. (2007) *The Last Days of Europe: Epitaph for an Old Continent*, New York, Macmillan Publishers.

Leydet, D. (2017) 'Citizenship', in Zalta, E. N. (ed) *The Stanford Encyclopedia of Philosophy*, Stanford, CA, Metaphysics Research Lab, Stanford University [Online]. Available at https://plato.stanford.edu/entries/citizenship/

See for metadata: https://plato.stanford.edu/cgi-bin/encyclopedia/archinfo.cgi?entry=citizenship (Accessed 15 March 2021).

Löwenheim, O. and Gazit, O. (2009) 'Power and Examination: A Critique of Citizenship Tests,' *Security Dialogue*, vol. 40, no. 2, pp. 145–167 [Online]. Available at https://doi.org/10.1177/0967010609103074 (Accessed 14 March 2021).

Maltz, E. M. (2018) 'The Constitution and the Trump Travel Ban', *Lewis & Clark Law Review*, vol. 22, no. 2, pp. 391–412.

Markku Juhani Läärä, Cotswold Microsystems Ltd and Oy Transatlantic Software Ltd v Kihlakunnansyyttäjä (Jyväskylä) and Suomen Valtio (Finnish State) [1999] Case C-124/97, European Court Reports 1999 I-06067.

McCrea, R. (2010) *Religion and the Public Order of the European Union*, Oxford, Oxford University Press.

Meer, N. (2014) *Key Concepts in Race and Ethnicity*, Newbury Park, CA, SAGE Publications [Online]. Available at https://doi.org/10.4135/9781473906051 (Accessed 15 March 2021).

Menjívar, C. and Ness, I. (eds) (2019) *The Oxford Handbook of Migration Crises*, Oxford, Oxford University Press.

Michalowski, I. (2011) 'Required to Assimilate? The Content of Citizenship Tests in Five Countries', *Citizenship Studies*, vol. 15, no. 6–7, pp. 749–768 [Online]. Available at https://doi.org/10.1080/13621025.2011.600116 (Accessed 15 March 2021).

Michalowski, I. (2010a) 'Citizenship Tests and Traditions of State Interference with Cultural Diversity', in Joppke, C. and Bauböck, R. (eds) *How Liberal Are Citizenship Tests?* Fiesole, European University Institute, pp. 5–8.

Michalowski, I. (2010b) 'Integration Tests in Germany. A Communitarian Approach?', in van Oers, R., Ersbøll, E. and Kostakopoulou, D. (eds) *A Re-Definition of Belonging? Language and Integration Tests in Europe*, Leiden, Brill-Nijhoff, pp. 185–210.

Miller, D. (2000) *Citizenship and National Identity*, Cambridge, Polity Press.

Ministry of Social Affairs and Employment (n.d.) 'Basic Civic Integration Examination Abroad' [Online]. Available at https://www.naarnederland.nl/en (Accessed 14 March 2021).

Mitrotti, A. (2019) 'Il rovesciamento di prospettiva sulla misura di revoca della cittadinanza nel "dibattuto" Decreto sicurezza "Salvini"', *Osservatorio Costituzionale*, vol. 13, no. 1–2, pp. 65–77.

Motilla, A. (2018) 'Security and Religious Radicalization. Securitization of Islam in Europe', *Stato, Chiese e Pluralismo Confessionale*, no. 1, pp. 1–20.

Motomura, H. (2020) 'The New Migration Law: Migrants, Refugees, and Citizens in an Anxious Age', *Cornell Law Review*, vol. 105, no. 2, pp. 457–548.

Murdoch, J. (2012) *Protecting the Right to Freedom of Thought, Conscience and Religion Under the European Convention on Human Rights*, Strasbourg, Council of Europe.

Murphy, C. C. (2019) 'EU Counter-terrorism Law: What Kind of Exemplar of Transnational Law?', *Cambridge Yearbook of European Legal Studies*, vol. 21, pp. 217–242 [Online]. Available at https://doi.org/10.1017/cel.2019.7 (Accessed 15 March 2021).

Netherlands. Princess Beatrix (2006) *Wet Inburgering in het Buitenland [Civic Integration Abroad Act]*. The Hague, The Royal Household [Online]. Available at https://wetten.overheid.nl/BWBR0023204/2006-03-15 (Accessed 14 March 2021).

Ninatti, S. and Gennusa, M. E. (2016) 'Cittadinanza europea e religioni', *Quaderni di Diritto e Politica Ecclesiastica*, vol. 19, no. 1, pp. 55–72.

Njaim, M. (2018) 'Migration Dilemma: Security versus Humanitarian Nexus', *Granite Journal: A Postgraduate Interdisciplinary Journal*, vol. 2, pp. 25–32.

Orgad, L. (2010) 'Illiberal Liberalism: Cultural Restrictions on Migration and Access to Citizenship in Europe', *American Journal of Comparative Law*, vol. 58, no. 1, pp. 53–105 [Online]. Available at https://doi.org/10.5131/ajcl.2009.0004 (Accessed 15 March 2021).

Pedroza, L. (2019) *Citizenship Beyond Nationality: Immigrants' Right to Vote Across the World*, Philadelphia, University of Pennsylvania Press.

Pillai, S. and Williams, G. (2017) 'Twenty-first Century Banishment: Citizenship Stripping in Common Law Nations', *International & Comparative Law Quarterly*, vol. 66, no. 3, pp. 521–555 [Online]. Available at https://doi.org/10.1017/S0020589317000021 (Accessed 15 March 2021).

Pin, A. (2019) 'Islam e Costituzione italiana: Il ruolo della cittadinanza', *Quaderni di Diritto e Politica Ecclesiastica*, no. 1, pp. 49–64 [Online]. Available at https://doi.org/10.1440/93549 (Accessed 14 March 2021).

Questore di Verona v Diego Zenatti [1999] Case C-67/98, European Court Reports 1999 I-07289.

Raimondo, F. (2019) 'Il privilegio della cittadinanza: La revoca come strumento di contrasto al terrorismo. La riforma italiana nel contesto europeo', *Quaderni Costituzionali*, no. 2, pp. 416–419 [Online]. Available at https://doi.org/10.1439/93595 (Accessed 15 March 2021).

Sager, A. (ed) (2016) *The Ethics and Politics of Immigration: Core Issues and Emerging Trends*, Lanham, MD, Rowman & Littlefield.

S.A.S. v France [2014] Case 43835/11, European Court of Human Rights.

Scholten, P. W. A., Entzinger, H., Kofman, E., Hollomey, C., Lechner, C., Vacchelli, E. and Kraler, A. (2012) *Integration from Abroad? Perception and Impacts of Pre-Entry Tests for Third Country Nationals*, Brussels, European Commission [Online]. Available at https://www.researchgate.net/publication/262344915_INTEGRATION_FROM_ABROAD_PERCEPTION_AND_IMPACTS_OF_PRE-ENTRY_TESTS_FOR_THIRD_COUNTRY_NATIONALS (Accessed 15 March 2021).

Shachar, A. (ed) (2020) *The Shifting Border: Legal Cartographies of Migration and Mobility: Ayelet Shachar in Dialogue*, Manchester, Manchester University Press.

Shachar, A. (2001) *Multicultural Jurisdictions: Cultural Differences and Women's Rights*, Cambridge, Cambridge University Press.

Shachar, A., Bauboeck, R., Bloemraad, I. and Vink, M. (eds) (2017) *The Oxford Handbook of Citizenship*, Oxford, Oxford University Press.

Shaw-Taylor, Y. and McCall, L. (2020) *Immigration, Assimilation, and Border Security*, 2nd edn, Lanham, MD, Bernan Press.

Soysal, Y. N. (1997) 'Changing Parameters of Citizenship and Claims-making: Organized Islam in European Public Spheres', *Theory and Society*, vol. 26, no. 4, pp. 509–527.

Stewart, E. and Mulvey, G. (2014) 'Seeking Safety beyond Refuge: The Impact of Immigration and Citizenship Policy Upon Refugees in the UK', *Journal of Ethnic and Migration Studies*, vol. 40, no. 7, pp. 1023–1039 [Online]. Available at https://doi.org/10.1080/1369183X.2013.836960 (Accessed 14 March 2021).

Temperman, J., Gunn, T. J. and Evans, M. D. (eds) (2019) *The European Court of Human Rights and the Freedom of Religion or Belief: The 25 Years Since Kokkinakis*, Leiden, Brill-Nijhoff.

The Local (2021) 'Citizenship: Foreigners in Denmark Could Face Interviews to Test "Danish values"', 9 February [Online]. Available at https://www.thelocal.dk/20210209/citizenship-applicants-should-attend-interviews-to-test-danish-values-proposal/ (Accessed 15 March 2021).

Torpey, J. (1999) *The Invention of the Passport: Surveillance, Citizenship and the State*, Cambridge, Cambridge University Press [Online]. Available at https://doi.org/10.1017/CBO9780511520990 (Accessed 15 March 2021).

Triandafyllidou, A. and Maroukis, T. (2012) *Migrant Smuggling: Irregular Migration from Asia and Africa to Europe*, London, Palgrave Macmillan.

Trump, D. J. (2017a) *Executive Order 13769: Protecting the Nation from Foreign Terrorist Entry into the United States*, Washington, DC, Executive Office of the President [Online]. Available at https://www.federalregister.gov/documents/2017/02/01/2017-02281/protecting-the-nation-from-foreign-terrorist-entry-into-the-united-states (Accessed 14 March 2021).

Trump, D. J. (2017b) *Executive Order 13780: Protecting the Nation from Foreign Terrorist Entry into the United States*, Washington, DC, Executive Office of the President [Online]. Available at https://www.federalregister.gov/documents/2017/03/09/2017-04837/protecting-the-nation-from-foreign-terrorist-entry-into-the-united-states (Accessed 14 March 2021).

Trump v Hawaii [2018] 138 S. Ct. 2392.

Uitz, R. (2007) *Freedom of Religion in European Constitutional and International Case Law*, Strasbourg, Council of Europe Publishing.

United States Congress (1917) 'An Act to Regulate the Immigration of Aliens to, and the Residence of Aliens in, the United States,' *U.S. Statutes at Large*, vol. 39, pp. 874–898.

United States Congress (1907) 'An Act to Establish a Bureau of Immigration and Naturalization, and to Provide for a Uniform Rule for the Naturalization of Aliens throughout the United States. Approved June 29, 1906', *The American Journal of International Law*, vol. 1, no. 1, Supplement: Official Documents, pp. 31–47 [Online]. Available at https://www.jstor.org/stable/2212339 (Accessed 15 March 2021).

van Hear, N., Brubaker, R. and Bessa, T. (2009) *Managing Mobility for Human Development: The Growing Salience of Mixed Migration*, New York, United Nations Development Program [Online]. Available at https://hdr.undp.org/content/managing-mobility-human-development (Accessed 15 March 2021).

van Oers, R. (2014) *Deserving Citizenship: Citizenship Tests in Germany, the Netherlands and the United Kingdom*, Leiden, Martinus Nijhoff Publishers.

Vedaschi, A. (2018) 'Il diritto alla verità e le misure antiterrorismo nella giurisprudenza della Corte di Strasburgo', in Forni, L. and Vettor, T. (eds) *Sicurezza e Libertà in Tempi di Terrorismo Globale*, Torino, Italy, G. Giappichelli Editore, pp. 167–190.

Viola, L. (2019) 'La revoca della cittadinanza dopo il decreto Salvini: Profili processuali e (nuovi) cantieri aperti', *Federalismi.it*, no. 13, pp. 1–19.

von Busekist, A. and Boudou, B. (2018) 'Language Proficiency and Migration: An Argument against Testing,' in Gazzola, M., Templin, T. and Wickström, B. (eds) *Language Policy and Linguistic Justice: Economic, Philosophical and Sociolinguistic Approaches*, New York, Springer, pp. 189–208.

Weinar, A., Bonjour, S. and Zhyznomirska, L. (2018) *The Routledge Handbook of the Politics of Migration in Europe*, Abingdon, United Kingdom, Routledge [Online]. Available at https://doi.org/10.4324/9781315512853 (Accessed 15 March 2021).

Welfens, N. and Pisarevskaya, A. (2020) 'The "Others" amongst "Them" – Selection Categories in European Resettlement and Humanitarian Admission Programmes', in Jesse, M. (ed) *European Societies, Migration, and the Law: The 'Others' Amongst 'Us'*, Cambridge, Cambridge University Press, pp. 81–104 [Online]. Available at https://doi.org/10.1017/9781108767637.006 (Accessed 15 March 2021).

Wonders, N. A. and Jones, L. C. (2019) 'Doing and Undoing Borders: The Multiplication of Citizenship, Citizenship Performances, and Migration as Social Movement', *Theoretical Criminology*, vol. 23, no. 2, pp. 136–155 [Online]. Available at https://doi.org/10.1177/1362480618802297 (Accessed 14 March 2021).
Wright, S. (2008) 'Citizenship Tests in Europe – Editorial introduction', *International Journal on Multicultural Societies*, vol. 10, no. 1, pp. 1–9.
Yvonne van Duyn v Home Office [1974] Case 41-74, European Court Reports 1974-01337.
Zanfrini, L. (ed) (2020) *Migrants and Religion: Paths, Issues, and Lenses*, Leiden, Brill.
Zedner, L. (2010) 'Security, the State, and the Citizen: The Changing Architecture of Crime Control', *New Criminal Law Review*, vol. 13, no. 2, pp. 379–403.

9

RELIGION, CITIZENSHIP REVOCATION, AND FOREIGN COMBATANT LAWS

The Illiberal Turn

Joshua M. Roose

1 Introduction

This chapter will view the intersection of freedom of religion and citizenship through an issue at the cutting edge of the national security paradigm: foreign combatants fighting for a religious cause in other nations. The rise and subsequent fall of the Islamic State Movement led to several legislative, judicial, and philosophical challenges across Western contexts. A small, but not insignificant number of locally born Muslim citizens not only would turn their back on their country of birth but would leave to fight, kill, and often die in the conflict in the name of a movement explicitly hostile to Western liberal democracy. This raised questions about not only the relationship between citizenship and loyalty, but how these concepts related to religious adherence and the management of potential threats carried out in the name of religion.

While some primarily European states adopted policies of reintegration, others including Australia and the UK introduced legislation to strip citizenship from those proven to have fought in said conflicts, a move designed to simultaneously punish and deter. This chapter demonstrates that in addition to targeting terrorism, these new laws, through their wide potential application, extend too far, threatening freedom of speech and freedom of religion. Furthermore, as found by the Australian High Court in June 2022, they were, in some forms, unconstitutional. While these laws may currently target Muslim communities, they have much wider potential applicability to other religious minorities. Citizenship laws are even more problematic in Asian contexts, justifying the extremes of exclusion and violence resulting in the persecution of Muslim communities. This chapter explores the legislative,

DOI: 10.4324/9781003453086-13

jurisprudential, and liberal philosophical challenges of this decision by a group of select Western and non-Western states and considers implications for freedom of religion on a global scale.

2 Islamic State

In examining the relationship between citizenship law and national security, it is important to first consider the stated reason for the mobilisation of new legislation on a global scale. The rapid rise and fall (and now imminent military defeat) of the Islamic State Movement has been one of the most significant developments in global politics this century, and in the context of Islamic politics, of the past 1,000 years. The declaration of the *Khilafah* (Caliphate) on 29 June 2014 by Islamic State leader *Abu Bakr al-Baghdadi* (a former detainee at Abu Ghraib) served as a beacon to Salafi jihadists worldwide, signalling the emergence of the first such entity since the fall of the Ottoman Empire almost 90 years earlier. *Al-Baghdadi* signalled the intent of the Islamic State to conquer Rome and Spain (past historical ambitions for Islamic armies) and subsequently urged Muslims to conduct *hijra* (immigration) to the Islamic State, centred in the Syrian city of *Raqqa*.

An estimated 30,000 men and women had heeded the call from around the world, including up to 6,000 from within Western Muslim communities in the UK, Europe, North America, and Australia. These men would become known as Islamic State "foreign fighters" and the phenomenon of Western-born Muslims joining the movement would cause considerable anger and angst amongst politicians, media figures, and the wider public alike. The Islamic State immediately became synonymous with extreme acts of savagery, atrocity, and the rape and forced marriages of women in conquered territories, most notably women of the *Yazidi,* a monotheistic, Kurdish-speaking people native to northern Mesopotamia. This violence against the Yazidi has been labelled as genocide by the United Nations and combined with attacks against other religious minorities indicates that the Islamic State stood antithetically opposed to religious freedom. It very quickly became clear to intelligence agencies, scholars, and the world's media alike that Western Muslims and in particular Western Muslim men who had migrated to join the Islamic State were firmly at the fore of many acts of atrocity, torture, rape, and sexual enslavement (Roose, 2020).

The Islamic State was quick to exploit the presence of Western Muslims, less for their fighting ability than for propaganda value. Footage and photos of Western Muslims burning their passports were used to demonstrate a rejection of their citizenship and loyalty to the countries of their birth. Western nations rushed to bolster national security legislation, in particular those who had joined the Islamic State Movement, with many, in particular the English-speaking anglophone countries, seeking to strip them of citizenship and to prevent them from returning. Muslims from non-Western nations including Tunisia, Central Asia, and Chechnya made up the majority of foreign fighters with the Islamic State Movement.

On first appearance, this appears to be a prima facie case of sovereign states introducing counter-terrorism legislation to deal with the clear and present danger of a terrorist threat from returning foreign fighters. However, as a reference to many other cases of foreign combatants indicates, this is an unprecedented and inconsistently applied approach and, notwithstanding the illegality of the actions of combatants, raises important questions about the intersection of freedom of religion, revocation of citizenship, and the place of minority Muslim communities on a global scale.

3 Foreign Fighters

Individuals fighting in another country for ideological purposes or financial remuneration as mercenaries has a long history. From the medieval Crusades to French, German, and Polish fighters in the American Revolutionary War and the involvement of international volunteer brigades in the Spanish Civil War, there are many examples in history of individuals fighting on foreign soil in wars in the service of a cause other than the national interest of their country of birth.

More recent examples include the attraction of Muslims around the world to fight in the Jihad against Soviet Forces in Afghanistan, the participation of Serbs and Bosnians from both sides of the religious divide in the Bosnian War (1992–1995), and Chechnya. Most recently, in addition to the Islamic State, we have seen young men from around the world participate in the Ukrainian conflict as volunteers.

In the movement of individuals to join conflicts, we have seen the institutionalisation, by states and corporations, of the "foreign fighter" from mercenary "contractor" armies such as Blackwater, with no national status aside from incorporation in a state, to the active incorporation of foreigners into national militaries, including the British Gurkhas, the French Foreign Legion, and inter-military exchanges, which has included participation in combat serving with other nations. In other cases, dual nationals serve in the armed forces of the birthplace of their parents, sometimes despite never having physically visited the nation, for example, Greece, Lebanon, and Israel. It is clear that the notion of two clearly defined combatant forces based solely on nationality in any conflict has never had a basis in reality.

It is perhaps for this reason that the concept of the foreign fighter has no clear-cut definition in international law. As Heinsch (2016) asserts, the 1998 Rome Statute of the International Criminal Court (ICC Statute) does not mention the term "foreign fighter" nor do the statutes of any other international criminal tribunals. While bearing similarities to the definition of mercenaries within the Additional Protocol I to the Geneva Convention, foreign fighters fight for ideological and/or religious reasons and the definition is focused on international state-based conflicts, putting foreign fighters beyond the scope of international criminal law (Heinsch, 2016).

It is for this reason, among others, including the difficulty of substantiating allegations when all activities were conducted in foreign conflict zones beyond the reach of surveillance and evidence gatherers and the risk of attack by highly trained returned fighters, that national governments have framed their responses to citizens fighting overseas in the context of national security. However, responses have differed significantly amongst the Western democracies between those seeking to repatriate and reintegrate individuals that joined and fought with the Islamic State Movement and those seeking to strip them of their citizenship and prevent their return. Traditionally, and particularly since the formation of the United Nations, the revocation of citizenship has been associated with totalitarian, not democratic states (Herzog, 2010, p. 88). Moves by liberal democratic states to do so require particular scrutiny.

4 Citizenship

The concept of citizenship is a central feature of the modern nation-state. It occupies a central political status and is inscribed in both constitutions and legislation that articulates who – and who may not – be granted it. Traditional notions of citizenship grounded in a sociological approach view citizenship as a "status bestowed on those who are full members of a community" grounded in equal rights and responsibilities. Citizenship is considered to be a human right – "the right to have rights" through an unwritten, but tangible social contract between the state and individual (Arendt, 1951).

Citizenship has traditionally been associated with a universalist approach, outlined in the work of sociologist T. H. Marshall (Leydet, 2017). Marshall regarded citizenship as a "status, bestowed on those who are full members of a community," stating further that "all who possess the status are equal with respect to the rights and duties with which the state is endowed" (Marshall, 1950, pp. 28–29).

A differentiated approach to citizenship has taken hold across Western liberal democracies since the late 1980s that has been grounded in the acknowledgement of the political relevance of differences including class, race, gender, and sexuality (Leydet, 2017). This has seen the emergence of a pluralist approach to citizenship, with recognition of difference essential to the demonstration of respect for citizenship rights. A vast body of law centred on countering discrimination and protecting minorities from the majority came into tension with cultural expectations of conformity, leading to tensions between progressives who promote diversity and differentiated citizenship and conservatives promoting a universalist citizenship centred on some form of national homogeneity. This has not been limited to Western contexts. Globalisation and the use of new technologies including social media has seen this broad division between those promoting differential citizenship and those promoting universalism of rights and responsibilities spread globally. In developing contexts approaches such as multiculturalism and differentiated citizenship are typically viewed by the political establishment as the imposition of Western liberal values and are associated with calls for the respect of human rights including freedom of religion.

5 The Illiberal Turn: Citizenship as Weapon

Over 130 nations have passed legislation making the revocation of citizenship possible for treason or fighting for a foreign government. The majority of these states identify national security grounds as the primary reason for such legislation. However, a number of researchers have claimed that such measures have limited efficacy and carry more symbolic than practical weight. Benton and Banulescu-Bogdan (2019) argue that citizenship revocation can serve to "allay public anxiety" and "sends a strong signal that people who have reneged on their obligations as citizens are no longer entitled to the protection of the state." Pillai and Williams argue that both rationales "take as their starting point the idea that recent events have produced an increased number of 'undesirable citizens,'" and that this requires a legislative response (2018, p. 855). This is clear across Western contexts. Speaking in 2014 British Prime Minister David Cameron stated:

> We will always take whatever action is necessary to keep the British people safe here at home...We are stopping suspects from travelling by seizing passports. We're barring foreign nationals from re-entering the UK. We're depriving people of citizenship and we are legislating so we can prosecute people for all terrorist activity, even where that activity takes place overseas.
>
> *(2014)*

In the second reading speech to the *Australian Citizenship Amendment (Allegiance to Australia) Bill 2015*, the Australian Minister for Home Affairs stated:

> The *Australian Citizenship Amendment (Allegiance to Australia) Bill 2015* implements the Prime Minister's commitment to address the challenges posed by dual citizens who betray Australia by participating in serious terrorism-related activities. This Bill emphasises the central importance of allegiance to Australia in the concept of citizenship.

> Australian citizenship is something to be treasured. It is a common bond which unites us all, whether we were born here or chose to make Australia our home. Australian citizenship involves a commitment to this country, its people and its democratic rights and privileges. Australian citizenship should not be taken lightly.
>
> We face a heightened and complex security environment. Regrettably, some of the most pressing threats to the security of the nation and the safety of the Australian community come from citizens engaged in terrorism. It is now appropriate to modernise provisions concerning loss of citizenship to respond to current terrorist threats. The world has changed so our laws should change accordingly.
>
> *(Dutton, 2015)*

Speaking at the Munk Debate, a policy debate held in Toronto in 2015, Canadian Prime Minister Stephen Harper, who introduced laws repealing citizenship, stated simply, "We will and have revoked the citizenship of people who are convicted of terrorist offenses who do not need to remain to be our citizens. There's no reason why we would not do that" (Maclean's, 2015).

The willingness to revoke citizenship on the grounds that foreign fighters have demonstrated disloyalty to their home country is common across Europe. Speaking in 2019, Danish Prime Minister Mette Frederickson, from the Social Democrats, a traditionally leftist party that has increasingly moved to the political right on social issues, would state the reasons for legislation targeting citizens of dual citizenship: "These are people who turned their back on Denmark and fought with violence against our democracy and freedom. They pose a threat to our security. They are unwanted in Denmark" (Skydsgaard and Jacobsen, 2019).

Citizenship in these contexts has been weaponised and turned against citizens of the nation that are considered to have demonstrated disloyalty by fighting for the Islamic State. This requires a paradoxical approach from primarily right-wing governments, who plead their right to revoke citizenship, yet do not want to meet the responsibilities as nation-states in dealing with illegal behaviour by their own citizens. Furthermore, other nationals fighting as mercenaries or with other groups have avoided the close scrutiny of these governments. These same governments demand protection of freedom of speech, whilst rejecting differentiated expressions of citizenship that challenge national homogeneity.

While some of this is grounded in legitimate national security concerns, all too often this is only the basis for an extended effort by modern nation-states to deny belonging to certain groups considered outside the ideal national community. Islam has become conflated with terrorism and Muslim communities, already subjected to surveillance, media hostility, and securitisation, have become the primary population group targeted by the new laws (Roose, 2016). This has resulted in a "guilt by association," no matter how removed, with implications for freedom of religious expression in public life.

6 Citizenship Revocation in the UK and Australia

In seeking to understand the impact of citizenship revocation upon freedom of religion, particularly as it impacts Muslims, it is important to examine the legal pathways in greater depth.

6.1 UK

The severe shortage of labour power in Britain following World War II was a key impetus for opening migration to Ireland and non-white nations. The increasing visibility of migration, first from the Caribbean and then from South Asia, caused considerable consternation, particularly from the political right. Many of these migrants moved after the partition of India and Pakistan in 1947. In 1968, the Labour government sought to introduce the *Race Relations Act* (1968), which was to supersede the *Race Relations Act* (1965). The 1968 Act made discrimination on the grounds of colour, race, ethnic, or national origin illegal, and it applied to the provision of housing, employment, and the provision of public services. This would again be replaced by the *Race Relations Act* (1976).

In the context of this increasing institutionalisation of multiculturalism, the number of British Muslims would grow from just 50,000 in 1961 (0.11% of the population) to an estimated 3.3 million (approximately 5% of the population) by 2017 (*Office for National Statistics*, 2018; Peach and Gale, 2003). Accompanying this growth, multiculturalism, integration, and the meaning of Britishness were increasingly scrutinised in public and political spheres and citizenship became a meta-issue (Mantu, 2015).

The *British Nationality Act* (1981) abolished the 1948 definitions of British citizenship, limiting the right to reside in the UK to those that possessed British citizenship. It has, because of successive expansions in scope, been dramatically expanded in 2001 (post-9/11), in 2006 (post the London bombings), and in 2014 (post Islamic State Foreign fighters emerging as a significant problem).

In its current form, the *British Nationality Act* enables the Secretary of State to revoke the citizenship of a naturalised individual, even if consequently they become stateless (Great Britain. *British Nationality Act 1981*, s. 40(4)). This legislation allows for such measures where they align with a very broadly defined "public good," namely, that an individual conducted themselves "in a manner seriously prejudicial to the vital interests of the United Kingdom." This is a significantly relaxed standard compared to previous manifestation of the legislation and places significant power in the hands of the Secretary of State.

The Act primarily targets dual citizens – individuals for whom another citizenship is already held, resulting in the creation of different forms of punishment. In this case, while avenues of appeal are open to a decision of the Home Secretary, the decision relies upon their ministerial discretion. Appeals are likely to be highly constrained if the individual is overseas when their citizenship is stripped (prohibiting their return to contest the appeal) or impacted. Furthermore, judges may refer to the Executive specifically secretive briefs that are not open to the wider public to make their decisions.

Between 1970 and 2001, the UK only revoked the citizenship of one person. Between 2016 and 2018, it revoked the citizenship of 138 individuals primarily under the "public good" definition. This concept of the "public good" has significant implications for how liberal democratic citizenship is defined and weighed not by courts, but by elected officials with a political motivation.

Amongst the most notable cases of citizenship revocation has been that of 21-year-old Shamima Begum, who joined the Islamic State Movement as a 15-year-old in 2015. Begum was found nine months pregnant in a Syrian Refugee camp in 2019 having previously lost two children. Her citizenship was revoked on national security grounds in 2019, and her right to be physically present in the UK to present her case was rejected by the Supreme Court. This has been considered a human rights violation, denying her human dignity, recourse to procedural fairness, and access to substantive justice (Masters and Regilme, 2020).

6.2 Australia

The Immigration Restriction Act (1901), known colloquially as the "White Australia Policy," effectively closed Australia to immigration from non-white nations from 1901 to 1972 (Roose, 2020). This received bipartisan support from across the political spectrum. It was not until December 1973 and the election of the Whitlam Labor government, after decades of Conservative rule, that the White Australia Policy was renounced and the official adoption of multiculturalism actively encouraging a differentiated form of citizenship commenced.

Until the end of World War II, numbers of Muslims in Australia fluctuated between approximately 2,000 and 4,000 until the influx of refugees from Europe in 1947 including Muslims that met the "white threshold" (Omar and Allen, 1996, p. 23). In 1947 the number of Muslims in Australia stood at 2,704 (0.04% of the population) (Australian Bureau of Statistics, 1947). By 2016 the Australian Muslim population stood at 604,200 (2.6% of the total population) (Australian Bureau of Statistics, 2016).

The move to make the revocation of citizenship a key platform in counter-terrorism legislation was initiated by the political right. Since 1948 there had been a total of just 44 revocations under section 24 of the Australian Citizenship Act 1948. A wide raft of national security legislation has been consistently introduced since the turn of the century in the context of the "war on terror." This has led to 66 new legislative measures being introduced at the federal level – more than any other nation on earth. This stood alongside the introduction of citizenship tests and an Australian "values statement" all designed to solidify the boundary around acceptable Australian behaviours.

In December 2015, the Australian Federal Parliament passed the *Australian Citizenship Amendment (Allegiance to Australia) Act 2015* bringing in an expanded scope of powers for the government to revoke citizenship within the *Australian Citizenship Act 2007*.

This legislation enabled the Minister to revoke an individual's citizenship where their actions are considered to "breach their allegiance to Australia," a concept not dissimilar to the UK framing of acting in a "manner prejudicial to the interests of the United Kingdom." The Second Reading speech of this *Allegiance to Australia* Act by the Home Affairs Minister Peter Dutton stated:

> In conclusion, this Bill deals with the threat caused by those who have engaged in terrorist-related conduct that is contrary to their allegiance to Australia. It formally removes a person from the Australian community when they themselves have breached their allegiance to Australia.
>
> *(Dutton, 2015)*

While direct acts of terrorism were covered by the laws, the broader language utilised and discretion available to the Minister across the suite of national security legislation has been widely critiqued. On the operation of the "advocating terrorism" offence introduced in 2014 into section 80.2C of the Australian Criminal Code by the *Counter-Terrorism Legislation Amendment (Foreign Fighters) Act*, for example, advocacy of terrorism (however conceived) can be grounds for criminality and, subsequently, loss of citizenship. The concept of advocacy is particularly problematic, enabling law enforcement to target any individuals *perceived* to be supporting terrorism at home or abroad. There is no criterion of proof beyond reasonable doubt as in a criminal proceeding; rather, the Minister must be satisfied on "reasonable grounds" (Brooks, 2016, p. 121). In his analysis of this small, but important change to the Criminal Code, Brooks argues:

> [U]nlike comparable offences abroad, s 80.2C seeks to conflate advocating terrorism with treason and derivative offences. The concepts embodied by terrorism and those embodied by treason, sedition or treachery overlap, but they are not congruent. Indeed, it is precisely those crimes against

> the state for which high thresholds should be retained. The criminalisation of advocacy in any form is likely to have a profound chilling effect on free speech – whether or not that speech is formally captured by the offence. That chilling effect is undoubtedly exacerbated by implications of subversiveness or disloyalty, and efforts to expand the laws of subversion should be treated with suspicion. Sedition and urging violence should be the low watermark of subversive speech, not the high watermark.... Between criminalising innocuous speech and toying with treason, there is little to commend the design of the new offence.
>
> *(2016, p. 121)*

Most concerning here was the use of ministerial discretion to revoke citizenship on broadly defined, often secretive national security grounds and, in the Australian context, the conflation of advocacy of terrorism (which could be broadly defined anywhere in the world) and treason. The use of these laws has been focused primarily on Australian Muslims accused of terrorism-related crimes; however, the ramifications extend well beyond these individuals towards the whole community, with the threat of revocation of citizenship for those that speak outside the boundaries of official acceptable narratives about the place of Islam in Australia or persecution of Muslims in other nations. Such speech is part and parcel of the concern with Islam (and indeed many faiths) for the political circumstances of shared holders of the faith.

A notable case of revocation in Australia is that of Melbourne-born and raised Islamic State propagandist Neil Prakash, a convert to Islam. Prakash grew up in Melbourne's outer south-eastern suburbs and became radicalised at a local Islamic bookshop before departing to join the Islamic State Movement. Specifically targeted by the new suite of legislation, this was a clear-cut case of the abdication of responsibility for the actions of an Australian citizen by the Australian government.

On 08 June 2022, the majority of the High Court of Australia invalidated the ability of the Minister to revoke the citizenship of dual nationals engaged in terrorism-related conduct (Parliament of Australia, 2022). This legislation has been challenged on constitutional grounds, including that it conferred upon the Minister the "exclusive judicial function of adjudging and punishing criminal guilt" (High Court of Australia, 2021). This ruling would only impact the new Labor government, with the previous government that had instituted the law voted out of power in May 2022. Tellingly, it did not stimulate any wider debate about the impact of these laws on Muslim communities.

7 Asia

Citizenship has been similarly weaponised on a global scale in recent years, no more so than in Asia. The rise of demagogic strongmen on the one hand

and established autocratic regimes on the other that have rolled back democracy, discarded it entirely, or enacted alternative autocratic systems of government have placed citizenship – who belongs to the imagined national community and who does not – as central to narratives of national progress.

Three examples, Myanmar, China, and India, stand as particularly poignant examples of how this preoccupation with citizenship and conflation with the notion of internal "threat" from Muslims has resulted in extremes of violence and subjugation of freedom of religion and human rights.

7.1 Myanmar

Rohingya Muslims have lived in Myanmar for over 1,000 years. However, Rohingya Muslims were denied citizenship during the British colonial period, and this continued through various iterations of government, most recently the military junta that has ruled over the country in one form or another (apart from a small period of time from 2015 to 2020) since 1962. Human Rights Watch (2000) has noted:

> Despite being able to trace Rohingya history to the eighth century, Burmese law does not recognize the ethnic minority as one of the national races. Many Rohingya families migrated to and settled in Arakan during the British colonial period which would immediately exclude them from citizenship. Even for those Rohingya whose families settled in the region before 1823, moreover, the onerous burden of proof has made it nearly impossible for all but a handful to secure citizenship.

The estimated one million Rohingya Muslims in Myanmar have been concentrated primarily in Rakhine State and have been represented by a Buddhist elite as Bengali Muslims. They are denied citizenship by the *Pyithu Hluttaw [Citizenship] Law No. 4* of 1982. This Act defines those ethnic groups that are considered citizens. It denies citizenship to children born to those considered non-citizens. Chapter 2, sections 3 and 4, states:

> Nationals such as the Kachin, Kayah, Karen, Chin, Burman, Mon, Rakhine or Shan and ethnic groups as have settled in any of the territories included within the State as their permanent home from a period anterior to 1185 B.E., 1823 A.D. are Burma citizens.
>
> *(Myanmar. [Citizenship] Law No. 4, 1982)*

The Council of State may decide whether any ethnic group is national or not.

Arraiza and Vonk (2017, p. 3) note that this law adopts

> an essentialist and dichotomist understanding of Burmese Society which pursues nation-building through the exclusion of the ethnic "other"

> (particularly persons of Indian descent – both Muslim, Hindu, Sikh and other religions) who are considered an inheritance of Burma's colonial past as a province of British India.

The uneven application of the law has had the effect of rendering entire communities stateless (Arraiza and Vonk, 2017, p. 13). It has been the Rohingya Muslims of Rakhine State that have been the core focus of the enactment of these laws. Human Rights Watch (2000) notes:

> Rohingya who cannot provide "conclusive evidence" of their lineage or history of residence find themselves ineligible for any class of citizenship. And because of their formal legal status as resident foreigners, Rohingya are subject to restrictions on their freedom of movement, are denied access to higher education, and are restricted from holding public office.

In late 2016 the Myanmar armed forces commenced a campaign against the Rohingya including arson of entire Rohingya villages, extrajudicial killing, rape, and infanticide, killing that has been described by the United Nations as Ethnic Cleansing and Genocide (Office of the United Nations High Commissioner for Human Rights, 2018). It has been estimated that up to 745,000 Rohingya Muslims (including over 400,000 children) have fled Myanmar, making them stateless in refugee camps in Bangladesh (*United Nations Office for the Coordination of Humanitarian Affairs*, 2018). In early 2020, the International Court of Justice at the Hague imposed emergency provisional measures on Myanmar instructing the government to abide by the provisions stipulated in the 1948 *Convention on the Prevention and Punishment of the Crime of Genocide* (*UN News*, 2020; United Nations, 1948).

7.2 China

Islam has existed in the nation we now refer to as China since the earliest days of the faith 1,400 years ago. The Xinjiang province was annexed to China in the 1880s, though it has historically been part of East Turkestan, in Muslim-majority central Asia. The attempt to settle Han Chinese in the Muslim-majority region of approximately 12.71 million Uyghur (of a total population of 24.86 million (Global Times, 2021; Yu, 2021)) has caused tensions over the years and a series of small but violent revolts against the central government. One such rebellion occurred in Xinjiang in 1990 where arms were supplied by the Afghan Mujahadeen. This is considered the first serious rebellion (Israeli, 2010, p. 91). Another rebellion in 1993 indicated a significant underlying discontent at the central government's attempts to control the region.

In subsequent years, the Chinese government would place the region's Muslims under severely oppressive laws under the guise of attacking "Islamist terrorists" including language and education restrictions and the demolition of Muslim holy sites. The Chinese state would claim that the region's Muslims were linked first to Al-Qaeda and later to the Islamic State and that militant Islam was spreading in the region, necessitating their intervention.

In recent years extensive international attention has been paid to the treatment of the Uyghur Muslim population in the Xinjiang province of China. Citizenship in China falls firmly within the concept of nationality. In this context, citizenship has been used not only to exclude, but to forcibly integrate a population portrayed as a national security threat. A new National Security Law from the Ministry of National Defence of the People's Republic of China titled *National Security Law of the People's Republic of China* was passed by the National People's Congress in 2015. Article 2 of the new law defines "national security" as:

> [A] status in which the regime, sovereignty, unity, territorial integrity, welfare of the people, sustainable economic and social development, and other major interests of the state are relatively not faced with any danger and not threatened internally or externally and the capability to maintain a sustained security status.
>
> *(China Info Services, 2018)*

This law demonstrates potentially limitless scope to any individual or group deemed to challenge the one-party Communist regime. The concept of "danger" is similarly extremely broad and could conceivably range from a physical armed threat to merely existing and practising an alternate value system to that propagated by the government. UN High Commissioner for Human Rights Zeid Ra'ad Al Hussein stated shortly after the law's adoption in 2015:

> This law raises many concerns due to its extraordinarily broad scope coupled with the vagueness of its terminology and definitions. As a result, it leaves the door wide open to further restrictions of the rights and freedoms of Chinese citizens, and to even tighter control of civil society by the Chinese authorities than there is already.
>
> *(Office of the United Nations High Commissioner for Human Rights, 2015)*

The very existence of the Uyghurs has become conflated with a threat to national security, enabling their citizenship rights to be not only restricted but repealed in what numerous scholars have termed a cultural genocide (Finnegan, 2020; Roberts, 2020; Smith Finley, 2020). The internment of Uyghurs on the basis of their religion under the rubric of "vocational re-education" and other measures including the destruction of mosques, rape, forced sterilisation, and forced co-habitation of Uyghur Muslim women with Han men (Hill et al., 2021; Emmerson, 2020) under the guise of securing "unity" and "welfare of the people" may, alongside Myanmar, constitute the most clear-cut attack on freedom of religion anywhere in the world today.

7.3 India

India is home to the world's largest Muslim-minority population with almost 200 million Muslims. One in ten of the world's Muslims live in India and this is projected to become the world's largest Muslim population (majority or minority) with 300 million by 2050 (Lipka, 2017).

The history of religious violence in India is well documented, particularly since the partition of Hindu-majority India and Muslim-majority Pakistan in 1947. While minorities including Sikhs and Christians have historically faced marginalisation based on their beliefs, animosity has primarily been directed towards Indian Muslims. This is a pattern that has grown in recent decades with the emergence of Hindu nationalist political parties including the *Bharatiya Janata Party* (BJP) led by Narendra Modi. Formerly the Chief Minister of Gujarat who was allegedly complicit in the 2002 Gujarat riots targeting Indian Muslims and killing 790 Muslims, Modi has enjoyed broad popular appeal nationally and internationally, amongst the Indian diaspora.

Religion and nationalism are inextricably linked in Indian politics. In an examination of the centrality of Hinduism in the Indian body politic, Rajagopal argues that it serves as a "surrogate category of political discourse used to mobilise recruits of the nationalist cause" (Rajagopal, 2001, p. 83). Muslim citizenship in India has, as in both Western and Asian nations, become conflated with a threat to national security. In 2019, India passed the *Citizenship Amendment Bill* granting citizenship to religious minorities (but excluding Muslims, including Muslim minorities facing persecution including the Rohingya and Ahmadis) from Pakistan, Afghanistan, and Bangladesh. The Bill amended the then 64-year-old citizenship laws prohibiting illegal migrants from becoming Indian citizens. Section 2 of the Act stated:

> 2. In the Citizenship Act, 1955 (hereinafter referred to as the principal Act), in section 2, in sub-section (*1*), in clause (*b*), the following proviso shall be inserted, namely: —
>
> "Provided that any person belonging to Hindu, Sikh, Buddhist, Jain, Parsi or Christian community from Afghanistan, Bangladesh or Pakistan, who entered into India on or before the 31st day of December 2014 and who has been exempted by the Central Government by or under clause (c) of sub-section (2) of section 3 of the Passport (Entry into India) Act, 1920

> or from the application of the provisions of the Foreigners Act, 1946 or any rule or order made thereunder, shall not be treated as illegal migrant for the purposes of this Act."
>
> *(The Gazette of India Extraordinary, 2019)*

The Act, which came into force on 10 January 2020, was argued by critics to violate India's secular constitution, making faith (Hindu, Sikh, Buddhist, Jain, Parsi, and Christianity) a precondition of citizenship for migrants from the Muslim-majority contexts of Pakistan, Bangladesh, and Afghanistan, while excluding Muslims, including those Muslim minorities including the Ahmadi and Rohingya that have faced persecution. Indian historian and essayist Mukul Kesavan (2019) has noted the motivation behind this law at length:

> [Its] main purpose is the de-legitimization of Muslim citizenship ...this institutional pincer will result in an Indian Inquisition designed to tell true citizens from false ones. And since the rules of the game will have been rigged by the new citizenship law, only Muslims will potentially be false citizens.

According to this perspective, religious status (and not being Muslim) will become the basis of citizenship. Delhi-based lawyer Gautam Bhatia would assert that by dividing migrants into Muslims and non-Muslims, the Bill "explicitly seeks to enshrine religious discrimination into law, contrary to our long standing constitutional ethos" (BBC News, 2019).

Just prior to the Bill passing into law, the Office of the United Nations High Commissioner for Human Rights would state the concern that the Act is fundamentally discriminatory (2019). The United States Commission on International Religious Freedom would call for sanctions against the Indian Home Affairs Minister, Amit Shah from the BJP (United States Commission on International Religious Freedom, 2019). This Bill became the *Citizenship* (Amendment) Act (2019) on 11 December 2019. After a year of often violent protests, Indian writer Arundhati Roy would summarise the impact of the law:

> It is an anti-Muslim law. That's not a perspective...It's an objective reality. And, when combined with the National Population Register (NPR) and the National Register of Citizens (NRC), it tears through even what's left of the pretense of India's secularism and constitution.
>
> *(Vaid, 2020)*

The legislation had not been implemented by the time of writing, with extensions granted for the process of rule writing to April and July 2021. The next

Indian election is due in 2024, giving the BJP Party at least three years to further its Hindu nationalist agenda.

8 Muslims at the Domestic Frontline

As this chapter covers both Western and Asian contexts (and approximately 40% of the world's population) and makes clear, Muslims have been at the front and centre of domestic debates and targeted legislation directly impacting their citizenship and belonging. This has had a direct impact on freedom of religion, at best forcing Muslims to dissociate themselves from perspectives that could be framed by prosecutors as supportive of the Islamic State and terrorism and at worst, as genocidal, seeking the annihilation of an entire Islamic culture and Muslim population.

This arguably extends globally. Writing in a comparative context examining the UK and Canada, Macklin suggests that "citizenship emerges as an enhanced form of conditional permanent residence, revokable through the exercise of executive discretion" (2014, p. 1). Anti-terror laws and particularly those symbolic laws targeting citizenship may send a symbolic message to voting (or captive) constituencies, but they also have the power to undermine trust amongst minority groups, suggesting that the loyalty of Muslims is in question and that citizenship is conditional. Denationalisation has often been a symbol of the abuse of government power and as a precursor to genocide (Benton and Banulescu-Bogdan, 2019).

In the UK and Australia, there has been the creation of two tiers of citizenship; those individuals who possess single citizenship and those who possess dual citizenship from migrant backgrounds. Dual citizenship has allowed national governments to reject the local citizenship and to, in effect, discard the problem to the other nation without making them stateless. This also leads to considerable inconsistencies. Those individuals using dual citizenship to fight for causes overseas, including Ukraine, militias in Iraq and Syria, and national armies, have not experienced the same pressure. The matter of former soldiers serving corporations as mercenaries where war crimes have been noted including across the Middle East and Africa has similarly avoided serious scrutiny.

Ministerial discretion offers extraordinary powers to politicians enacting a political agenda with limited rights of appeal. Combined with decades of securitisation and media scrutiny, the cumulative effect of national security legislation is to threaten citizenship and to silence dissent, particularly where this can be conceived of as support for terrorist movements. Citizenship provisions target public speech that can be interpreted as advocacy for terrorism. This has the impact of setting boundaries around speech for some groups (Muslims) including discussions about defending members of religious communities in foreign contexts or arguing for foreign territorial claims, whilst creating a situation in which entire communities can be scapegoated as sympathetic to terrorism without any similar penalty.

9 The Loss of Western Legitimacy?

National security laws have been primarily framed as threatening citizenship rights including freedom of speech and freedom of movement. However, these overlook the significant impact on freedom of religion. Contemporary national security legislation has been driven by political agendas. Governments are adopting illiberal tactics, withdrawing from concern with the rule of law, transparency, and inclusion to weaponise citizenship, largely against Muslim minorities. The potential for this to be easily applied to other faith communities based on political contingency has strong historic precedent and, in a context defined by increasing religious intolerance globally (*Pew Research Centre*, 2019), in the contemporary era.

This has significant impacts on freedom of religious practice and expression, including political opinions drawn from religious texts (fundamentalism) and broader concern with the status of foreign communities of fellow believers. In the context of the global authoritarian populist turn, where there is a strong history of anti-Semitism and willingness to use force against civilian populations, there are strong detrimental implications for freedom of religion on a global scale. Through its illiberal treatment of Muslim populations, making them in effect responsible for the actions of a tiny minority, many Western nations are losing any legitimacy to address concerns about freedom of religion in other contexts. The concept of citizenship as a revocable status is incompatible with democratic citizenship (Lenard, 2016).

In Asian contexts citizenship legislation is increasingly intertwined with national security legislation to demarcate the national community and to exclude Muslim populations. Once a religious or ethnic group is posited as non-citizens, they are, in effect, an "enemy within" to be controlled, expelled, or exterminated. When considered "non-citizens" that are external to the nation, we see governments capable of enacting and replicating the worst behaviours of the Islamic State Movement: re-education, rape, imprisonment, execution, and cultural and physical genocide.

10 Conclusion

This chapter explores the legislative, jurisprudential, and liberal philosophical challenges of this decision by a group of select Western and non-Western states and considers implications for freedom of religion on a global scale.

Whilst ostensibly developed to ensure national security and national unity, citizenship, or, in the case of some Asian contexts, nationality laws have been used to target religious minorities, in particular Muslim communities, impacting their freedom of speech and religion. This has ranged from effectively being denied the right of citizenship to acts of genocide aimed at eradicating national communities.

In applying these fundamentally *illiberal* laws, Western nations undermine their capacity to promote freedom of religion in other contexts and to adequately challenge the treatment of religious minorities in non-democratic contexts. Western nations must not only take responsibility for the actions of their citizens and bear the burden of their participation in movements promoting terrorism including the Islamic State, but they must also retract provisions that inhibit (under threat of coercive state attention) freedom of religious expression including the holding of strong political views that align with text and highly conservative manifestations of religion where these do not cross a threshold into the advocacy or enactment of violence.

There is no dispute that groups such as the Islamic State and Al-Qaeda are transnational terrorist organisations responsible for tens of thousands of deaths over the past three decades. These are fundamentally illiberal actors responsible for grave violations and abuses of human rights, including attacks on freedom of religion. Equally indisputable is that the vast majority of the West and Western Muslims reject these views. While some condemn them directly, the majority do so through their contributions as citizens to the countries in which their forebears have settled.

In a political epoch defined by an authoritarian shift and the rise of global right-wing populism, it is more important than ever for liberal democracies to lead by example in protecting religious minorities. The retraction of revocation of citizenship laws is an important potential first step to this end.

References

Arendt, H. (1951) *The Origins of Totalitarianism*, New York, Harcourt Brace and Co.

Arraiza, J. M. and Vonk, O. (2017) *Report on Citizenship Law: Myanmar*, Fiesole, Italy, European University Institute.

Australian Bureau of Statistics (2016) *Census of Housing and Population*, Canberra, Australian Bureau of Statistics.

Australian Bureau of Statistics (1947) *Census of Housing and Population*, Canberra, Australian Bureau of Statistics.

BBC News (2019) 'Citizenship Amendment Bill: India's New "Anti-Muslim" Law Explained', 11 December [Online]. Available at https://www.bbc.com/news/world-asia-india-50670393 (Accessed 23 February 2023).

Benton, M. and Banulescu-Bogdan, N. (2019) 'Foreign Fighters: Will Revoking Citizenship Mitigate the Threat?', Migration Policy Institute, 3 April [Online]. Available at https://www.migrationpolicy.org/article/foreign-fighters-will-revoking-citizenship-mitigate-threat (Accessed 23 February 2023).

Brooks, B. (2016) 'Treason, Terrorism and Imprecision: Locating s 80.2C of the Criminal Code (Cth) in the Taxonomy of Crimes Against the State', *Sydney Law Review*, vol. 38, no. 1, pp. 121–140.

Cameron, D. (2014) 'Threat Level from International Terrorism Raised: PM Press Statement', Speech, Prime Minister's Office, 29 August [Online]. Available at https://perma.cc/T66A-E6QG (Accessed 23 February 2023).

China Info Services (2018) 'National Security Law of the People's Republic of China (2015) [Effective]', China Daily, 11 December [Online]. Available at https://govt.chinadaily.com.cn/s/201812/11/WS5c0f1b56498eefb3fe46e8c9/national-security-law-of-the-peoples-republic-of-china-2015-effective.html (Accessed 23 February 2023).

Dutton, P. (2015) 'Second Reading Speech to the Australian Citizenship Amendment (Allegiance to Australia) Bill 2015', Australian Parliament, 24 June [Online]. Available at https://www.homeaffairs.gov.au/foi/files/2017/FA170500435-documents-released.pdf (Accessed 23 February 2023).

Emmerson, B. (2020) 'Foreword', in Roberts, S. R. (ed) *The War on the Uyghurs*, Princeton, NJ, Princeton University Press, pp. ix–xvii.

Finnegan, C. (2020) 'The Uyghur Minority in China: A Case Study of Cultural Genocide, Minority Rights and the Insufficiency of the International Legal Framework in Preventing State-imposed Extinction', *Laws*, vol. 9, no. 1 [Online]. Available at https://www.mdpi.com/2075-471X/9/1/1 (Accessed 23 February 2023).

Global Times (2021) 'An Analysis Report on Population Change in Xinjiang', 7 January [Online]. Available at https://www.globaltimes.cn/page/202101/1212073.shtml (Accessed 23 January 2023).

Great Britain. *British Nationality Act: Queen Elizabeth II*, Chapter 61 (1981), London, The Stationery Office.

Heinsch, R. (2016) 'Foreign Fighters and International Criminal Law', in de Guttry, A., Capone, F. and Paulussen, C. (eds) *Foreign Fighters under International Law and Beyond*, Berlin, Springer, pp. 161–186.

Herzog, B. (2010) 'Dual Citizenship and the Revocation of Citizenship', in Wejnert, B. (ed) *Democratic Paths and Trends*, Bingley, Emerald Group Publishing, pp. 87–110.

High Court of Australia (2021) *Delil Alexander (By His Litigation Guardian Berivan Alexander) v. Minister for Home affairs & Anor*: Case S103/2021.

Hill, M., Campanale, D. and Gunter, J. (2021) '"Their Goal Is to Destroy Everyone": Uighur Camp Detainees Allege Systematic Rape', BBC News, 2 February [Online]. Available at https://www.bbc.com/news/world-asia-china-55794071 (Accessed 23 February 2023).

Human Rights Watch (2000) 'Discrimination in Arakan' [Online]. Available at https://www.hrw.org/reports/2000/burma/burm005-02.htm (Accessed 23 February 2023).

Israeli, R. (2010) 'China's Uyghur Problem', *Israel Journal of Foreign Affairs*, vol. 4, no. 1, pp. 89–101.

Kesavan, M. (2019) 'The Greatest Threat to Indian Democracy Today', The Telegraph Online, 28 July [Online]. Available at https://www.telegraphindia.com/opinion/nrc-and-the-citizenship-bill-are-the-greatest-threat-to-indian-democracy-today/cid/1695315# (Accessed 23 February 2023).

Lenard, P. T. (2016) 'Democracies and the Power to Revoke Citizenship', *Ethics and International Affairs*, vol. 30, no. 1, pp. 73–91.

Leydet, D. (2017) 'Citizenship', in Zalta, E. N. (ed) *The Stanford Encyclopaedia of Philosophy* (Fall 2017 Edition), Stanford, Metaphysics Research Lab at Stanford

University [Online]. Available at https://plato.stanford.edu/archives/fall2017/entries/citizenship/ (Accessed 23 February 2023).

Lipka, M. (2017) 'Muslims and Islam: Key Findings in the U.S. and around the World', Washington, DC, Pew Research Centre, 9 August [Online]. Available at https://www.pewresearch.org/fact-tank/2017/08/09/muslims-and-islam-key-findings-in-the-u-s-and-around-the-world/ (Accessed 23 February 2023).

Macklin, A. (2014) 'Citizenship Revocation, the Privilege to Have Rights and the Production of the Alien', *Queen's Law Journal*, vol. 40, no. 1, pp. 1–54.

Maclean's (2015) 'Tale of the Tape: Transcript of the Munk Debate', 28 September [Online]. Available at https://www.macleans.ca/politics/ottawa/tale-of-the-tape-transcript-of-the-munk-debate-on-the-refugee-crisis/ (Accessed 23 February 2023).

Mantu, S. (2015) Citizenship in Times of Terror: Citizenship Deprivation in the UK, Nijmegen Migration Law Working Papers Series, no. 2.

Marshall, T. H. (1950) *Citizenship and Social Class, and Other Essays*, Cambridge, Cambridge University Press.

Masters, M. and Regilme, S. F. (2020) 'Citizenship Revocation as a Human Rights Violation: the Case of Shamima Begum', E-International Relations, 28 November [Online]. Available at https://www.e-ir.info/2020/11/28/citizenship-revocation-as-a-human-rights-violation-the-case-of-shamima-begum/ (Accessed 23 February 2023).

Myanmar. Pyithu Hluttaw (1982) [Citizenship] Law No. 4. Naypyidaw.

Office for National Statistics (2018) 'Muslim Population in the UK' [Online]. Available at https://www.ons.gov.uk/aboutus/transparencyandgovernance/freedomofinformationfoi/muslimpopulationintheuk/ (Accessed 23 February 2023).

Office of the United Nations High Commissioner for Human Rights (2019) 'Press Briefing on India', United Nations, 13 December [Online]. Available at https://www.ohchr.org/en/NewsEvents/Pages/DisplayNews.aspx?NewsID=25425&LangID=E (Accessed 23 February 2023).

Office of the United Nations High Commissioner for Human Rights (2018) 'Myanmar: UN Fact-finding Mission Releases Its Full Account of Massive Violations by Military in Rakhine, Kachin and Shan States', United Nations [Online]. Available at https://www.ohchr.org/EN/HRBodies/HRC/Pages/NewsDetail.aspx?NewsID=23575&LangID=E (Accessed 23 February 2023).

Office of the United Nations High Commissioner for Human Rights (2015) 'UN Human Rights Chief Says China's New Security Law Is Too Broad, Too Vague', United Nations [Online]. Available at https://www.ohchr.org/en/NewsEvents/Pages/DisplayNews.aspx?NewsID=16210&LangID=E (Accessed 23 February 2023).

Omar, W. and Allen, K. (1996) *The Muslims in Australia*, Canberra, Australian Government Publishing Service.

Parliament of Australia (2022) 'Invalidity of the Minister's Power to Revoke Citizenship', Parliament of Australia Website. Available at: https://www.aph.gov.au/About_Parliament/Parliamentary_Departments/Parliamentary_Library/FlagPost/2022/June/Power_to_revoke_citizenship.

Peach, C. and Gale, R. (2003) 'Muslims, Hindus and Sikhs in the New Religious Landscape of England', *Geographical Review*, vol. 93, no. 4, pp. 469–490.

Pew Research Centre (2019) 'A Closer Look at How Religious Restrictions Have RISEN around the World', Washington, DC. [Online]. Available at https://www.pewforum.org/2019/07/15/a-closer-look-at-how-religious-restrictions-have-risen-around-the-world/ (Accessed 23 February 2023).

Pillai, S. and Williams, G. (2018) 'The Utility of Citizenship Stripping Laws in the UK, Canada and Australia', *Melbourne University Law Review*, vol. 41, no. 2, pp. 845–889.

Rajagopal, A. (2001) *Politics After Television: Hindu Nationalism and the Reshaping of the Public in India*, Cambridge, Cambridge University Press.

Roberts, S. R. (2020) *The War on the Uyghurs*, Princeton, NJ, Princeton University Press.

Roose, J. M. (2020) *The New Demagogues: Religion, Masculinity and the Populist Epoch*, London, Routledge.

Roose, J. M. (2016) *Political Islam and Masculinity: Muslim Men in Australia*, New York, Palgrave.

Skydsgaard, N. and Jacobsen, S. (2019) 'Denmark to Strip Foreign Fighters of Danish Citizenship', Reuters, 15 October [Online]. Available at https://www.reuters.com/article/us-syria-security-denmark/denmark-to-strip-foreign-fighters-of-danish-citizenship-idUSKBN1WT1RN (Accessed 23 February 2023).

Smith Finley, J. (2020) 'Why Scholars and Activists Increasingly Fear a Uyghur Genocide in Xinjiang', *Journal of Genocide Research*, vol. 23, no. 3, pp. 348–370 [Online]. Available at DOI: 10.1080/14623528.2020.1848109 (Accessed 23 February 2023).

The Gazette of India Extraordinary (2019) 'The Citizenship (Amendment) Act, 2019', 12 December [Online]. Available at http://egazette.nic.in/WriteReadData/2019/214646.pdf (Accessed 23 February 2023).

United Nations (1948) 'Convention on the Prevention and Punishment of the Crime of Genocide', New York [Online]. Available at https://www.un.org/en/genocideprevention/documents/atrocity-crimes/Doc.1_Convention%20on%20the%20Prevention%20and%20Punishment%20of%20the%20Crime%20of%20Genocide.pdf (Accessed 23 February 2023).

United Nations Office for the Coordination of Humanitarian Affairs (2018) 'Rohingya Refugee Crisis' [Online]. Available at https://www.unocha.org/rohingya-refugee-crisis (Accessed 23 February 2023).

United States Commission on International Religious Freedom (2019) 'USCIRF Raises Serious Concerns and Eyes Sanctions Recommendations for Citizenship (Amendment) Bill in India, Which Passed Lower House Today', United Nations, 9 December [Online]. Available at https://web.archive.org/web/20191210093153/https://www.uscirf.gov/news-room/press-releases-statements/uscirf-raises-serious-concerns-and-eyes-sanctions (Accessed 23 February 2023).

UN News (2020) 'Top UN Court Orders Myanmar to Protect Rohingya from Genocide', United Nations, 23 January [Online]. Available at https://news.un.org/en/story/2020/01/1055841 (Accessed 23 February 2023).

Vaid, D. (2020) 'One Year of India's Citizenship Amendment Act', Deutsche Welle, 11 December [Online]. Available at https://www.dw.com/en/one-year-of-indias-citizenship-amendment-act/a-55909013 (Accessed 23 February 2023).

Yu, M. (2021) 'Chinese Statistics Reveal Plummeting Births in Xinjiang during Crackdown on Uyghurs', Voice of America, 27 March [Online]. Available at https://www.voanews.com/east-asia-pacific/voa-news-china/chinese-statistics-reveal-plummeting-births-xinjiang-during (Accessed 23 February 2023).

CONCLUSION

Freedom of Religion as Shield, Sword, and Contributor in Relation to National Security

Joshua M. Roose and G. P. Marcar

Freedom of religion—along with its conceptual siblings of thought, opinion, belief, and conscience—remains a fundamental human right, enshrined in the Universal Declaration of Human Rights and International Covenant for Civil and Political Rights (ICCPR) (Article 18), the European Convention on Human Rights (ECHR) (Article 9), and other legal treatises. While there may be international agreement as to its protection, however, there is no consensus on the scope of religion's protection. This is particularly notable in respect to national security. Under both Article 18 UDHR/ICCPR and Article 9 ECHR, manifestations of religion (unlike the neighbouring right of freedom of expression) are not subject to limitations based on national security or 'public order' (*ordre public*). Where they diverge, however, is on the issue of derogations: Article 15 ECHR *enshrines* the possibility of derogations from freedom of religion or belief (FORB) "[i]n time of war or other public emergency threatening the life of the nation", while, in contrast, the ICCPR (Article 4) explicitly *exempts* FORB (but not freedom of expression) from such derogation.

The European context, then, retains the possibility that FORB (including, theoretically, the supposedly inviolable inner sanctum of the *forum internum*) can be intruded upon when 'the life of the nation' is threatened. This, in conjunction with the proclivity of the European Court of Human Rights to afford a generous 'margin of appreciation' to states and their restrictions on FORB, accentuates the need for consultation with a wide variety of European and non-European perspectives—such as those represented in the present volume.

Whether in Europe or elsewhere, domestically or internationally, debates over freedom of religion are at the fore of the relationship between religion and politics. Freedom of Religion or Belief is inscribed in international human rights instruments and is a critical protective mechanism, or 'shield',

DOI: 10.4324/9781003453086-14

particularly for religious minorities that have historically experienced persecution, violence, and genocide. It enables states and activists alike not only to label, but to mobilise against abuses of this fundamental human right. In a domestic sense, it encourages pluralism and the acceptance, respect, and recognition essential to peaceable, modern, and democratic societies.

Yet as numerous contributions to this volume have capably demonstrated, as a fundamental human right, Freedom of Religion or Belief very often stands in direct contrast to conceptions of national security that are grounded in political narratives of an internal or external 'threat' to the national community. This threat is very often understood in terms of 'us', the homogenous national community with shared moral and political values, and 'them', the enemy within or external group who are at fundamental odds with those values. In this sense, particularly against the 'threat within' or 'fifth column', exceptional measures may be taken to secure the safety and freedom of the people. These exceptional measures include disregarding the fundamental human rights of the potential 'threat' or 'enemy' and subjecting entire minority communities to securitisation, hostile political and media discourse, and pressure to conform. For those seeking asylum, the situation is often even worse. In addition to long-standing attacks on multiculturalism (Akbarzadeh and Roose, 2011), as Pagotto notes in this volume, Western European nations have sought to select only 'desirable' migrants, whilst controlling 'undesirables' through the prisms of crime, class, race, ethnicity, gender, or religion. At its extreme, as has been seen in the narratives of far-right populists, entire religious communities are represented as a sub-human threat to national security and rejected entirely, opening the door to attacks on their human rights and, in some cases, existence.

In Western contexts in recent times, this threat has been primarily framed in terms of Salafi Jihadist terrorism, with entire Muslim communities being securitised and held to account for the actions of a tiny minority. We witnessed the equation of Islam, a religion with over almost two billion adherents globally, with all the diversity that entails, with terrorism and extremism. In other contexts, however, where the threat is external, such as the threat faced by Ukraine from Russian invasion and infiltration of political, economic, cultural, and religious institutions, the religious minority may be separated by purely denominational differences within the same faith. Targeting the perceived enemy within can cause deep societal divisions that undermine the efforts to repel the invader. As Vasin emphasised, the problem was not religious freedom, but a lack of it.

Further to Salafi Jihadism and invasion, the spectre of antisemitism once again casts a dark shadow over Europe, whilst religious minorities from China and Russia to India and the United States continue to face persecution for their beliefs. In this context, it is a perverse development that textualist Christian movements that hold enormous institutional and political sway, even given the secular context in which they are situated, have sought to wield FORB as a sword, asserting the need for the right to discriminate to circumvent human rights-based legislation, including anti-discrimination laws. Such actors, who enjoy significant tax breaks as charitable institutions, frame Christianity as under attack from secularism and as requiring protections to protect them from an imagined horde of activists bent on subverting their values. Schools and children are seen as a frontline in the battle for FORB, as the churches, and increasingly other faiths, seek to mobilise to prevent the exposure of their students to LGBTIQ materials and protect their hiring practices.

Freedom of Religion or Belief operates most effectively and fulfils its purpose most powerfully, as a shield against persecution on the one hand and as a peacebuilding mechanism on the other. The protection of religious freedom empowers communities not only to live without fear, but also to contribute to the development of their community and wider society as citizens. As researchers at Georgetown and Brigham Young University have identified in a 2014 study, the presence of Freedom of Religion is related to less corruption, more peace, less economically harmful regulation, and more economic growth (Grim, Clark, and Snyder, 2014). Between 2008 and 2012, countries with very high religious diversity outpaced the rest of the world in economic growth (Grim and Tucker, 2014).

With this in mind, it is important to move beyond the purely negative conceptions of the relationship between national security and religious freedom that predominate in authoritarian states or with governments focused primarily on mobilising against the 'other' and to consider the positive role that enhanced religious freedom can have on improving national security. To do this we need to look beyond the literature on Freedom of Religion or Belief. Whilst discussions about FORB are typically grounded in human rights and legal frameworks, it is important to bring these into conversation with the interdisciplinary fields that examine pathways to radicalisation and patterns of participation. These include security and terrorism studies as well as the social sciences including politics, sociology, and criminology. The traditional framing of radicalisation to violent extremism and terrorism is understood as constituted by external 'push' and internal 'pull' factors. While this frame is not without its critics, the concept suggests that, in contrast to the deterministic framing of religions as inherently bloodthirsty and violent, governments can act to challenge and prevent the appeal of extremist narratives and the pre-conditions that might push individuals to violence. In this context, religious justifications are but some of the many potential influences shaping the attraction to terrorist organisations and violent extremism. Research in these fields demonstrates that the most important preventative work is carried out by governments in cooperation and concert with minority communities and is grounded in building mutual trust, respect, and recognition and in developing upward social trajectories.

Domestic terror threats are very often reported by members of the alleged offenders' communities well before they can escalate to become successful.

Those successful plots are very often from those ostracised by their communities in the first place, or as in the case of Islamic State terror attacks in Europe such as the Bataclan attacks, from foreign infiltrators with few, if any, organic links to local communities. In Australia, Canada, New Zealand, the United Kingdom, and across Europe, dedicated government departments, academics, and community leaders and advocates work together to build these relationships, as well as other initiatives including interfaith work, creating face-to-face networks between faith leaders who can then offer each other mutual support in the event of an attack on any of their communities. These are often far from perfect examples of policy best practices elucidated by Rodrigo Alves in his exploration of the United Nations approach and former Special Rapporteur Martin Scheinn, which included the importance of ensuring consistency between anti-terrorist legislation and approaches with human rights instruments and protection of freedom of expression. The Prevent Program in the United Kingdom was specifically criticised for targeting Muslim communities by the United Nations Special Rapporteur on the promotion and protection of human rights while countering terrorism, as per Fionnuala Ní Aoláin. However, in strong contrast to many other contexts where human rights are largely ignored, an emphasis remains on working with rather than against communities. Considerable effort is made to engage with community leaders, from the first and second and third generations, and funding often goes to community organisations including sporting clubs and youth clubs.

In relation to national security and challenging terrorism and violent extremism while also addressing foreign threats, it becomes apparent that Freedom of Religion or Belief is an important contributor to social cohesion, peacebuilding, and economic development. It fosters a sense of acceptance, respect, and recognition between different communities while contributing to the cohesion necessary for the predictable social and political circumstances that provide certainty for private sector growth and opportunity. Most importantly, in the context of this book, these are the foundation stones of a viable and sustainable national security policy.

References

Akbarzadeh, S. and Roose, J.M., 2011. Muslims, multiculturalism and the question of the silent majority. *Journal of Muslim Minority Affairs*, 31(3), 309–325.

Grim, B.J., Clark, G. and Snyder, R.E., 2014. Is religious freedom good for business?: A conceptual and empirical analysis. *Interdisciplinary Journal of Research on Religion*, 10(4), 1–18.

Grim, J. and Tucker, M.E., 2014. *Ecology and religion*. Island Press.

INDEX

Note: Page numbers followed by "n" denote endnotes.

For Product Safety Concerns and Information please contact our EU representative GPSR@taylorandfrancis.com
Taylor & Francis Verlag GmbH, Kaufingerstraße 24, 80331 München, Germany

www.ingramcontent.com/pod-product-compliance
Ingram Content Group UK Ltd.
Pitfield, Milton Keynes, MK11 3LW, UK
UKHW020009200926
475702UK00015B/2556

* 9 7 8 1 0 3 2 5 9 1 2 4 7 *